Animals and War

Animals and War

Confronting the Military-Animal Industrial Complex

Edited by

Colin Salter
Anthony J. Nocella II
Judy K.C. Bentley

LEXINGTON BOOKS
Lanham • Boulder • New York • Toronto • London

Published by Lexington Books
A wholly owned subsidiary of Rowman & Littlefield
4501 Forbes Boulevard, Suite 200, Lanham, Maryland 20706
www.rowman.com

Unit A, Whitacre Mews, 26-34 Stannary Street, London SE11 4AB

British Library Cataloguing in Publication Information Available

Library of Congress Cataloging-in-Publication Data
The hardback edition of this book was previously cataloged by the Library of Congress as
follows:

Animals and war: confronting the military-animal industrial complex / edited by Anthony
J. Nocella II; Colin Salter and Judy K.C. Bentley.
    pages cm. -- (Critical animal studies, theory, pedagogy, and methodology)
  Includes bibliographical references and index.
  1. Animals--War use. 2. Animal welfare. I. Nocella, Anthony J. II. Salter, Colin, 1957-
III. Bentley, Judy K. C.
  UH87.A54 2013
  355.4'24--dc23
                                2013037460

ISBN 978-0-7391-8651-0 (cloth : alk. paper)
ISBN 978-1-4985-2086-7 (pbk : alk. paper)
ISBN 978-0-7391-8652-7 (electronic)

Printed in the United States of America

DEDICATION

This book is dedicated to all those who suffer as a consequence of violent military conflict throughout history, and seeks to give voice to the hidden victims of war.

Critical Animal Studies and Theory

Series Editors

Dan Featherston and Anthony J. Nocella II

The *Critical Animal Studies and Theory* series for Lexington Books addresses human relations with other animals in the context of socio-political relations and economic systems of power. *Critical Animal Studies and Theory* sees liberation not as a single-issue phenomenon, but rather as inseparably related to human rights, peace and justice, and environmental issues and movements. Rather than emphasizing abstract theory, the series links theory with practice and emphasizes the immense importance of animal advocacy for a humane, democratic, peaceful, and sustainable world. Taking an interdisciplinary approach to questions of social change, moral progress, and ecological sustainability, the *Critical Animal Studies and Theory* series connects with disciplines such as feminism, globalization, economics, science, history, education, critical race theory, environmental studies, media studies, ecopedagogy, art, literature, disability, gender, political science, sociology, religion, anthropology, philosophy, and cultural studies. The series will serve as a foundational project for one of the fastest growing and most exciting new fields of scholarship, Critical Animal Studies. Rooted in critical theory as well as the animal advocacy movement, the *Critical Animal Studies and Theory* series argues for an interdisciplinary approach to understanding our relationships with nonhuman animals. Rejecting the notion that nonhuman animals do not have a voice, the series stresses that nonhuman animals do have agency and thus argues for an animal standpoint. In keeping with the principles of Critical Animal Studies, the series encourages progressive and committed scholarship and views exploitation of nonhuman animals, such as animal research and studies, as interrelated with other oppressions such as classism, sexism, and racism. Against apolitical scholarship, for example human-animal studies, the series encourages engaged critical praxis, promotes liberation of all animals, and challenges all systems of domination.

Titles in Series

Animals and War: Confronting Animal Studies and Theory, edited by Anthony J. Nocella II, Colin Salter, and Judy K.C. Bentley

WHAT PEOPLE ARE SAYING ABOUT
ANIMALS AND WAR

One day, thanks in part to books like these, we will stop saying, "Let's respect each other, for we are all human beings" and say, "Let's respect each other, for we are all living beings. Peace begins at breakfast with what's on our plates."

> — *Ingrid Newkirk*, author of *Free the Animals*

In this breakthrough volume, leading animal rights activists and peace anti-war activists shed a crucial light on the important connection between critical animal studies and peace studies. The leading scholar-activists in this volume are at the cutting edge of the struggle to resist the exploitation of nonhuman animals in the military. All social justice educators and activists would do well to read this book!

> — *Dr. Peter McLaren*, Professor, Graduate School of Education and Information Studies at University of California, Los Angeles

Animals and War is a wonderfully original contribution to the world of activism, social justice, and peace studies. An enlightening read for everyone!

> — *Dr. Jason Del Gandio*, author of *Rhetoric for Radicals: A Handbook for 21st Century Activists*

Animals and War: Dismantling the Military-Animal Industrial Complex is a seminal book for those who oppose war, those who fight for animal liberation, and those who do both. This essay collection powerfully exposes the use of animals as unwitting instruments and casualties of the battles that humans continue to wage against each other. If ever a text could move the animal liberation movement beyond its unjust categorization as "single issue," this is it. *Animals and War* demands that all give attention to the ways in which manifestations of abuse, exploitation and domination are interwoven during war time, and it serves as a much needed rallying cry to put a cog in the machine that is the military-animal industrial complex.

> — *Dr. Kim Socha*, author of *Women, Destruction and the Avant-Garde: A Paradigm for Animal Liberation*

In a world that has seemed to value things over life/people, this book brings to the public's notice the often unheard voice of animals—animals who are treated in inhumane ways just to continue the war machine. This book gives us a much-needed insight into an area of study rarely gone. *Animals and War* is the premier reader for animal studies and violence.

> — *Dr. Daniel White Hodge*, Director of Center for Youth Ministry Studies and Assistant Professor of Youth & Popular Culture, North Park University

Animals and War takes us beyond critical theory's usual concerns about war, amplifying our understanding—and our concerns—about human suffering to appreciate the impact on other animals of this most human, most destructive of practices.

> — *Dr. Toby Miller*, author of *Makeover Nation: The United States of Reinvention*

Given the awful destructiveness of war, it is all too easy to think that its horrors are limited to its effect on human beings. This book makes the much-needed point that animals, too, have been both "instruments" of war and its victims, a trend that threatens to continue, even in our highly technological age. *Animals and War* is an important contribution to a previously neglected arena.

> — *Dr. David P. Barash*, editor of the book *Approaches to Peace: A Reader in Peace Studies*

Discarding the anthropocentrism inherent to conventional antimilitarist analyses, *Animals and War* exposes the very bedrock upon which the reality of contemporary militarism has been constructed. As the contributors amply demonstrate, the lives of "lesser" species have been so utterly devalued in the name of tactical utility that, inevitably, the same degree of devaluation would be applied not only to "lesser" races, nations, and peoples, but ultimately to all forms of life. For anyone wishing to understand the thanatophoric nature of the societal dynamic we now confront, the connections made in this book are of profound importance.

> — *Ward Churchill*, author of *A Little Matter of Genocide*

Animals and War is an eye-opening exploration of the profoundly destructive consequences of human chauvinism on nonhuman populations, and indeed the entire planet. This book is extraordinary in its theoretical depth and breadth, and in its engagement with the material reality of systematized death dealing and suffering, and yet it manages to inspire both hope and action.

> — *Dr. David Naguib Pellow*, Professor of Sociology, University of Minnesota

As if war weren't already evil enough in terms of human suffering, this collection documents what's hidden in plain view: the wholesale and horrifying forced conscription and torture of animals by the military-industrial complex.

— *Chris Hannah, Propagandhi*

Excellent! The central arguments in *Animals and War* burn brightly, and illuminate a truth that will stay with you long after you have finished reading this challenging, timely and valuable addition to the literature.

— *Dr. Richard J. White,* Editor of the *Journal for Critical Animal Studies*

A great read! *Animals and War* is an original contribution that documents how in horrific ways in war and in peace we humans dominate, exploit and horribly abuse all other species.

— *Dr. Piers Beirne,* author of *Confronting Animal Abuse* and other books on law and criminology

Congratulations to the writers and editors of *Animals and War: Dismantling the Military-Animal Industrial Complex* for exposing and criticizing this most appalling form of exploitation of other animals by the human species.

— *Ronnie Lee,* veteran animal liberation campaigner

Animals and War offers a holistic and in-depth analysis of the important social and military contributions nonhuman animals play, a contribution all too frequently born in blood and exploitation. This book represents the best of the emerging literature and facilitates new strides in critical animal studies and peace studies.

— *Dr. Jason J. Campbell,* Founder and Director, Institute for Genocide Awareness and Applied Research

CONTENTS

FOREWORD

Colman McCarthy

When opening a discussion in my high school, college and law school classes on Peace Studies classes, I ask students to call out the varicolored ways animals are preyed upon by humans. It doesn't take long. In only a minute, the list is long: food, clothing, recreation, jewelry, rodeos, horse and dog races, bull or cock fighting, circuses, zoos, hunting and trapping, entertainment, testing, scientific research—among others. I can't recall anyone ever mentioning militarism and how, in the name of national security, the Department of Defense, which was once more correctly called the Department of War, tortures and kills animals.

The unawareness isn't surprising. Only rarely do the media, print or electronic, include military violence to animals as a topic worth reporting. When it does, the coverage is likely to favor the military. In the early 1990's, CBS's *60 Minutes* told the story of an ongoing army-funded medical experiment in which some 700 cats were locked in vises and shot in the head. In the thirteen-minute segment, narrator Mike Wallace, someone ever touting himself as Mr. Tough Guy Interviewer, was limp and lame in reporting the controversy involving the $2 million research project. Inaccurate quoting, innuendo, and shifty editing prevailed. Wallace and *60 Minutes* markedly sided with Michael Carey, a professor of neurosurgery at Louisiana State University Medical School who was paid by the army to shoot anesthetized cats to supply information that could be used for treating soldiers' combat brain injuries. Animal rights groups opposing the experiment as medically specious and exceptionally cruel, found themselves disdained by Wallace as "zealots" and extremists opposed to breakthrough science. In the program, Carey was pictured as the hero, while the heavy was Dr. Neal Barnard, of the Washington-based Physicians Committee for Responsible Medicine. In the end, thanks to pressing the issue by Barnard, as well as a Louisiana member of Congress, the General Accounting Office found the experiment to be flawed. It was eventually canceled. The main finding for the army was that when shot in the head cats feel pain.

Animals and War: Dismantling the Military-Animal Industrial Complex is a worthy attempt at easing the imbalance between what the Pentagon, high-rolling defense lobbyists, and their bankrolled servants in Congress are doing, and what citizens and the media need to know about. The research in these pages is credible. The facts are grounded and the conclusions are sound. What's here is a strong tailwind that can help push forward a morally based movement that promises to offer humane alternatives to abusing and killing animals.

Much of the public suffers from outrage overload when it comes to the effects of American militarism, whether it is the high rates of suicide among soldiers and war veterans, the incessant reports of sexual assaults and harassment, the waste and fraud by military contractors, the uncountable killing of civilians in Iraq and Afghanistan, the maintaining of more than 700 military bases around the world and, since 1991, the extravagant funding by Congress to wage wars in Iraq and Afghanistan that can't be explained, can't be won and can't be afforded. By the latest tote, military and security spending is reaching well beyond $900 billion a year, more than $2.5 billion a day and close to $30,000 a second—all of it bringing to mind the thought of Martin Luther King Jr. on April 4, 1967, in New York City's Riverside Church: "A nation that continues year after year to spend more money on military defense than on programs of social uplift is approaching spiritual death."

When it comes to decreasing abuse to animals, whether by the military or corporate America, is anyone really innocent and guilt-free? We dwell in homes or work in sites that once displaced animals, we pay federal taxes that legalize the slaughter of animals for profit or pleasure, we travel in cars with leather seats over roads unfenced to prevent roadkill, we attend schools that allow animal experiments in biology classes, we take drugs once tested on animals, we buy newspapers that carry adds for the meat, egg, dairy and fur industries, we shop in stores that profit from the sale of animal products, we vote for politicians who pass laws favoring the meat, dairy, egg and hunting lobbies, we pay the salaries of federal and state judges who interpret a constitution that says nothing about the welfare or rights of animals and we embrace religions that give humans dominion over animals; and it's a rare sermon where the sacredness of animals is sounded.

These pages offer a place to pause, step back and examine our complicity, as difficult as that may be. If our path has no difficulties, it probably isn't leading anywhere.

PREFACE

Andrew Tyler
Director, *Animal Aid*

"War is hell", said the American Civil War general William Sherman. For many years I thought this was a remarkably trite statement and wondered why it is recited so often, so approvingly. But war, I came to understand, really does let loose the devil (or whatever we might wish to call it) in human beings. Sherman also said: "War is at best barbarism. Its glory is all moonshine." That's true too.

Most people are familiar with the varied and peculiarly savage treatment humans are capable of meting out to each other during even "low-level" wars: the use of systematic rape and amputations; the burning of villages; parents forced to watch or even participate in the slaughter of their own children....

Until recent years, the suffering of animals as a consequence of human conflict attracted scant consideration, and rarely the kind of systematic analysis to be found in the pages of this important volume.

We can point to, at least, five distinct war-related categories of harm that befall animals.

Collateral damage: Some of the most indelible images of the 1991 Gulf War showed the scorched and bloated bodies of camels abandoned in the shadow of burning oil wells. Photographer Steve McCurry describes "driving through the oilfields for several weeks after the hostilities ended and often [coming] across cattle, camels and horses wandering around like zombies. I guess most died eventually—all the water holes and vegetation were covered in oil" (*Guardian*, 2003 February 1, para. 2).

Willful assaults: During the Serbian conflict—also in the early 1990s— bored or hyped-up soldiers amused themselves by taking shots at wild animals. Zoo inmates were starved, beaten, fired upon and even attacked with grenades.

The deserted ones: These include the farmed animals abandoned in their sheds or in fields once the shooting starts. And dogs, cats, fish, guinea pigs and birds left alone in people's houses after those people take off to escape the mayhem. The animals starve and cry out for water, while the terrifying din of gunfire and explosions sound around them.

Front line victims: We can go back to the ancient Greeks and their use in pitched battles of Indian elephants—or consider the recent deployment of German Shepherd dogs, parachuted into Taliban strongholds in Afghanistan to search buildings for the enemy. A new generation of animal conscripts is even more expertly controlled and manipulated than those in the past—dolphins trained under extreme psychological and physical duress; and rats with gadgets implanted into their brains so that they can be directed, punished and rewarded at the tap of a keyboard.

Animals in weapons research: In Britain, most war-related vivisection is conducted by the Ministry of Defence in Porton Down, Wiltshire. Animals have been poisoned by chemical warfare agents, subjected to blast injuries, force-fed sensory irritants and deliberately wounded and killed by bacterial toxins. Porton scientists have described how monkeys, dosed with the nerve agent soman, became prostrate with violent convulsions, made attempts to crawl about the cage and then lost consciousness.

The impulses that draw people into war are deeply embedded. They are a product of weakness, greed, ambition, fear, stupidity, a lack of empathy and imagination, and much else. But while the impulses are raw, the project of warfare is often propelled by "sophisticated" ideology. We see at work a doctrine that requires enemies and heroes, as well as a mission of necessity. Within this framework, animals are many things. They are simultaneously expendable and heroic. They might be killed with impunity or awarded medals. Or both. Often, they are not thought about at all but are simply invisible.

In industrialized economies, where the populations manifest a high level of individual autonomy, those who orchestrate war have an increasingly difficult task in gaining majority consent. Most people no longer want to march off to battle. They are also more reluctant to sanction large numbers of home-bred professional warriors being killed in protracted campaigns. True progress would be if they also rejected the killing and suffering of "others"—the enemy across the hill, and members of kindred species.

As far as nonhuman animals are concerned, there are hopeful signs. *Animal Aid* has been pressing for a wider recognition of the suffering of animals in war for some fifteen years. In 2005, we introduced the purple poppy and encouraged people to wear it on November 11, Armistice Day. Uncertain as to the reception it would receive, that first year we produced 1,000. In 2011, we distributed 50,000. Together with our purple poppy wreaths, they have been displayed at sites of First and Second World War battlefields in France and Belgium. They are worn in Canada, the United States of America and other countries. Many people do now recognize the suffering of animals in wartime. The monumental Portland stone and bronze Animals in War memorial in London's up-market Park Lane is testimony to that fact.

What we are determined to guard against, however, is perpetuating the idea of animals as fallen heroes.

A British national newspaper ran a feature in 2011 on what eight million horses had to endure during the insane bloodbath that was the First World War. One million were sent from Britain alone to the Western Front. Just 60,000 survived—and even those would have ended up in French and Belgian abattoirs if not for compassionate people who fought for them to be brought home.

Among the photographs published in that newspaper feature was one of a cavalry horse standing over the body of his rider. The caption spoke of a "poignant vigil for his dead master." But this wasn't a vigil. The rider had fallen with the horse's reins still clasped in his dead hands. The horse could go nowhere. Stoic and long-suffering these animals were, but we should never pretend that they volunteered to their fate. They were conscripts. They didn't volunteer their lives; their lives were taken from them. And, no matter how many medals are handed out, they are not heroes but victims.

The suffering of animals and of vulnerable humans too will end only when the glorification and justification of war ends. Will that ever happen? The track record of human beings suggests it won't come about any time soon. But we must, in any case, do everything in our power to make it happen. People of conscience must reject war and we must refuse to be part of its glorification. We owe at least that to the animal victims ... and we owe it to ourselves.

ACKNOWLEDGMENTS

We would like to thank the reviewers of this book, and the Institute for Critical Animal Studies for believing in this project and for being so passionate for its completion during the editing stages. We would also like to thank Steve Hutton (and Animal Aid UK) for granting permission to reproduce his artwork on the cover of this book. We would like to also thank Colman McCarthy for his foreword and Andrew Tyler for his preface. It goes without saying that *Animals and War* would not have been possible without the fine contributions of John Sorenson, Shalin Gala, Ian Smith, Justin Goodman, Ana Morron, Julie Andrzejewski, Rajmohan Ramanathapillai, Bill Hamilton and Elliot M. Katz. We would also like to thank Ingrid Newkirk, Peter McLaren, Jason Del Gandio, Kim Socha, Toby Miller, Daniel White Hodge, David P. Barash, Ward Churchill, and David Pellow, Chris Hannah, Richard White, Ronnie Lee, Piers Beirne, and Jason Campbell for their support of this book. The support of our university departments, colleagues, many friends, and of course our families were invaluable and if it was not for them we would not be where we are today. Our gratitude goes to the *Journal for Critical Animal Studies*, LibNow.org, *Peace Studies Journal, Transformative Justice Journal, Social Advocacy and Systems Change*, the *Central New York Peace Studies Consortium*, and *Green Theory and Praxis Journal* for their willingness to review and promote this book.

INTRODUCING THE MILITARY-ANIMAL INDUSTRIAL COMPLEX

Colin Salter

Of all the strange changes happening in war in the 21st century, one of the most odd has to be the return of animals to the battlefield. War is not just about hardware and software, it is also now involving what some researchers call "wetware."
— P. W. Singer

At its core, this volume is about peace in both its negative and positive conceptions. To put it simply, negative peace is the absence of war, of violent conflict. Positive peace, on the other hand, is a broader, progressive and affirmative vision of the world we want to see, and how we can live that change (Galtung & Jacobsen, 2000). A vision of positive peace is one that embraces conflict: an embrace of the idea that conflict happens for a reason. Conflict has the potential to facilitate inclusive and transformative change, change rooted in an understanding of peace as justice. Conflict transformation is an ongoing and long-term process in which those enmeshed in a conflict come together, working toward building healthy relationships and communities. Conflict transformation is not about resolution. There is no endpoint. A central element of conflict transformation is a rejection of limited, and most-often superficial, attempts by a third party to impose "solutions" on parties to a conflict.

In seeking to highlight the exploitation of nonhuman animals as tools of war for human ends, on human terms and at the whim of anthropocentric, speciesist and human chauvinist notions, this volume forms an interjection into the discourse of war. What is provided is another layer of critical intervention, another set of voices that are more than antiwar. The chapters included here expand on the critique of the military-industrial complex in relation to the broader animal industrial complex—a concept first introduced by Barbara Noske in 1989, suggesting a military-animal industrial complex. Use and extension-refinement of Noske's concept—which identifies permeable and dynamic boundaries in the ways and means through which nonhuman animals

1

are exploited for profit—in this volume seeks to move beyond monolithic and "almost rhetorical" reference in critical discourse, identifying specific aspects of "the myriad complexity of the multiple relations, actors, technologies and identities that may be said to comprise the complex" (Twine, 2012, p. 15). In seeking to increase engagement with Noske's concept, Richard Twine (2012) has offered "an initial basic and succinct definition" of the animal industrial complex (with the agriculture placed in brackets to express his specific interests) as:

> a partly opaque and multiple set of networks and relationships between the corporate (agricultural) sector, governments, and public and private science. With economic, cultural, social and affective dimensions it encompasses an extensive range of practices, technologies, images, identities and markets (p. 23).

In challenging the intersection of the military-industrial and animal industrial complexes, the arguments presented here are critical of pro-war and negative peace narratives, alongside those that may be considered as promoting a form of positive peace, albeit without addressing the nonhuman animal question.[1,2] In many ways, this volume provides a number of tools for strategic peacebuilding, exposing questions central to self- and societal-transformation toward a more just society.

Nonhuman animals have had a forced role in human warfare, as with most human-centered activities, for millennia. With a focus on the nonhuman animal question, this book diverges from many critical works on war: the causes of war are not explicitly engaged with here. What are highlighted are some of the horrors in our collective histories, and a possible future seeking to build negative peace as a foundation from which a positive peace can emerge. A central premise of this book is that a vision of a peaceful world is just on one in which there is total liberation: a world where one's gender, ability, sexuality, body, intellect and species are not used to dictate how they are considered. The ontological dualism in the distinction between human and animal is exposed and rejected as a falsehood. This is a world free of structural violence, which is exploitation and violence embedded in the very fabric of a society, where systems, institutions, policies or cultural beliefs can and do meet the needs and rights of some at the expense of others (Schirch, 2004)[3]

Animals and War: Dismantling the Military-Animal Industrial Complex explicitly draws attention to the species boundary, to the ongoing implications of ideologies of dominionism (speciesism and human chauvinism) which enable systematic (structural and direct) violence to be perpetrated against nonhuman animals, to the benefit of the human at the expense of all others. Benefit here is a little dubious a term, as in war there is often little or limited benefit (beyond that to the military-industrial complex). A fundamental aspect of war is dehumanization, the relational construction of someone as *other*. Othering has a long history that extends beyond traditional conceptions of warfare, being central to colonial imperialism, imperialism more generally, some religious doctrines, capitalist economic frameworks and the social world shaped biopolitically in various ways by some and all of these (Foucault, 1988). We use the term biopolitics here to refer to the politics of the body and the politics of the social: the social construction of the biophysical self and its implications. To be positioned as the *other* is to be marginalized as less-than-human, an absent referent, be it based on the color of one's skin, their class, culture, religious persuasion, moral values or more simply their geographic circumstance.[4] This is often akin to positioning the *other* as closer to nature, as we have seen in the history of colonialism and, albeit at times differently, patriarchy (Plumwood, 1993). In being closer to nature, one is positioned as animal-like in a derogatory sense. Such dualistic positioning enables different treatment, a different moral relationship that is counter to a mutually beneficial relationship, a positive peace.

In embracing difference, there is an implicit and explicit rejection of implied negative connotations—rooted in and emerging from species hierarchy constructed on (selective) self-validating human characteristics—as false. Contributors to *Animals and War* embrace that we are all animals, that humans are part of the natural world: one part and not separate from ecosystems however we act counter to ecological integrity. In envisioning positive peace and a means to work toward this, rejection of such constructed hierarchies with an embrace of diversity and connectedness is a foundation from which total liberation can emerge. This is an essential cornerstone for a positive peace-based existence.

In extending the critique of the military-industrial complex, we delineate and position a framework for engaging with and challenging past, present and potential future exploitation of nonhuman animals in warfare. The implications are substantively more far-reaching, and challenge the very fabric of entrenched structural violence in society today. The use of nonhuman animals for human ends is speciesist, and rooted in human chauvinism. Widespread exploitation of the nonhuman animal is a central feature of the animal industrial complex.

Industrial Complexes

Animals and War: Dismantling the Military-Animal Industrial Complex provides an exploration of the linkages between the military-industrial complex, a term that became popular after its use by former president Dwight D. Eisenhower in his January 17, 1961, farewell address, and the animal industrial complex introduced by Barbara Noske (1997) in 1989.[5] To define exactly what we consider to be the military-animal complex, we must first outline and explore the military-industrial and animal industrial complexes.

Carl Boggs (2005) considers the work of C. Wright Mills (1999) as the "most systematic and critical earlier recognition of the implications of the emerging military-industrial complex, providing more nuance and detail missing in many later works" (p. xxii). What is simply described as a war economy is the perpetual preparedness that has become ubiquitous in a number of countries, none other as large as the United States of America (USA). State military institutions and the corporations providing the technologies and weapons of war have become economic and political powerhouses—where they directly shape domestic and foreign policies. Mills was able to see and foresee these implications well before most. For example, according to US government figures, 20 percent of US Gross Domestic Product (GDP) is directed to the Department of Defense (DOD). The actual figure is considered to be much higher.[6] Figures published by the Stockholm Institute for Peace Research for 2010 place the United States of America as comprising 43 percent of the $1630 billion in global military expenditure, significantly more than the remaining top ten countries combined, and six times more than second-placed China (Stockholm International Peace Research Institute [SIPRI], 2010).

Boggs (2005) proposes that *Pentagon system* is a more appropriate term than the more-common permanent war economy, which is an "intricate and vast web of political, bureaucratic, social and international, as well as economic, institutions and processes" (p. 23). Whereas the US military-industrial complex, or Pentagon system, dominates most (Western-centric, and at times more broadly) discussion and critique of militarism, the impacts are more far-reaching and enmeshed in the economies of many countries. As such, we consider military-industrial complex, and *ipso facto*, military-animal industrial complex to be appropriate terminology.

One example of the breadth of the military-animal industrial complex (and the military-industrial complex) is the increasing permeation of Pentagon funds into the academy. Continued support for research funds, the livelihoods and professors and departments, is often tied directly to the militarization of research. For example, funding from the US Defense Advanced Research Projects Agency (DARPA) is much easier to obtain than from any other source. A number of scientists refuse to accept such research funding, adopting principles across the negative peace-positive peace spectrum. Others take what they believe to be an apolitical stance: seeking to remain willfully ignorant of the implications of their work and, in effect, perpetuating the status quo and (indirectly) supporting the war machine (Singer, 2009).[7]

The addiction to militarism and which is war central to the military-industrial complex is only surpassed by the epistemological and ontological normativity of carnism: the ideology, or belief system, that the exploitation of nonhuman animals is natural, ethical and appropriate (Joy, 2010). Carnism, alongside the total commodification of the natural world is central to the modern industrial system (Boggs, 2011). The exploitation of nonhuman animals often goes hand in hand with the exploitation of the racialized human *other*: historically in the exploitation of Aboriginal labor as "inferior" on Australian cattle stations (who routinely received no pay), through to the use of migrant and undocumented workers in dehumanizing and extremely unsafe conditions in slaughterhouses (Broome, 1994; Gouveia & Juska, 2002). Noske (1997) locates the roots of the animal industrial complex with the expansion of Taylorism, the scientific management of labor, to produce the most capitalist-economically efficient processes. What has resulted is an increasing corporate commodification of animal use in the (factory) farming sector. The base principles of Taylorism are to reduce the tasks of an employee to their simplest form, and remove any economically unnecessary elements, crossing into the biopolitical. A direct result of this hyper-reductionism is a deskilling of labor alongside increasingly mechanized processes, rendering workers as infinitely replaceable. The outcome is a normalization of job insecurity, with an associated forced-competitive individualization.

In outlining the process and implications of Taylorist processes, Noske (1997) draws on a Marxist analysis of alienation of both the human workers engaged in the mechanized and routinized slaughter of nonhuman animals, and the nonhuman animals themselves. The alienation of nonhuman animals is rooted in the long history of domestication, or to draw from David Nibert's (2011) work domesecration. Both workers and the commodified nonhuman animals are alienated from the commodities they produce. For the workers, it is the body parts of nonhuman animals. For nonhuman animals, it is their offspring and/both their milk, eggs and other fetishized "products." They are alienated from productive activities: skill and creative capacity for the workers; all activities beyond reproducing *commodities* for nonhuman animals. They are alienated from life and each other (relationships), their own and collective potential—the essence of a rewarding and fulfilling life. And they are alienated from the natural world, constrained by the mechanized (factory) farming operations to which they are imprisoned (Noske, 1997).[8]

Whereas alienation is central to the animal industrial complex, it is also comprised of much more. This alienation is founded upon, drawing from the work of Jaques Ellul, "the totality of methods rationally arrived at and having absolute efficiency ... in every field of human activity" (1990, p. 1). These are comprised and exist across a network (the complex) of relations of corporate and governmental actors and agencies, which are multiply intersecting. What is constructed—and often unmarked, non-considered and unquestioned—is an anthropocentrically justified ideology based on and built around human chauvinism. In other words, drawing from Richard Routely (1973, later Sylvan) and Val Routley (1979, later Plumwood), human chauvinism is the ideological underwriter of "the modern economic-industrial superstructure," of which the animal industrial complex is a key aspect (Routley & Routley, 1979. p. 57). What we directly draw from this is that the military-industrial complex is a military-animal industrial complex. We are not suggesting that a military-industrial complex cannot exist without an animal industrial complex, rather it is foundational and a central feature of the military-industrial complex as it exists today. The exploitation of nonhuman animals is a key feature of war: whether this be direct or indirect uses.

Human Chauvinism

The use of nonhuman animals in warfare, their exploitation, has a long and human chauvinist history. Before we define human chauvinism, it is pertinent to explore the magnitude of this sustained and widespread exploitation of nonhuman animals as discardable and replaceable weapons of war. In *Animals and War* you will find key explorations, engagements and grounded critiques of the use of animals in times of war—as well as what radical post-structuralists such as Michael Hardt and Antonio Negri refer to as the perpetual and "general state of war" in which we exist today (Hardt & Negri, 2004, p. 5). In essence, what we are talking about here is a permanent war economy enmeshed with the military-industrial complex.

Systematically, the majority of people in the West continue to remain strategically ignorant of the horrendous experiments that approximately 10 billion nonhuman animals suffer through every year. To make this figure more comprehensible, this equates to more than 19,000 nonhuman animals per minute.[9] In using the term strategic ignorance, we draw from critical race theory and the valuable work of many scholars on epistemologies of ignorance (Sullivan & Tuana, 2007). As the combination of terms suggest, the vast majority of us are strategically and willfully ignorant of the pain, suffering and murder of these billions of individual nonhuman animals. This has clear benefits for the human, and these benefits are at the root of such ignorance. Being aware of the sheer scale of this exploitation, even for those who embrace human chauvinism, would require some level of reflection as to what level of suffering and murder can be attempted to be justified—and on what terms, if any. Noam Chomsky has referred to such epistemological ignorance as Orwell's problem: "the problem of explaining how we can know so little, given that we have so much evidence" (1987, p. xxv).

Billions of nonhuman animals painfully experimented on every year suffer and die to fuel the coffers of corporate-capitalist interests invested in the military-animal industrial complex. This expanding profit-and-pain-generating industry has a very long history. Unfortunately, it appears to have an ever-increasing present and future. A just and consistent resistance to the exploitative, violent and social destructiveness that is war requires equally tenacious, creative and unrelenting action against the use of all animals—in all forms. *Animals and War*'s focus on the nonhuman animal in no way takes away from the exploitative physical, psychological and social implications of war on the human animal and society more broadly. The engagements presented here add another layer to the expanding and solidly founded critique of all war—a pillar upon which positive peace can and must be founded. As many before us have identified, until we cease the exploitation of nonhuman animals, violence within our own species will continue apace: all species will continue to suffer.

Building on these foundations, we can now explore what it is that human chauvinism exposes and defines. What we are referring to is a form of anthropocentrism that is more insidious than speciesism. The term anthropocentrism is etymologically derived from the ancient Greek term anthrōpos, which is used in prefix form for words relating to humans. Anthropocentrism is human-centerdness, the placing of human interests at the center of thought, with preference ascribed above and at the expense of all else (nonhuman animals and all that encompasses the natural world). It can be very difficult, and some suggest impossible, to fully escape the implications of anthropocentrism. If we accept this inescapability, we can still, and must, locate human interests in the milieu of all interests encompassed by all species and ecosystems. We can do this by reframing our anthropocentrism with an acknowledgment that we are not superior to nonhuman animals, rather we are part of the amalgam of ecosystems in which all species exists. Paralleling this reframing is an awakening to the arbitrariness of the criteria human chauvinism appropriates, in seeking to socially construct a species hierarchy with humans situated above all else. This does not imply a sameness amongst species. Rather, again drawing from scholarship in critical race studies, an acceptance of a shared ecological togetherness in difference (Haggis, 2004).

Speciesism is a term first coined by British psychologist Richard Ryder in 1970, and popularized by Peter Singer's (1975) groundbreaking treatise *Animal Liberation*. Speciesism is an ideology. It is a socially constructed belief system to justify certain actions at the expense of members of other species in much the same way that racism is mobilized by those (socially) positioned as white people. Singer's exposition on speciesism is rooted in a preference utilitarian, or consequentialist, framework. Utilitarianism is most simply described as seeking the greatest good for the greatest number. Actions that tend to maximize good are preferable. Such a framework is consequentialist as these actions have consequences: it is from an awareness of these consequences that the maximization of good can be determined. Of key importance here, harm to animals, human and nonhuman, can be justified if a greater good emerges. Whereas Singer's extrapolation of Ryder's initial ideas were groundbreaking and seen as liberatory for nonhuman animals, the implications of his framework, the permissibility of harm, are considered by many as problematic and inconsistent with interest- or rights-based approaches to the animal question. One root of concerns lies with where demarcation, the line that differentiates justifiable harm under a common, or maximization of the, good, rests. Others have exposed anthropocentric scientific reductionism implicit in calculations about maximization of good and minimization of suffering (Noske, 1997; Routley & Routley, 1979). These concerns, in part, locate the specific applicability of human chauvinism as a combination of terms to describe the long and disastrous history of the exploitation of nonhuman animals at the whim of human desire. The ideological basis for the use of animals very specifically extends beyond species privilege to one of chauvinism.

The combination of the two terms, and the attribution of specific meaning to, human and chauvinism was first undertaken by Richard Routley in 1973, and further explored with Val Routley in their groundbreaking paper "Against the Inevitability of Human Chauvinism" (Routley, 1973; Routley & Routley, 1979; 1980). These ideas were developed during a time of broad and significant reflection on the ecological question, of seeking to reinterpret and challenge the socially and politically constructed notion of human separateness and superiority to the natural world. It was this period that contemporary environmental ethics was born, an ethics that continues to influence ecological and socially just thought and action today. Human chauvinism itself refers to a variant, an extension of, a basic anthropocentrism, in which "humans, or people, come first and everything else a bad last." In this fundamentalist species bias, human interests come first, with actions that harm nonhuman animals (and ecosystems) being morally permissible as long as human (self) interests are not harmed. This extends beyond utilitarian principles, where nonhuman animals are only given consideration pertaining to their interests being aligned with human interests. The distinction is important, perhaps more-so today, given the rise in human-centric notions such as locavore and conscientious omnivore: concern for animals raised for human consumption rest with assuaging guilt (and, at times, the claims of health benefits for those consuming them) and seeking to render one's actions socially acceptable in the wake of increasing awareness of the morally impermissible use of animals (Sanbonmatsu, 2011a, 2011b). In other words, we can consider such actions as an attempt to reclaim a level of strategic ignorance through the reconstruction of a chauvinist species distinction. Such distinctions, once again, seek to identify arbitrary criteria as the point of demarcation and constructions of human superiority.

It is here that we locate the use of nonhuman animals in war, at the foundational level. Nonhuman animals are often used, in a rather disposable fashion, to augment and at times replace humans—be it for menial, dangerous or otherwise undesirable tasks. In *Animals and War* you will find numerous expositions of how disposable nonhuman animals are considered and treated. Examples range from the deployment of dogs as non-consenting and remotely detonated suicide bombers—trained through a denial of food to hide under tanks and other vehicles, through to the wholesale murder of animals exploited for warfare (many of whom have saved countless human lives) at the cessation of violent conflict as it was cheaper than transporting them back to their countries of origin.

The horrific example of "tankdogs" is matched, and exceeded in many ways, in the "imaginative" ideas behind tests carried out during WWII by the Office of Strategic Services (OSS), the predecessor of the Central Intelligence Agency (CIA) in the United States of America. Based on a "suggestion" that cats always land on their feet and will do whatever they can to avoid water, it was hypothesized that strapping bombs to cats would virtually ensure that bombs dropped above ships would hit their targets. The explosive cats, it was argued, would guide the bomb to the deck of the warship below in an act of desperation to avoid landing in water. Tests carried out did not live up to their rationalized outcomes, with cats "even unattached to high explosives ... likely to become unconscious long before a Nazi ship seemed an attractive landing place" (Harris & Paxman, 1983, p. 206).

The emergence of the permanent war economy, what is widely referred to as the military-industrial complex, and the underexplored (until now) military-animal industrial complex are rooted in human chauvinism. Whereas there are historical and contemporary accounts of deep emotional ties between "handlers" and the nonhuman animals they used as tools of war, the hybridization of the nonhuman has increased apace. This has taken form in physical mounting of technological apparatus onto animals from ferrets through to dolphins and seals, haptic feedback technologies that create a linkage between a distant handler and the nonhuman animal as weapon, and direct neural connections of computing devices into the brains of what are essentially neo-Cartesian hybrids—once limited to the realm of science fiction. The amalgam of the military-industrial complex, where profit generation is a rapidly increasingly manifestation, is driving such excursions in human chauvinism and manifests in many different ways. We need not look beyond the phenomenal rise of Private Military Companies (PMCs), deeply rooted in disaster capitalism, to see the economic capitalization on pain and suffering, which is a cornerstone of exploitation—human and nonhuman (Klein, 2008; Scahill, 2008). We must not stop at PMCs, which have become the public face of the privatization of war. The companies that provide the multimillion and multibillion dollar weapons of contemporary warfare have for decades had substantial influence economically and politically both inter- and intra-State. Such companies are a cornerstone of the military-industrial complex, and play a significant role, alongside research institutions, in the normative (pre) formative hybridized biopolitics of the military-animal industrial complex.

Nonhuman Animals and War

The chapters to follow document the use of nonhuman animals in war, ranging from mass historical mobilizations through to more covert operations in contemporary warfare. Roles have included the transport of supplies, the movement of human troops, as messengers, as weapons, for medical "training," and objects of weapons testing. The historical uses of animals are often well known, a small number of uncommon examples aside. Contemporary, trialed, and proposed uses illustrate the extent of human chauvinism and the military-animal industrial complex, and many aspects of the changing nature of warfare. Mechanization in warfare replaced the widespread use of nonhuman animals following World War I, with the use of nonhuman animals becoming increasingly specialized. For example, in the 1980s the US Navy captured and trained dolphins to locate sea mines, expanding on the use of beluga, orca and pilot whales as part of the U.S. Navy Marine Mammal Program. Human chauvinism is explicit in a *National Geographic News* article describing the justification for placing dolphins directly in harm's way, replacing humans: "dolphin's unrivalled underwater sonar abilities, and great intelligence, make them uniquely suitable for locating mines in cluttered shallow-water environments where military electronic hardware is rendered virtually useless" (Pickrell, 2003, March 28, para. 3).

The use of dogs stretch back to the early days of warfare, with them increasingly forced into tasks far removed from natural activities, and continues today. In 2010, there were more than 2800 dogs (referred to as Military Working Dogs, or MWD) in use by the US Army in Iraq and Afghanistan. These dogs can be *deployed* from aircraft and helicopters, including tandem parachute jumps and being thrown by their handlers into the ocean. The US Navy is seeking the development of bulletproof vests for dogs, to further increase their use as weapons of war (Frankel, 2011). Alongside this, the US Marines planned to increase the number of bomb-sniffing dogs to 600 by late 2012, more than doubling the size of the training program established in 2006 (Kovach, 2010). Apparently, the irony of using dogs to detect bombs, after using them as unwitting and nonconsensual suicide bombers (i.e., tankdogs) in WWII, is lost in this new form of exploitation (Biggs, 2008).

The military-animal industrial complex is increasingly adopting genetic engineering to generate profit and produce hybrid nonhuman animals. The K-9 Vapor Wake Detection Program is one example, with dogs genetically manipulated to detect the "scent plume" from explosives (Yager, 2010). This is a neo-Cartesian melding of nonhuman animals with increasingly pervasive technology. On the small-scale, DARPA developed a Hybrid Insect Micro-

Electro-Mechanical Systems program seeking to manufacture insect-cyborgs: "You might recall that Gandalf the friendly wizard in the recent classic *Lord of the Rings* used a moth to call in air support," DARPA program manager Amit Lal said at a symposium in 2007. Later, he said, "this science fiction vision is within the realm of reality" (*Weiss,* 2007, October 9).

Amongst all the research towards building neo-Cartesian Frankesteinian nonhuman animals for human ends, there is a growing awareness of the implications of war on nonhuman animals: both those forced into "service," and those directly and indirectly impacted in other ways. The majority of dogs deployed in Vietnam who were not killed in combat were left behind when Western troops withdrew. Similar situations have emerged in Iraq, with the Society for the Prevention of Cruelty to Animals (SPCA) International successfully organizing a campaign to raise the funds necessary to transport seven "retired" dogs to the United States of America (SPCA International, 2011, March 12). In another example, a Marine bomb-sniffing dog named Gunner was "declared excess" as the effects of Post-Traumatic Stress Disorder (PTSD) manifested themselves. He was adopted by the family of a young soldier who sacrificed his life to save the lives of two other Marines and was awarded the Medal of Honor. After his adoption, the extent of Gunner's injuries became clearer: "even the sight of cameras sent him slinking behind the sofa" (Phillips, 2010, October 6, para. 8).

The story of a young springer spaniel named Theo, deployed in Afghanistan with British troops similarly made headlines. In February 2011 Theo, with his "handler," Lance Corporal Liam Tasker, held the record for finding the most improvised explosive devices (IEDs) and weapons. His tour was subsequently extended. On March 1, Tasker was shot and killed north of Nahr-e-Saraj in Helmand Province. Hours later Theo was the sixth "British Military dog" to die whilst deployed in Afghanistan or Iraq. Different reports attribute Theo's death to a heart attack, seizure, stress and a broken heart (Drury, 2011, March 5).[10] Canine PTSD, first defined in 2010 and emerging in large part due to the contemporary use of dogs in warfare, is increasingly being recognized. Veterinarians are now being taught how to detect it, often with the aim of treating dogs so they can be redeployed into war zones (Dao, 2011; Mendoza, 2010). A catch-22.

The use of nonhuman animals in medical and other testing (vivisection) has long been controversial (Twine, 2010). Similarly, the use of nonhuman animals for combat trauma training courses (for military physicians, surgeons, medics, corpsmen, and infantry) has met significant internal and external resistance. Techniques include the repeated and forced exposure of vervet monkeys to chemical agents, seeking to simulate chemical weapon attacks; the severing of limbs on goats, one after one, to cause severe hemorrhaging; and gunshot wounds, burns and other wounds to pigs. One example, reported in the *New York Times*, details a pig being shot twice in the face with a 9-millimeter pistol, six times with a Kalashnikov (AK-47) assault rifle, and twice with a 12-gauge shotgun. The pig was kept alive for fifteen hours (Chivers, 2006).

On November 11, Remembrance Day (known as Veteran's Day in the United States of America) 2011, the Physicians Committee for Responsible Medicine (PCRM, n.d.) published a letter calling on the United States Congress to draft and enact "legislation that would improve frontline care and end the cruel and unnecessary killing of thousands of animals each year" (para. 2). Opposition is based on the inherent cruelty of the practice, and the efficacy of approaches using human subjects and human analogues over and above nonhuman animals. Our aim here is not to challenge the "effectiveness" of such training, rather to expose the use of nonhuman animals in combat training, a subset of the military-animal industrial complex, as rooted in human chauvinism.

Challenges to the use of nonhuman animals in combat training is having some effect. For example, Doctors Against Animal Experiments (DAAE) Germany became aware of a mid-2010 request by the US Army to use live nonhuman animals in trauma training at Grafenwöhr Training Area (Robson & Kloeckner, 2010). After a call to action, "the Headquarters of the U.S. Army in Germany were flooded with letters and emails from the public," with the US Army withdrawing the application one day later. A subsequent application was denied as the use of nonhuman animals "for the development or testing of arms, ammunition or military equipment are forbidden. In addition animal use in education and training is prohibited, if its purpose can be achieved by non-animal means" (Doctors Against Animal Experiments, 2010). There are legal moves in the United States of America as well. For example, the Battlefield Excellence through Superior Training Practices Act (*aka* Best Practices Act), referred to Committee in November 2011, requires a complete phase-in of human-based methods in combat trauma training courses funded by the Department of Defense. The phase-in is to be immediate for biological and chemical weapon simulations, and by October 1, 2013 for other injury simulations (Lovley, 2010).

There is also the more direct, if widely nonconsidered, impact of war on nonhuman animals who are not a part of the war machine. In his 2010 documentary *The War You Don't See*, renowned journalist, war correspondent and filmmaker John Pilger interviewed independent photojournalist Guy Smallman (Pilger & Lowery, 2010). Smallman recounted the outcome of a 4 May 2009 attack by a $283 million US B-1 Lancer Bomber on Granai in Farah Province, Afghanistan, intentionally coinciding with evening prayer. During the interview, there was a profound moment in which the largely nonconsidered (or reported) impact of industrially deterministic military attacks on nonhuman animals was starkly expressed. Smallman, the first Westerner to witness the carnage after the bombing, recounted: "The first thing that struck me when I was going in there was the silence. The Afghan countryside is usually a symphony of birdsong. And it was absolutely *dead quiet...*"[11] We can look to pictures of battlefields, such as between the trenches in World War's I and II to see the utter devastation of the landscapes and reflect on the wholesale impacts on ecological communities.

Ironically, there are also examples of animals flourishing in post-conflict arenas. The 180 km long (346 square kilometer) United Nations buffer zone in Cyprus and the 250 km by 4km strip of land running across the Korean Peninsula have become refuges for wildlife: "In these enclosed linear enclaves, the negative impact of war and separation has allowed the power of nature to reclaim its original territories, inserting a positive dimension into these landscapes and allowing them to become havens of natural biodiversity" (Grichting, 2007, p. 4). The situation in the Falklands is more tenuous in its positives, and (at least potentially) indicative of implications of (more recent) warfare. It is estimated that over 15,000 land mines, alongside an unknown number of cluster munitions dropped by British forces, remain scattered across at least eighty-three areas. This number represents what is left, following a 2009-10 pilot project near Port Stanley, Port Howard, Fox Bay and Goose Green in which 678 mines were manually removed.[12] The presence of mines has assisted in protecting penguin—including Gentoo, Southern Rockhopper, Magellanic, and King—habitats. The weight of the penguins is apparently too light to set off the mines, and they now congregate in the fenced-off minefields away from humans and other animals (Pearl, 2006).

Facing the Challenge

At the least, the examples of the penguins in the Falklands and the reclamation of demilitarized zones provide a stark illustration of the multiplicitous impacts of war on nonhuman animals, and human chauvinism in the broad sense. The contributions to this volume add to a necessary and critical mosaic, helping to lay the foundation for a stronger intersectional analysis of exploitation and the shift toward a society moving away from war (a negative peace) and the embracing of a positive peace. Examples such as explosive cats and tankdogs seem quite far-fetched, even ridiculous today—not to mention horrific. Yet much of the research, ideology and practice central to the contemporary military-animal industrial complex will similarly be seen as such in the not-to-distant future. History has provided numerous examples of science fiction becoming science fact. Various forms of genetically engineered and hybridized animals are already in existence.

The chapters that follow include the voices of philosophers in critical animal studies, animal activists and antiwar activist-scholars. John Sorenson explores the use of nonhuman animals as vehicles in warfare, engaging with politics of dominionism and processes of commodification that enable such use. The diverse and perverse machinations of human chauvinism are highlighted in breadth of human imagination for exploitation and alienation, highlighting unforseen and even unintended extensions. Sorenson provides a substantive deconstruction of the implications of nonhuman animals as absent referents in the military-animal industrial complex, a common element of the remaining chapters. Contrasting with the use of nonhuman animals as transport Justin Goodman, Shalin Gala and Ian Smith providing an empirically deep and situated engagement with the exploitation of nonhuman animals in U.S. Military Medical Training Exercises. The obstinate hyper-masculine and chauvinist traditionalism in the continued use of animals in medical training earmarked to save lives is counterpoised with a range of internal policy contradictions. The nuance presented, developed through what can only be gained via long-term immersion in challenging the rampant speciesism of the training practices adopted, underscores contradictions within the military-animal industrial complex. Such contradictions extend across techno-industrial capitalism, and directly expose central elements of human chauvinism.

Ana Morrón's chapter shifts from the (more) contemporary examples of the exploitation in U.S. Military Medical Training Exercises presented by Goodman, Gala and Smith to explore the historical use of nonhuman animals as weapons of war. The intersectionality of exploitation across species, reflected on by Sorenson in the construction of the nonhuman animal other, is made evident in the interlinked oppression of nonhuman animals and select humans positioned as inferior (i.e., slave and dog). Morrón similarly illustrates the process in which select nonhuman animals are socially constructed as symbols of status and the role that nonhuman animals have played in changing social structures. Ever-present elements of the use of animals in war are the perceived and actual (anthropocentric) benefits situated alongside what we might consider as dangers. One clear example is of elephants stampeding when frightened, often killing those whom they were trained to support-protect. Whereas such an example may be seen as a fight or flight reaction in the heart of the moment, we must also reflect on such acts as strategic resistance. [13]

Julie Andrzejewski explores the aftermath of the (human) activities of war, drawing direct parallels with the manifestation of colonialism and imperialism. The implications of war on nonhuman animals are exposed through the positioning of nonhuman animals as absent referent, and a further process of indivisiblization: the lives and concerns of nonhuman animals receive little to no consideration whatsoever, being collateral damage in the most extreme and invisible sense of the term. Andrzejewski focuses on longterm, and routinely nonconsidered, effects of war on nonhuman animals, directly exposing the centrality of human chauvinism to the waging of war.

Rajmohan Ramanathapillai provides a contrast with the indivisibility of nonhuman animals, albeit in many ways illustrating nonhuman animals as absent referent. The juxtapositon of nonhuman animals positioned as worthy of worship, valored instruments of war, and fetishized commodities across and within cultures parallels aspects of Sorenson's engagement. Ramanathapillai explores five stages of human and nonhuman relationships, highlighting a shift from sacred status (itself a contradictory, speciesist and human chauvinist construction) to those of exploited (non)lives and absent referents. Drawing the implications of the stages together, he identifies that a positive peace approach to conflict and its transformation has the necessary elements to transcend human chauvinism and associated nonconsideration of all species.

In the final chapter, Bill Hamilton and Elliot Katz provide an at times frightening account on the role of science (fiction and fact) in the past and potential futures with respect to the use of nonhuman animals in war.

Notes

1. For example, David Barash, in *Approaches to Peace: A Reader in Peace Studies*, refers to "the peculiar, complex elephant that is war" (Barash, 2010). Whilst critical of war and promoting approaches to positive peace, Barash's use of a nonhuman animal metaphor, with an elephant derogatorily equated with the scourge of war, is indicative of an effective nonconsideration of the animal question.

2. The term "nonhuman animal" is used, or inferred, through this volume to expose and challenge the socially constructed false binary between human and nonhuman animals. This is a key and at times contradictory element of colonialism and capitalism: the juxtaposition of various classed and "raced" humans as closer to the nonhuman to enable-justify exploitation.

3. Brian Martin (1993) has suggested the term structural exploitation in place of Johan Galtung's notion of structural violence: "The main problem with the expression 'structural violence' is that it adds an enormous burden onto the term violence. Most people think of violence as direct physical violence. For much communication, terms such as exploitation and oppression may be clearer than 'structural violence.'" Whereas, Martin's analysis has broad applicability, the term structural violence has specific relevance here, reflecting that violence (and exploitation) perpetrated against nonhuman animals is normative and enmeshed in the very structure of societies.

4. See Adams (1997) for an engagement with nonhuman animals as absent referents in the specific context of the animal industrial complex, and Adams (2000) for a broader and more detailed engagement.

5. Noske does not include the animal research industry within the animal industrial complex. At the time of writing, the form of animal research industry was not considered profitable enough to be a self-perpetuating complex (Noske,

1997). Here we consider it a key aspect of the military-animal industrial complex.

6. The War Resisters League considers government figures as a distortion, citing 48 percent of US Federal funds diverted to military expenditure in the US Federal budget (including 18 percent on past military activities including veterans' benefits and interest on military spending debt) (War Resisters League, 'Where Your Income Tax Money Really Goes: U.S. Federal Budget 2012 Fiscal Year,' 2011). The Center for Arms Control and Non-Proliferation, in analyzing the proposed 2012 budget, also notes that government figures "do not include nuclear weapons related spending in the Department of Energy (DoE) or other defense related funding" (Olson, 2011a; Olson, 2011b).

7. Alongside increased difficulty in securing research funding, those who do not engage in or refuse to support military-focused research and agendas face broader sanctions. See, for example, Rupert (2010).

8. Lourdes Gouveia and Arunas Juska (Gouveia & Juska, 2002) examine some of the implications of "the fictional distance separating production from consumption" in slaughterhouses, adopting the socially banal term "meatpacking industries." Alongside the implications for undocumented workers, the separation enmeshed in the animal industrial complex further enables the unquestioned normativity and hegemony of carnism.

9. This mind-boggling figure is dwarfed by the number of nonhuman animals killed for human consumption each year: 56 billion (a conservative figure), which translates to 106,000 per minute.

10. See also Celia Haddon (2011): "The surprise is not that a dog can die of a broken heart—as in poor Theo's case—but that so many humans still dismiss the notion of animals expressing emotion as sentimental, anthropomorphic rubbish."

11. Locals expressed to Smallman that 147 people were killed in the attack, an attack based on "false intelligence." Smallman noted over seventy fresh graves in the town, including those in which entire families were buried together. One mass grave, around 30 m across, included the remains of fifty-five people whose bodies were so devastated that their pieces could not be identified. The North Atlantic Treaty Organization (NATO) listed the casualties at twenty-five.

12. See also the United Kingdom's 2011 *article 7* report filed to the United Nations pursuant to the *Ottawa Convention*, also known as the *Convention on the Prohibition of the Use, Stockpiling, Production and Transfer of Anti-Personnel Mines and on their Destruction* (Casey-Maslen, 2009). Controversially, the UK successfully sought to extend its 1 March 2009 mine clearance deadline by ten years in 2008 (Chayer, 2008; Crawford, 2008).

13. We can draw from the empirical detail and engagement presented in Jason Hribal's (2010) *Fear of the Animal Planet: The Hidden History of Animal*

Resistance for a multitude of examples (albeit unrelated to the use of nonhuman animals in war).

CHAPTER ONE

ANIMALS AS VEHICLES OF WAR

John Sorenson

While nothing can match, in terms of sheer numbers, the deliberate savagery that humans have directed against other animals in our determination to exploit them for food, clothing, entertainment and objects for experimentation, the suffering that has been imposed upon them as "collateral damage" in wars directed at others of our own species remains very impressive. Ideologies of speciesism and dominionism and processes of commodification have all shaped the Othering of nonhuman animals. The dualistic thinking that characterizes patriarchal attitudes towards nature have devalued animals (Plumwood, 1993) and have allowed humans to treat other animals as mere things to be used and this is as evident in the context of warfare as it is in our other everyday uses of nonhuman animals. In all of these contexts, we have regarded nonhuman animals as vehicles through which we can obtain our own objectives. In warfare, nonhuman animals have been used as vehicles not only in the direct sense of serving as devices of transport but also in the more general sense as the means by which humans have carried themselves forward into war. Human ingenuity seems limitless in the ways in which we have conscripted other animals to meet our own objectives, giving little thought to theirs. Throughout history we have forced other animals to serve us in our violent pursuits, using them as vehicles of war to propel ourselves onward to ever-greater feats of destruction.

For thousands of years, humans have considered it their "right" to enslave other animals such as buffalo, camels, dogs, donkeys, elephants, horses, mules, and oxen in order to send equipment into battle (Curry, 2003). Prior to the development of mechanized transport, animals were essential to the conduct of war. Without the use of other animals, humans could engage in limited local skirmishes but in order to carry out more extensive campaigns of destruction, animals were necessary to carry soldiers themselves as well as the food and equipment required for their activities. Large, powerful animals provided greater speed and mobility and allowed for the greater elaboration of more sophisticated techniques of attacking and killing other humans. Indeed, throughout history, without the forced conscription of other animals, it would have been impossible for humans to carry out wars as we have known them (Kistler, 2011).

The human imagination seems to have almost no limits when it comes to the exploitation of other animals during wartime. In World War I, soldiers used the light given off by glowworms to send signals or read maps in their trenches (CNN, 2004). Pigeons were pressed into service to carry messages. During World Wars I and II the British alone used hundreds of thousands of pigeons and thirty-two pigeons received the Dickin Medal for their service, which saved many human lives (BBC News, 2009; Daily Mail, 2010). The medal is administered by the People's Dispensary for Sick Animals (PDSA), a charity established in 1917 by Martha Dickin to provide the poor of London's East End with free medical care for their animals and now among the country's largest (PDSA, n.d.). Numerous dogs and horses also received the medal for the work in helping soldiers. More recently, in 2010 the medal was given to a Labrador, Treo, for his work for the Royal Army in locating hidden bombs in Afghanistan (BBC News, 2010).

Larger animals such as camels, elephants and horses have been widely used as mounts for soldiers. Impressed by the remarkable strength and endurance of these animals, humans have not only made them into beasts of burden, but forced them to labor under frightening conditions where they are often deliberately targeted by enemy forces who want to eliminate them precisely because they are so useful. Similarly, the ancient Romans particularly enjoyed abusing elephants in public spectacles of violence, precisely because they were identified with the power of the natural world, and also with human military enemies who used these impressive and terrifying animals. Thus, abusing and dominating elephants symbolized Rome's control of the natural and political world (Shelton, 2006).

Since ancient times, humans have recognized that mounting warriors on animals such as elephants and horses provides enormous advantages of speed and movement for attacks and retreats and for maneuvers against enemy forces on foot. By riding atop such large animals, these mounted soldiers had the advantage of superior height and speed, allowing them to crash through enemy lines, crush their opponents and chase down those who tried to flee. Obviously, a thundering troop of large animals conveyed a sense of overwhelming shock and awe (Gowers, 1947; Rance, 2003; Schafer, 1957).

Elephants have long been used in warfare to attack and frighten enemies (Charles, 2008). Armored elephants were used to drive through enemy defenses and fortifications and they also bore carriages or turrets upon their backs, from which archers could rain down arrows. The turreted elephant has been a symbol of strength since antiquity and the derived elephant and castle symbol has long featured in European iconography, even though elephants were not widely used there in warfare. However, the use of elephants in war is known from ancient India, Sri Lanka, Burma, Cambodia, Thailand as well as Persia, Egypt, The military significance of elephants was clear, and obtaining them became a priority, with far-reaching consequences. For example, Ptolemy II, the king of

Egypt from 284-246 BCE, organized massive hunts for elephants throughout the Horn of Africa at great expense, involving large numbers of soldiers and the establishment of ports and shipyards to transport the captured animals. Along with ivory hunting, this contributed to the depletion of elephants in the region, and led to military operations in Nubia, and clashes with groups who hunted them for food. By the time of his death, Ptolemy had established a powerful elephant corps that was used in several campaigns (Burstein, 2008; Casson, 1993). In some cases, thousands of elephants were mobilized for battles. Doubtless, these attacks were almost as terrifying for their human targets as for the enslaved elephants. However, armies soon developed tactics to resist such attacks, usually involving painful and deadly violence directed at these animals. As cannons and artillery were developed, the use of elephants in battle declined. Nevertheless, elephants continued to be used in battles in Asia during the nineteenth century and, because they can move in areas that mechanized vehicles cannot traverse, they were still used for transporting supplies and military construction projects in the wars of the twentieth century (Kistler, 2007). In order to be put to military use, many elephants have been captured from the wild, which typically has involved abducting young animals after killing their older family members who try to protect them (Begley, 2006). The captives are then subjected to brutal training methods to subdue them and make them obey commands.

In World War I, the German army took Jenny, an elephant imprisoned in the Hagenbeck Zoo in Hamburg, for use as forced labor in France (Wylie, 2008). During World War II, the British army maintained a company of 700 elephants in Burma under the command of Lt. Col. J.H. Williams, who became widely known as "Elephant Bill." Williams later wrote about his experiences and the use of elephants in building the famous Burma Road in his 1954 book *Bandoola*; Williams reported that Bandoola was the first Burmese work elephant raised from birth in captivity and described Bandoola's impressive feats of labor in extracting hundreds of tons of teak from the forests. In 1944 (April 10), *Life* magazine reported on "Elephant Bill" and the use of elephants in Burma by both the British and Japanese military, describing how they were put to work to build bridges and culverts and to transport supplies to troops stationed in areas inaccessible to motorized vehicles or even to horses and mules; previously, these elephants had served as forced labor in the logging industry. In 1942 British tea planter Gyles Mackrell used elephants to transport hundreds of sick and starving refugees fleeing Japanese troops more than 160 kilometers through the jungle and then across the monsoon-flooded Dapha River near the Indian border (Hui, 2010).

The military use of elephants and connections with the logging industry in Burma has continued into the present. In 2010, *The Independent* newspaper reported that Burma's military dictatorship was "desperately" engaged in a hunt for a wild white elephant that had been sighted in 2008 in the western part of the country by an elephant handler working in the timber industry (Kennedy, 2010). Buddhist mythology maintains that a white elephant presented Buddha's mother with a sacred lotus flower before his birth. Throughout southeast Asia white elephants have been considered a sign of power and good fortune; discovering one symbolizes prosperity and indicates that a nation is ruled by wise and good leaders. Recognizing the power of such a symbol, Burma's military leader, Senior General Than Shwe, sent a company of soldiers, elephant handlers and veterinarians to capture the elephant. The military also forced local villagers to work without pay for months searching for the elephant. Another three white elephants had been captured between 2000 and 2002, dressed in full military uniform, were kept at a private temple in Rangoon by the country's previous leader General Khin Nyunt, Secretary One of the State Peace and Development Council. During his rule, hundreds of high-ranking military officers, government officials and wealthy businessmen paid daily visits to the temple but after Khin Nyunt was purged, the visits stopped and the elephants, no longer considered auspicious, were largely ignored. A commemorative stone plaque celebrating Khin Nyunt was replaced by a large photograph of the wife of the new leader General Than Shwe blessing the elephants, accompanied by an inscription reading: "White elephants are only found during the reign of a glorious king. It is an omen that augurs the country's prosperity" (Aung Thet Wine, 2010, p. 7).

Camels have been used for military purposes in arid and rugged conditions. In World War I, the Allied forces created the Imperial Camel Corps to operate in Palestine and the Sinai. Since camels can travel for longer distances without water than horses can, they were considered very useful in desert campaigns. Camels also provided much of the means of transportation during the 1916 Arab Revolt against the Ottoman Turks, especially in the Hejaz campaigns and the capture of Aqaba in 1917 by mounted forces led by Auda abu Tayi and the British officer, T. E. Lawrence. As "Lawrence of Arabia," the latter became a celebrity for his role in these military campaigns and was frequently depicted in Arab dress and mounted on a camel. In the Horn of Africa, the British also used the Somaliland Camel Constabulary against the "Mad Mullah," the anti-imperialist leader Sayyid Muhammad Abd Allah al-Hassan and against the Italians in World War II (Katagiri, 2010; Lawrence, 1997). After World War II, the former Italian colony of Eritrea was federated with Ethiopia instead of receiving independence like other European colonies. During Eritrea's ensuing nationalist struggle, one of the longest wars of the twentieth century, camels and donkeys played a vital role in transporting equipment and supplies, including food aid as famine gripped the Horn of Africa, across the rugged terrain (Last, 2000). The camel's strength and endurance and the essential role this animal played in the history of the Eritrean nationalist movement was explicitly acknowledged in 1993 after independence when the camel was selected as an emblem of the nationalist struggle and, along with an olive wreath to symbolize the achievement of peace, incorporated into the country's coat of arms

(Ghebrehiwet, 1998). Despite such symbolism that recognizes the camel's positive attributes and the animal's importance in the nation's history, Eritrea's beasts of burden endure extremely difficult lives; donkeys, for example, are abused, neglected, receive little veterinary care and are abandoned when no longer useful.

Ancient Egyptians, Greeks, Persians and Romans used dogs in warfare in various ways, often as scouts, sentries and messengers but were also used to haul carts bearing supplies (Lemish, 1996). Dogs were also transformed into weapons themselves: war dogs wore spiked collars and were trained to attack and kill, as exemplified in the savagery of the Spanish invasion of the Americas after the sixteenth century and genocidal assaults on indigenous cultures (Varner & Varner, 1983). In addition to burning people alive, whipping them to death, cutting off arms and legs, the Spanish used dogs to tear people to shreds. Traveling as they did with packs of armored wolfhounds and mastiffs that were raised on a diet of human flesh and were trained to disembowel Indians, the Spanish used the dogs to terrorize slaves and entertain the troops (Stannard, 1992).

During World War II, the Soviets used dogs to carry explosives for use against German tanks. The dogs were first trained to seek and expect to receive food underneath military vehicles. Then they were deliberately starved and, loaded with explosives, were let loose during combat. Seeking food, the dogs ran toward German tanks and the explosives would be detonated as the animals crawled under them (Benedictus, 2011). No doubt, German troops would have quickly recognized this strategy and would have shot dogs on sight to avoid being subjected to any such attacks.

In Iraq, insurgents also used dogs as weapons, loading them with explosives and detonating these as the dogs approached the intended targets and in Afghanistan, donkeys and camels have been used in the same way by the mujahidin against the Russians and the Taliban against the United States (Telegraph, 2005, May 27; Fox News, 2006). The US military deployed over a thousand dogs in Iraq to search out explosive devices planted by insurgents. In the Vietnam war, the US military used thousands of dogs. Many of those animals were killed in combat and those who survived the war also had a grim fate (Ravitz, 2010). The US military ruled that those dogs who had been used in war should not be returned to the United States of America, presumably because they were considered dangerous or diseased, so many of them were killed when the US military withdrew from Vietnam (Lemish, 1996; O'Donnell, 2001). This was a poor reward for their services but not an unusual one: many military forces have considered it too uneconomical to bring animals back from distant regions where they have been forced into service. Considered property, the animals have been disposed of either by killing them or selling them to slaughter.

John Lilly (1996) claims that the US military paid Sandia Corporation to develop a portable nuclear bomb that could be carried by a mule who would be controlled by electrodes implanted in his brain. Using satellites and by stimulating pain or pleasure centers of the brain, the military could steer the mule across enemy territory so that the bomb could be delivered to whichever location the military desired. Lilly also maintains that the CIA and the US Navy used other techniques to train dolphins and killer whales to carry explosives— including nuclear warheads—to enemy ships or to ports located in enemy territory. The navy had been training dolphins since the 1960s and created "warrior dolphins" to attack enemy divers in Vietnam in the early 1970s and in the Persian Gulf in the 1980s; in 2003 the Navy used them for mine-detection in Iraq (Pickrell, 2003).

Horses have been among the most widely used animals in war (Hyland & Skipper, 2010). Almost as soon as horses were domesticated, humans recognized the utility of these animals in helping them to kill their enemies. Horse-drawn chariots were used in warfare in ancient empires such as Assyria, Babylon and Egypt. Alexander the Great used cavalry to conquer Persia and northern India and there were some small cavalry forces used in ancient Greece and Rome although the Roman army relied on its infantry (Greenhalgh, 2010). China incorporated the mounted military tactics of nomadic barbarian armies they encountered and deployed thousands of warriors on horseback (Creel, 1965). Arab armies also used light cavalry in their military conquests. In the thirteenth century, the Mongol army relied on horses for the ability to travel over great distances quickly and outmaneuver European troops, including more heavily armored cavalry (Piggott, 1974; Saunders, 2001). Horses played a vital role in allowing small groups of Spanish soldiers to overthrow the Aztec and Inca empires in the Americas (Diamond, 1997).

The highpoint of Europe's heavy cavalry was in the sixteenth century, before the development of gunpowder weapons led to the greater importance of infantry, although Morillo (1999) argues that it was not technological change that affected the relative significance of cavalry and infantry, but rather political changes and the power of centralized government over wealthy warrior classes. Infantry was cheaper to maintain and could more easily be replaced, whereas it was expensive to maintain heavily armored and trained cavalry. Indeed, the cavalry and the mounted warrior have been seen as markers of elite status in the military because it is expensive to breed and maintain horses. In feudal times, peasant armies might be led by a nobleman on a horse. Cavalry officers have typically come from the upper classes and in some cases were required to pay their own costs in order to maintain their elite status (Morillo, 1999). An exception to this was the "Buffalo Soldiers" of the US Army formed in the nineteenth century (Kenner, 1999; Leckie, 1985; Texas Parks and Wildlife, n.d; Texas State Historical Association, n.d.). These cavalry units were composed of black soldiers who were themselves the targets of racism but who were used extensively in the genocidal "Indian Wars" of 1866-1891, as well as in the Spanish-American War for control of Cuba, the colonial conquest of the Philippines and attacks on Mexico. The Buffalo Soldiers struggled for recognition within a racist society while taking part in the oppression of indigenous peoples. These contradictions continue to reverberate, exemplified by recent controversy over a special Texas license plate intended to recognize the Buffalo Soldiers. Noting that many African-Americans had opposed a Confederate flag license plate because it would remind them of "a legalized system of involuntary servitude, dehumanization, rape and mass murder" Steve Melendez, president of Houston's American Indian Genocide Museum said "I feel the same way about the Buffalo Soldiers. When we see the U.S. Cavalry uniform, we are forced to relive an American holocaust" (Scharrer, 2011, November 26, para. 6). Although his opposition to the cavalry had not prevented him from serving in the US military during the Vietnam war, Melendez was correct in identifying the genocidal character of that institution, exemplified by such notorious atrocities such as the 1864 Sand Creek massacre of Cheyenne and Arapaho by the 1st and 3rd Colorado Calvary led by the fanatical Colonel John Chivington and praised by President Theodore Roosevelt as a "righteous and beneficial act" (Stannard, 1992, p. 134) or the 1890 Wounded Knee massacre of Lakota Sioux by US 7th Calvary.

The cavalry remained important into the late nineteenth century, not only for killing indigenous people abroad but for quelling political dissent among domestic populations as well, as in the case of the 1819 Peterloo massacre in Manchester, where the 15th Hussars attacked citizens calling for parliamentary reform, killing fifteen people and wounding hundreds (Poole, 2006; Read, 1958; Walmsley, 1969). The use of horses remained critical for the military well into the twentieth century. All the warring nations entered World War I with supplies of draft animals and cavalry units. It should have been clear at the outset of this conflict that there had been a revolution in military affairs that had now rendered the cavalry obsolete. The infamous "Charge of the Light Brigade" at Balaclava in 1854 during the Crimean War provided a particularly striking indication: due to errors in military planning, a British cavalry unit had charged straight into Russian artillery fire that tore them to shreds, killing or wounding most of the soldiers and hundreds of horses. Nevertheless, both Britain and Germany actually built up their cavalry forces prior to World War I. Some obstinate traditionalists within the military insisted on the continued importance of the cavalry and a few mounted charges did take place in World War I but the new killing technologies of more advanced rifles and machine guns, along with the system of trench warfare and the extensive use of barbed wire all meant disaster for those who persisted with these now outmoded tactics (Bethune, 1906). Horses were used with some greater success in the Palestine campaign under Field Marshall Allenby against the Turkish forces, such as at the 1917 Battle of Beersheba in which the Australian 4th Light Horse Brigade scored a significant victory, as depicted in the 1987 Australian film *The Lighthorsemen* (Wincer, 1987). However, by the end of the war most cavalry units had been dismounted and transformed into infantry or other troops. Nevertheless, some cavalry units were still deployed in battle even toward the end of the war. For example, in the March 30, 1918 battle of Moreuil Woods in France, the Canadian cavalry of Lord Strathcona's horse regiment was ordered to charge directly into German machine gun positions. As if in a replay of the "Charge of the Light Brigade," the Canadian forces were nearly decimated, although the Germans were eventually driven back through a savage combination of air and artillery attacks as well as hand-to-hand combat (Dube, 2010).

Although the role of the cavalry declined, draft animals continued to play a central role in World War I (Singleton, 1993). While mechanized vehicles were being developed, they were often irrelevant because they could not operate in the vast fields of mud. Military commanders thus considered it essential to use animals (Baillie, 1872; Phillips, 2011). Horses were divided into various categories according to the functions they were forced to serve. Light draft animals were assigned to pull ambulances and wagons while heavy draft animals pulled artillery. Although we do not know for certain how many horses died in transit or on the battlefield, it is evident that huge numbers of animals suffered unimaginable torments because of the war. Many died before they ever reached the battlefield. Rounded up quickly for military service, horses died of harsh treatment and injuries. Some horses were in transit for several weeks and, shipped in tightly packed, filthy conditions and deprived of food and water, many died of disease or exposure. Once they had started their military service, horses could be worked to death. After horses had reached the battlefield, it was often difficult to supply them with food or shelter. These animals were then subjected to a grueling regimen of labor under harsh conditions. Many horses became trapped in the mud and drowned or were shot. Horses and other animals used by the military were subject to all of the same dangers endured by human soldiers, such as from mines, artillery attacks, poison gas, sniper fire and so on, but they were also at additional risk. Knowing that horses were vital to military operations and, indeed, that horses were far more important than common soldiers, each side deliberately targeted the other's animals in order to reduce their opponent's mobility. Thus, the life expectancy of horses in the military was drastically shortened.

This was no exception: animals are often explicitly targeted by military forces not only for food but also because they are seen as a threat. For example, in November 1935, Italian forces invading Ethiopia captured the important caravan town of Makale, and deliberately bombed and machine gunned a camel caravan bringing ammunition and other supplies from the port of Berbera, to what was then British Somaliland to Harrar. More recently, in Eritrea's war for independence, the Ethiopian air force deliberately killed herds of goats and camels to starve the civilian population into submission and to deprive their military enemies of food transport (Human Rights Watch, 1990). In another example of the same pattern, in Vietnam, US forces deliberately killed elephants, bombing them from airplanes because their enemies might use them to transport supplies (Kistler, 2007). Of course, uncounted millions of animals have been killed as "collateral damage" either through bombing or destruction of their habitat. For example, from 1961 to 1969, US forces used chemical and biological weapons extensively in Vietnam, spraying over 100,000 tons of concentrated defoliants and herbicides as well as napalm and cluster bombs across that country as well as through wide areas of Laos and Cambodia, killing huge numbers of animals, human and nonhuman, and destroying the environment (Mydans, 2003; Wilcox, 2011). Similarly, the World Wildlife Fund reported that one result of the US bombing of Afghanistan after 2001 was a huge decrease in the number of migratory birds coming from Siberia and Central Asia to Pakistan and India via Afghanistan (Benham, 2010; Resources News, n.d.). Among the migratory birds affected are flamingos, ducks and cranes, who are very sensitive and will not use a route if they sense danger. War in Afghanistan also contributed to the rise of bird hunting and smuggling there, resulting in greater numbers of insects and mice, who then ate farmers' crops (Behnam 2010). Similarly, the International Snow Leopard Trust (n.d.) expressed its concern that those animals would not survive the bombing conducted across their territories. Once rich in flora and fauna, Afghanistan's environment has been depleted of forests and now offers little to animals.

Many soldiers have described the nightmarish situations they were forced to endure in combat. In many respects, these situations must have been even worse for horses. Horses are sensitive animals, well known for their flight reflexes, and in combat the noise, smells and explosions must have been indescribably frightening. Obviously, humans suffered greatly in these conditions but they could at least understand what was happening around them and some were able to console themselves with thoughts of patriotism, heroism, glory and sacrifice for their nation. Horses had no such consolations but, prevented from escaping, simply had to endure the incomprehensible terrors inflicted upon them.

In wartime, those animals we have forced to work for us as beasts of burden are threatened by even greater dangers than those they normally face. In all wars, animals' lives are cut short by direct violence, overwork, exhaustion, disease and starvation. As more animals are killed, their importance to the war machine becomes all the more apparent and the military forces of embattled nations desperately try to replace them.

For example, during the Civil War in the United States, over a million horses were killed and this created a huge demand for replacements, drawing these animals away from other uses; and in World War I, 8 million horses, donkeys and mules were killed (Battersby, 2012).

Horses, like men, were conscripted by the military and while they had long been considered property, the war intensified their commodification and created higher prices for them. In World War I the demand for horses to be used in warfare led to serious shortages of these animals in significant peacetime activities in agriculture and transportation. As domestic supplies were depleted, European militaries began to purchase horses from other countries. They turned to Argentina, Australia and North America. Governments, industry, and animal dealers all competed for horses, although in North America, specific areas were reserved as purchasing zones for particular European governments. Margaret Derry (2006) describes how warfare shaped the contours of an international market for horses. The resulting shortage of horses for other purposes led the War Department and the Department of Agriculture to push for legislation that would increase and improve breeding operations. As the huge military market expanded into an international industry, breeding, selling, transporting and training horses became major businesses although motives sometimes clashed. Farmers regarded the military as a means to get rid of the horses they didn't want. Animal breeders and dealers saw this as a chance to make huge profits but complained that government purchasers were too selective about the type of animals they purchased and that they did not pay enough for the horses they supplied. Although breeders consistently complained about the prices they received, war provided a further impetus to further breeding of horses and a globalized market. Australian breeders at the time of the Boer War asked if they were breeding the right type of horse to supply the British army's demands for cavalry, mounted infantry and gun horses.

Considering that the Empire spent at least 100,000 pounds on horseflesh in Australia during the war it is well worth the while of Australians to see that they are breeding the right sort of animal to supply this large demand, as no such chance of turning our horses into money is likely to occur in any other way; the Indian market is a steady market; but for wholesale transactions the army is likely to be our best customer, and it is worth our while to try and produce such animals as the army is likely to need. And that introduces the first question, namely, what sort of horses are required? (Australian Light Horse Association, n.d.)

Horses who did not meet military specifications were considered useless and as the demand for horses intensified and breeders scrambled to profit from it, the problem arose of an excess of unsuitable and unwanted horses, especially by the end of the war. For example, although many soldiers wanted to keep the horses they had used in the war, the Australian government insisted on quarantine regulations that made it impossible to repatriate tens of thousands of horses that had been conscripted in World War I, and followed this with an order that all poor quality horses were to be shot and skinned so their hides could be sold for leather (Australian Light Horse Association, n.d. b.). The problem of unwanted horses was solved by the promotion of the slaughterhouse industry and advertising campaigns that praised the tastiness of horseflesh. Government promotion of horse breeding business also contributed to the growth of the recreational equestrian industry. Here we see clearly the flexibility and the utter ruthlessness of the animal-industrial complex: alive or dead, horses, like other animals, were commodities; and there was little recognition of them as individual sentient beings, although some individual soldiers might form emotional bonds with particular animals (*Daily Mail, 2007*).

The breeding and supplying of horses has long been a part of national militarization programs. In 1775, the United States military created its Quartermaster Department to provide horses for the army and to train them. In Europe, the military demand for horses had led to the creation of state-run breeding operations, although the British preferred to leave horse breeding to private entrepreneurs. In 1887 the British had established their Remount Department to create a steady supply of horses by purchasing horses from breeders at fixed prices and in the same year the Commission on Horse Breeding was created to improve production operations to supply horses for the military. In 1899, the Boer War found the British largely unprepared, with poor quality horses and an unreliable supply and the success of their opponents convinced them of the necessity of improving their system of acquiring suitable animals. However, the Remount Department was incompetent and thousands of horses died in transport, due to starvation and filthy conditions. Many of the horses who actually reached their destination did so in severely weakened condition and died soon afterwards; untrained soldiers had no idea of how to treat them and veterinary services were inadequate (Swart, 2010a). During that war, hundreds of thousands of horses were lost to disease, starvation and poor treatment as well as to wounds suffered in battle. The British lost 69 percent of their horses in the Boer War and the Transvaal lost 75 percent of its total horse population (Swart, 2010b) and eyewitnesses described the loss of horses as a "holocaust" (Swart 2010a, p. 349).

The Ottoman sultans had encouraged the breeding of Arabian horses to supply the needs of their cavalry and these horses soon became coveted by the military forces of other nations, which imported them to use in their own breeding programs (Derry, 2006). Governments set up networks of breeding stations and selective breeding policies intended to produce the types of horses they desired. These breeding programs were considered an important part of national defense and military readiness. The military's interest in producing specific types of horses obviously had an impact on the development of these animals over generations as they have been physically shaped by the human desire for war.

Although horses had been essential to the war effort and had been rounded up by the millions to serve in these various roles, at the end of the conflict the survivors were considered a burden. Although a number of military monuments may acknowledge the vital role that these horses played in the war and valorize the idea that these animals, too, engaged in a "sacrifice" of their own interests for those of the nation, it is abundantly clear that the military regarded them as even more expendable and disposable than human soldiers. While the British army did ship some horses to India for further military service there, many of the animals who survived the war, especially those who were in poor health, were shot. Others were sold to slaughterhouses in Europe. Although the United States sold millions of horses to European militaries and used millions when it joined the war, only 200 horses returned there after the war ended (*Daily Mail,* 2007).

It may be imagined that by the end of World War I, animals had been completely replaced by mechanized vehicles but in fact animals continued to serve in important roles. In World War II, huge numbers of horses were forced to work for the militaries of the combatant nations but especially by Germany and Russia, which each used millions. Germany suffered from a lack of oil supplies and used horses extensively for transporting supplies and to maneuver artillery. The military also used horses in some areas that were not accessible by mechanized transport and irregular and guerrilla forces also carried out operations using horses. This has continued into the twenty-first century. For example, US Special Forces used horses to conduct attacks in Afghanistan in 2001 (Quade, 2001; Stanton, 2009). In Sudan, the janjaweed militia are often described as "devils on horseback;" largely drawn from nomadic pastoralist groups, they have launched attacks while mounted on horses and camels against their enemies, resulting in hundreds of thousands of human deaths amidst charges of genocide (Belloni, 2006). Donkeys also have played an important role in contemporary conflicts. For example, in May 2000, Ethiopian troops used thousands of donkeys to launch a decisive offensive in western Eritrea, skirting well-armed Eritrean soldiers in defensive trenches and unexpectedly attacking by a mountainous route, allowing them to drive deeply into Eritrean territory (Last, 2000).

Although horses are no longer used extensively in the military, they are still used for ceremonial purposes by the armies of various nations, serving in military parades, for example, as a means to express statements about power. The very act of riding a horse confers a message of domination and power over the natural world (the horse, after all, must be "broken" in order to be ridden). The horse has been widely viewed as a symbol of power and nobility and riding a horse indicates that one has usurped those qualities and absorbed them into oneself. The powerful image of a man on horseback is a popular theme for military memorials, as if to suggest that, rather than being squalid and savage, war is a noble and aristocratic endeavor. The symbolic transfer of power from horse to rider is seen in such paintings as Anthony van Dyck's Charles I on Horseback (1620) or Jean-Louis David's Napoleon Crossing the Alps (1801), which is believed to be a depiction of Napoleon on his favorite horse, Marengo. Marengo was captured by the British and after he died of natural causes, the military continued to regard his body as a kind of magical power-fetish: his skeleton is on display at London's National Army Museum and one of his hooves was made into a snuff box and given as a trophy to the elite Guard's Brigade (Hamilton, 2000; National Army Museum, 2011).

Similarly, the bones of Traveller, the famous horse ridden by Confederate general Robert E. Lee during the U.S. Civil War, were placed on public display in various venues after his death. The corpse of another famous military horse, Commache, who had been ridden by U.S. Army captain Miles Keogh and who survived the 1876 Battle of Little Big Horn, also was preserved after his death and was placed on display at the University of Kansas Natural History Museum (University of Kansas Natural History Museum, n.d).

Paintings, sculptures and memorials featuring our animal vehicles of war have tended to use them as devices to glorify the exploits of human warriors and build a sense of national identity.

For example, several statues in Australia, along with books, poems, paintings, postage stamps and now Facebook and Youtube, celebrate the efforts of "Simpson and His Donkey." John Simpson (John Simpson Kirkpatrick) was a stretcher-bearer for the Australian and New Zealand Army Corps (ANZAC) at Galipoli in 1915; he used a donkey, Duffy, to carry wounded soldiers away from the front lines for three weeks until he was killed. Simpson and Duffy became important icons as part of the so-called ANZAC Legend, celebrating the virtues of independence, courage, resourcefulness and mateship that are said to define Australian national identity (Australian War Memorial, n.d.; Pearn & Gardner-Medwin, 2003; Tsolidis, 2010).

Similarly, a monument to the Buffalo Soldiers of the US Army at Fort Leavenworth, Kansas, depicts a soldier mounted on horseback and the Buffalo Soldiers National Museum (n.d.) in Houston, Texas, presents their history of imperialist conquest and killing as a gallant and heroic one, while marketing items such as Buffalo Soldier barbecue sauce, to be slathered on the bodies of other dead animals while celebrating American patriotism and militarism. Canadian country singer Corb Lund's album *Horse Soldier! Horse Soldier!* mawkishly romanticizes the military, using the theme of a ghost soldier who rides with Genghis Khan, Napoleon, the anti-Bolshevik White Russian army, Custer's troops at Little Big Horn and US forces in Afghanistan.

Most commemorations of animals in war use them to create pro-military sentiments. For example, during Veterans' Week 2006, the Canadian government's Veterans Affairs Department produced a web-page for children aged 5-10 on "Tales of Animals in War" that portrays a group of happy-looking cartoon animals and feature stories about the brave sacrifices made by various animals who were used by the Canadian armed forces. The stories, such as that of Bonfire the horse who served in World War I helping Canadian Dr. John McCrae, are ostensibly written by other animals who are the relatives of those used in war, presumably as a way of attracting children to the military and instilling patriotic feelings in them. However, in recent years there has been some recognition that animals' own experiences in war must be acknowledged.

For example, in the Czech Republic, a war memorial to animals was erected in 2010 at the site of the 1805 battle of Austerlitz. The monument depicts a riderless horse who has just been shot and is reeling in pain; while this memorial seems to use the image of the riderless horse as a means to comment on the suffering of these other animals, the riderless horse (often with a pair of boots placed backward in the stirrups) is a symbol used at funerals, typically to honor the death of a high-ranking military officer or US president (Kovach, 2008).

In 2004, the Animals in War monument outside Hyde Park in London was created by the English sculptor David Backhouse. The monument includes two life-sized bronze mules carrying supplies, as well as statues of a horse and a dog and bas-relief carvings of other animals such as camels, elephants and birds who have been used in warfare. The inscription reads: "Animals in War. This monument is dedicated to all the animals that served and died alongside British and allied forces in wars and campaigns throughout time. They had no choice." Jonathan Burt (2006) objects to the memorial, writing that the inscription is "wholly inappropriate" to describe the situation of animals in war because "choice, with its all-too-human connotations of individualism and consumption, is not a word one would use for animals, even when they act freely, and it raises disconcerting questions about whether some beings are more deserving of sympathy than others" (pp. 70-71). But Burt is surely wrong in his complaint: animals are individuals and choice is not something limited to consumerist decisions. Recent findings in cognitive ethology (e.g., Balcombe, 2010; Bekoff & Pierce, 2010; Peterson, 2011) suggest that Burt's view of other animals' consciousness is too limited. Burt does not clarify why he thinks animals do not make choices when they act freely but it is certain that the animals commemorated in the memorial were forced into war, which is the obvious meaning behind the statement that "they had no choice." It is indeed the case that many humans, especially those who are poor and powerless, are also victimized by war but many others, eager to kill for excitement, glory or loot, willingly participate or fail to resist. Burt's misplaced alarm that the monument might suggest that "some beings are more deserving of sympathy than others" seems to reflect his anxiety that the suffering of other animals might be given anything like the sympathy we claim to have for humans killed in war. Similar complaints followed the release of Steven Spielberg's (2011) film *War Horse*, based on Michael Murpurgo's (2010) book of the same name, which depicted some of the horrors inflicted on horses in World War I. For example, reviewer Kevin Martinez (2012) complained "are there not greater tragedies taking place in the world that should be explored?" In reality, these sympathies for other animals that seem to so trouble many people are usually subordinated to practical needs. For example, one model for the *War Horse* film was Warrior, who was sent to war in 1914 with his owner, General Jack Seeley. Both survived and Warrior was considered a hero but rather than being memorialized upon his death in 1941 his body was used for meat during World War II (Battersby, 2012).

In fact, this seems to be another version of the standard speciesist response used to delegitimize animal advocacy: "You care more about animals than you do about people," delivered as if to suggest that such concerns must be mutually exclusive. The monument's inscription accurately captures the fact that animals have always been forced to serve as vehicles for human wars and that they are indeed worthy not only of our profound sympathy for their plight but also our efforts to relieve them.

For thousands of years, nonhuman animals have been forced to carry human soldiers, transport supplies and build infrastructure but they have been vehicles of war in more than just the literal sense of the term. Mechanization and sophisticated technology that facilitates long-distance killing has reduced our dependence on other animals for transportation and labor but we still use them in numerous ways to carry ourselves into war and achieve our violent objectives.

We use animals to test our weapons and to harden ourselves for killing. The US military alone uses hundreds of thousands of animals every year in its medical training programs, subjecting them to gunshot wounds, stabbings, burns, radiation and poisonings. While these experiments cause extreme suffering, the military typically does not provide medication to alleviate pain. Military research also includes the development of biological weapons and thousands of animals are deliberately infected with parasites, diseases and a wide range of deadly viruses. In addition to such direct physical abuse, the military also conducts other forms of research on animals such as sleep deprivation studies, exposure to excessive noise and hypothermia (Department of Defense, 2003). In all of these experiments, animals are victimized in order to perfect more effective ways of killing other humans, although the military justifies such experiments on the grounds of defense and treatment against weapons developed by enemies. However, it is clear that the military is interested in creating more effective weapons, many of which will be used against civilian populations. For example, the American Anti-Vivisection Society (AAVS) reported in 2003 that the United States Naval Board was testing Pulsed Energy Projectiles on animals to determine how effective such weapons were in creating excruciating pain and temporary paralysis in those targeted; the AAVS noted that these weapons were being developed for crowd control purposes.

Despite rhetoric from the vivisection industry about its dedication to finding alternatives, animal testing, including military research, is increasing. In 2006 *The Independent* reported that British military testing on animals had doubled during the previous five years (Woolf, 2006) and the *Daily Mail* (2011, July 14) reported a "huge rise in vivisection" with 3.7 million experiments per year being conducted on animals in the U.K. As is the case with corporate vivisection, many of the military experiments are redundant, repeating tests that have been done already. Tens of thousands of animals were subjected to biological and chemical warfare experiments. *The Independent* (Woolf 2006) reported that "monkeys in the secret Wiltshire military labs have been exposed to anthrax. Pigs have had 40 per cent of their blood drained and been injected with E coli. Others have been exposed to poison gas and lethal nerve agents. *Porton Down* has in the past shot anaesthetised pigs to help develop body armour." The British Union for the Abolition of Vivisection reported that the experiments involved such things as "chemical agent-induced burns left for days, poison gas experiments, applying fatal doses of nerve agent to animals' skins and monkeys given sarin and anthrax" and demanded for details of these experiments to be made public (Woolf, 2006). Unsurprisingly, the government and military representatives refused to provide this information and claimed that the experiments were done to develop forms of treatment.

Other forms of animal experimentation have been useful to the military. For example, psychologist Martin Seligman is notorious for his experiments in the 1960s in which he psychologically destroyed caged dogs by repeatedly subjecting them to electric shocks without hope of escape. The dogs were reduced to a condition that Seligman called "learned helplessness" (p. 407) and would not even try to escape further pain when the cage door was left open. Under the Bush II presidency, Seligman's research proved attractive for CIA and military interrogations and torture of prisoners in the so-called *War On Terror* (Allen & Raymond, 2010). According to a 2009 report from the Justice Department's Office of Professional Responsibility, "the express goal of the CIA interrogation program was to induce a state of 'learned helplessness'" (Benjamin, 2010, para. 8). Although Seligman denied that he condoned the use of torture, he was involved at the inception of the Survival, Evasion, Resistance and Escape program to train US soldiers to resist torture and was associated with a group of psychologists who agreed to reverse-engineer these training methods into interrogation techniques. In 2010 the US Army awarded Seligman a non-competitive $31 million contract to conduct training to help soldiers cope with the stress of war (Physicians for Human Rights, 2010).

In addition to using animals to develop new weapons and treatments that will allow soldiers to carry out their missions, the military also uses animals to encourage a warlike state of mind. By encouraging cruelty to animals, the military is able to produce more efficient killers who will feel less compunction about attacking other humans. For example, in Nazi Germany, elite SS soldiers were each assigned a German Shepherd dog during their training; after twelve weeks of working closely with them, the soldiers were required to break their dogs' necks in front of their commanding officers as a demonstration that they had acquired the necessary qualities of discipline and obedience (Arluke & Hafferty 1996). In 2002, the World Society for the Protection of Animals released videos it had obtained of the "bravery" tests given to Peruvian army cadets. Video taken at Otorongo Command Group 125 showed dogs tied up between two poles, unable to move; each cadet charged forward and stabbed the dog, some doing so repeatedly. The *Sunday Times* reported:

Once the animal is dead, its [sic] flesh is ripped apart and the soldiers pull out its [sic] heart and drink its [sic] blood ... Finally, one of the soldiers is selected to perform a "lap of honour" around the training ground with the lifeless animal draped around his neck like a medal. The *Times* noted that the objective of the exercise was to transform humans "into ruthless killing machines who relish the sight of blood" (Kirkham, 2002, December 15). These squalid scenes provide a clear example of how nonhuman animals are used as vehicles to drive humans into depravity.

As well as using direct violence against other animals as a means to make humans more violent, the military mentality is created through the symbolic use of animals. To encourage soldiers to kill people, it is useful to dehumanize or animalize the enemy. Just as animal images are used consistently in racist discourse, we see demeaning animal images encouraged by the military (where we also typically find racist discourse): enemies are described as dogs, vermin, lice, rats, monkeys, etcetera in order to create hatred toward them and to conceptualize them as being unworthy of ethical consideration. Here we can clearly see not only the devaluation of nature but also that the ideologies of dominionism and speciesism have negative effects on humans as well as other animals. The devaluation of other forms of life and the creation of hierarchies is an open invitation to move other humans into those "inferior" categories and to treat them accordingly.

Our assertion that nonhuman animals exist only as property has allowed us to exploit them in countless ways. Ideologies of speciesism and militarism have allowed us to transform nonhuman animals into our vehicles of war. Under our assumed "right" to do as we please with them, we have consigned uncounted millions of other animals to terror without end as we have used them as means to improve our chances of killing ever-greater numbers of our fellow humans. Recently and to a small degree, we have acknowledged their suffering in our wars through public memorials which recognize that "they had no choice" but it is only through a combined anti-militaristic, anti-speciesist stance, one that takes seriously an animal rights approach, that we will prevent such suffering in the future.

CHAPTER TWO

FRONT TOWARD ANIMALS: ANIMAL EXPLOITATION IN U.S. MILITARY MEDICAL TRAINING EXERCISES

Justin R. Goodman, Shalin G. Gala and Ian E. Smith

Upon returning home from Vietnam, Sergeant Joe Bangert testified about his experiences serving in the military at a hearing organized by Vietnam Veterans Against the War. The focus of the Winter Soldier hearings, as they were called, was to document atrocities and war crimes committed by the U.S. military against the people of Vietnam. In addition to crimes committed against the Vietnamese, Bangert relayed a startling experience that occurred before he was shipped overseas: the rabbit lesson.

The rabbit lesson, according to Bangert, consisted of a talk about evasive maneuvers and survival in a jungle environment. This presentation was given while the speaker was holding a live rabbit to whom the audience of inexperienced soldiers gradually grew attached. At the conclusion of the talk, the officer takes the rabbit and, "they kill it, and they skin it, and they play with the organs as if it's trash, and they throw the organs all over the place" (Winterfilm Collective & Lesser, 2008). The next day Bangert was sent from Camp Pendleton to Vietnam where he would see similar cruelties carried out on other humans.

Sadly, the shameful legacy of the rabbit lesson has lived on.

In what may be called the dog lesson, as recently as 2008, Bolivian military forces would slice open yelping, fully conscious dogs with knives and remove their hearts. In video of these training sessions that surfaced on the Internet, soldiers are seen laughing and cheering while less enthusiastic soldiers are ridiculed and taunted (People for the Ethical Treatment of Animals [PETA], n.d.). A commanding officer is seen holding a freshly severed dog's heart and demanding that soldiers literally bite into the organ as he smears its blood into their faces. A Bolivian soldier has stated that the Bolivian School of Condors began the dog lesson at the school's creation in the early 1980s when several instructors "received scholarships at the most prestigious courses for Special Forces in America" (Dubcovsky, personal communication, February 23, 2009). This training partnership is corroborated by a written memorandum signed by the two countries in 1967 (Bolivian Army, 1967, April 28). International outcry following the release of these videos by PETA in 2009 led the Bolivian Minister of Defense to approve Resolution 217 banning the military from harming and killing nonhuman animals in training exercises (La Prensa, 2009, March 31).

While Bolivia took swift and decisive action to end what it deemed unjustifiable cruelty, the United States has sadly not followed suit. Though it no longer offers the rabbit lesson—which is apt to be described as gratuitous violence or a military excess that does not serve what can be claimed as a legitimate function—the U.S. military continues to stab, dismember, shoot, burn, and otherwise maim and kill nonhuman animals under the guise of "medical" training even though, as we will discuss, the practice has demonstrated limited benefit for the actual treatment of injured soldiers and demonstrably superior non-animal training methods like high-fidelity human patient simulators are available. For example, a recent survey found that 22 of 28 member nations of the North Atlantic Treaty Organization (NATO) do not use any nonhuman animals for military medical training purposes (Gala et al., 2012).

The continued use of nonhuman animals for these purposes also appears to violate U.S. Department of Defense animal welfare regulations that state, "Alternative methods to the use of animals must be considered *and used* [emphasis added] if such alternatives produce scientifically valid or equivalent results to attain the research, education, training, and testing objectives" (U.S. Department of the Army, Navy, Air Force, Defense Advanced Research Projects Agency, & Uniformed Services University of the Health Sciences, 2005, p. 2). Yet, the U.S. military has continually refused to enforce this regulation despite petitioning from veterans, physicians, animal protection organizations, the general public and members of Congress.

Because medical training is clearly of vital importance many people see the abuse of nonhuman animals in that context as a "necessary evil," and the perceived necessity of the practice has allowed it to evade the kind of outrage sparked by Bolivia's dog lesson. In reality, the harm done to nonhuman animals under the pretext of military medical training is only superficially different than the senseless atrocities of the rabbit and dog lessons. Like these lessons, the nonhuman animal abuse that passes for medical training in the United States of America is mainly intended to initiate soldiers into a culture of violence, callousness and hyper-masculinity, rather than providing the most effective means of imparting vital medical skills.

While ethical concerns alone are certainly more than sufficient to justify ending the military's exploitation of nonhuman animals, regardless of any hypothetical benefits to the armed forces, this article will challenge the suggestion that this training is "necessary" from a scientific and educational perspective, and deconstruct some of the many unsatisfactory justifications the U.S. military has provided in defense of its abuse of nonhuman animals. Further, it documents the complicated web of relationships between the military, private contractors, the public-at-large, the media and animal rights activists, and how military policy and practice regarding the exploitation of animals is challenged and shaped by these various interactions.

"Live Tissue Training"

Since the 1950s, the U.S. Department of Defense has operated what used to be known as "wound labs" to train medics and soldiers how to treat traumatic injuries in humans (Barnard, 1986, p. 5). In these exercises, nonhuman animals who are sometimes conscious or semiconscious—at one time, dogs were the species of choice—are inflicted with serious traumatic injuries and then trainees are ordered to repair those wounds as if they were attending to fallen soldiers on the battlefield. According to the *Associated Press* (1984, January 24), in a response to public pressure in 1983, then-U.S. Secretary of Defense Caspar Weinberger ordered an end to all procedures in which nonhuman animals were, "shot in experiments related to research or training on wound treatment" (para. 4); however, in 1984, then-U.S. Assistant Secretary of Defense for Health Affairs William Mayer replaced this policy with a watered-down directive that only excluded the use of dogs and cats, thereby allowing the continued use of goats and pigs for what the U.S. military now calls "live tissue training," in which these nonhuman animals are shot, burned, mutilated, and killed.

In 2008, at least 7,500 nonhuman animals of eight different species were used for a diversity of U.S. military medical training exercises by the Department of Defense (Foster, Embrey, & Smith, 2009, p. 4). Independent research by the Physicians Committee for Responsible Medicine ([PCRM], n.d.) puts this number much higher, finding that a minimum of 15 U.S. military bases and at least 3 privately owned U.S. training contractors use and kill nearly 9,000 pigs and goats each year just in live tissue training exercises, which is now a pre-deployment requirement for all U.S. military medical providers.

Documents obtained from the U.S. military and its private training contractors through the U.S. Freedom of Information Act (FOIA), along with insider witness accounts, reveal that during live tissue training nonhuman animals are burned, shot with firearms, stabbed with knives, have bones broken with bolt cutters, and may even be dismembered with metal gardening shears. In 2006 (November 2), the *New York Times* quoted U.S. Navy corpsman and trauma medic Dustin Kirby whose trauma training experience included severely mutilating a pig: "They shot him twice in the face with a 9-millimeter pistol, and then six times with an AK-47, and then twice with a 12-gauge shotgun. And then he was set on fire" (Chivers, 2006, para. 35). Kirby indicated that the pig lived for fifteen hours after these wounds were inflicted before dying.

In the live tissue training protocol created and used by Tier 1 Group (2008), an Arkansas-based company that is operated by former military personnel and owned by Cerberus Capital Management—an international investment firm that counts former treasury secretary John Snow and former vice president Dan Quayle as employees, owns defense contractor DynCorp International Inc. and formed the Freedom Group to gobble up ammunition companies like Remington Arms—conducts exercises for the U.S. military, the company reveals that pigs and goats, the latter of whom are chosen for this abuse because of their "traits of gentleness, ease in handling and transport, intelligence, friendliness, cleanliness, and hardiness" (p. 4), are forced to endure the following violence in military medical training exercises: "[g]unshot wound may be inflicted to the extremities, face, thorax, or abdomen"; "limb is fractured using a blunt wounding tool, gunshot wound, or blast injury;" "limb is traumatically amputated by utilizing a sharp edge of the wounding tool or blast injury model"; "animal models may receive actual burns to not more than 20 percent of body surface or airway using propane torch"; "[c]ommon objects (sticks, metal rods, etc.) may be implanted abdominally or in muscle to simulate impalement"; "lacerations may be created over any portion of the skin"; and, "large vessels…may be lacerated…to induce massive hemorrhage" (pp. 11-16).

And without a hint of irony, Tier 1 Group concludes the list of ways detailing how pigs and goats may be mutilated with a sentence in bold font, stating: "The utmost care must be exercised to insure [*sic*] the safety of both the animal model and the wounder" (2008, p. 16).

In 2012, PETA released disturbing video taken by a whistleblower during a live tissue training session conducted by Tier 1 Group for members of the U.S. Coast Guard showing live goats who were repeatedly stabbed with scalpels, had their limbs cut off with tree trimmers, and shot (Aegerter & Bolack, 2012, April 19). In the footage, the goats moaned and kicked during the mutilations—signs that they had not received adequate anesthesia. One instructor is even heard cheerfully whistling as he cuts off goats' legs, and a Coast Guard participant callously jokes about writing songs about mutilating the animals. Following an official complaint from PETA, the U. S. Department of Agriculture cited Tier 1 Group for violating the federal Animal Welfare Act for failing to provide adequate anesthesia to the goats depicted in the video (Kimberlin, 2012, June 30).

Like many U.S. military facilities themselves have done, Tier 1 Group claims in its live tissue training protocol that, "Total replacement [of animals] is not feasible" (2008, p. 6). In truth, some U.S. military facilities and contractors have already completely replaced their use of nonhuman animals for trauma training with simulators, cadavers and other non-animal methods.

The U.S. Army's Alfred V. Rascon School of Combat Medicine at Fort Campbell uses only non-animal training methods and quotes the base's spokesperson, Cathy Grambling, as publicly stating: "Training on dummies is more realistic to providing care for a person than training on animals" (Hogsed, 2010, January 20 para. 5). The Department of the Navy (personal communication, December 19, 2008) and the Department of the Air Force (FOIA 08-0051-HS, August 28, 2008) have also confirmed that the U.S. Navy Trauma Training Center and the U.S. Air Force Expeditionary Medical Skills Institute's Center for Sustainment of Trauma and Readiness Skills, respectively, do not use nonhuman animals in their trauma training programs. The U.S. Department of Agriculture (memo, 2010, July 29) also reports that Tactical Medics International, a private contractor that provides live tissue training for Camp Lejeune—the largest U.S. Marine Corps base on the East Coast—no longer uses nonhuman animals in its Tactical Combat and Casualty Care (TCCC) course, which is the most widely offered trauma training course in the military; yet, other U.S. military bases and contractors continue to use nonhuman animals for this course.

The U.S. military has explained its lack of medical training harmonization as follows:

> The decision to use animals is autonomous and based frequently on the medical training officer or physician tasked with conducting the training ... Senior leadership is frequently not aware of what is being trained or how it is being trained. (Foster, Embrey & Smith, 2009, p. 6)

Regardless of the reasoning behind these inconsistencies, it is in cases such as this, where the U.S. military largely uses antiquated animal-based medical training methods while several U.S. installations and the overwhelming majority of U.S. military allies use only modern animal-free methods, that U.S. military claims of the "necessity" of nonhuman animal use to teach these medical skills quickly become transparently false.

Indeed, peer-reviewed research studies have repeatedly demonstrated that high-tech human simulators, human cadavers and other non-animal methods are equivalent or superior to the use of live nonhuman animals for training medical professionals to perform lifesaving procedures, including the vital trauma treatment methods that military medics are currently trained to perform (Aboud, et al., 2011; Bowyer, Liu, & Bonar, 2005; Block, Lottenberg, Flint, Jakobsen, & Liebnitzky, 2002; Hall, 2011). This is because simulation models—unlike animals—offer accurate anatomy, repeatability, and objective feedback and assessment (Ritter & Bowyer, 2005). Most importantly, simulators impart skills that have been proven to transfer directly to the treatment of human patients.

Since 2001, the American College of Surgeons (ACS) has approved the use of simulators to replace nonhuman animals in the most widely offered civilian trauma training course, Advanced Trauma Life Support (ATLS) (Cherry & Ali,

2008, p. 1189), which covers many of the surgical skills central to the U.S. military's TCCC course. A Physicians Committee for Responsible Medicine (2011a) survey found that more than 95 percent of U.S. and Canadian facilities teaching ATLS use exclusively non-animal methods—mainly human patient simulators and human cadavers—to teach these skills to physicians, emergency first responders and others. Even the U.S. military uses simulators to teach ATLS on many of its bases, while continuing to harm nonhuman animals to teach the same skills in other courses.

The response from the U.S. military to the availability of non-animal models for trauma training has frequently been that they do not have the luxury of providing several years of education as is provided to medical school students and other medical professionals, hence the purported need for using nonhuman animals. In reality, few military medical professionals need an education on par with that provided at medical schools; most are medics who need to be able to stabilize a wounded soldier until treatment can be provided. Further, using nonhuman animals who possess a radically different anatomy and physiology from humans does not represent a shortcut to competence, and it does not allow the military to achieve medical school quality results in a fraction of the time. For military personnel who do need an advanced medical education there will be no substitute for clinical experience. For those who do need accelerated preparation for the battlefield, there are more effective and ethical avenues to achieve this than cutting, shooting and blowing up animals. The Israeli Defense Force has developed a simulation- and scenario-based curriculum for rapidly preparing reserve military medical teams for deployment that participants have found to be extremely realistic and, after deployment, have expressed that it improved their ability to treat patients in real life settings (Lin et al., 2003). These Israeli researchers explicitly noted that the use of nonhuman animals for this training is not suitable "for diagnosis and decision-making" (p. 52).

U.S. military medical training experts have also noted that using nonhuman animals is "inadequate for combat training" (Allen, 2010, p. 15). The U.S. Medicine Institute for Health Studies (2002) published a transcript of a forum attended by various U.S. military medical training experts, such as the National Capital Area Simulation Center's Dr. Alan Liu who notes:

> [Animal laboratories are] not really a very good method [for medical training]. Animals obviously have the wrong anatomy... If you train with animals all day long, at the end of the day you become very good at saving goats and pigs. You haven't saved your first human yet. (U.S. Medicine Institute for Health Studies, 2002, December 3, p. 32)

Other military medical experts have raised similar criticisms, stating:

> Problems with [animal use for hemorrhage treatment training] are multiple and include differences in anatomy, differences in the force required on the tourniquet to arrest bleeding, ethical concerns for the animals, and lack of

repeatable training as erroneous management frequently results in death of the animal. (Ritter & Bowyer, 2005, p. 230).

During a panel discussion about appropriate medical responses to battlefield injuries, Dr. Craig Llewellyn, a retired U.S. Army surgeon, professor and former Chair of the Department of Military and Emergency Medicine at Uniformed Services University of the Health Sciences criticized what he called a "myth" about military medical training (as cited in Butler, Hagmann & Richards, 2000). He stated, "It is absolutely crazy to presume that if your medic training has involved a goat lab that you are prepared to open one of your team member's bellies if there is no opportunity to get him to surgery" (p.37).

Conversely, U.S. military research using simulators has found that non-animal training methods can effectively teach hemorrhage control and improve treatment times (Mabry, 2005). Simulation offers a less stressful learning environment that allows trainees to hone psychomotor skills without the risk of harming an animal. Once basic technical skill has been acquired, real life scenarios that generate anxiety and stress can be simulated and realistic stress reactions can be induced to help trainees develop the decision-making and stress management skills necessary for successful performance in a combat environment (Lin, et al., 2003). Oddly, while great detail is taken in replicating realistic environments for training sessions including accounting for realistic sounds and even smells that would be present on the battlefield, the use of nonhuman animals has not been entirely eliminated. To adequately induce emotions it would be preferable that a manikin with human form be used rather than a pig or a goat. The presence of nonhuman animals serves as the most glaring reminder that the environment is staged.

Live tissue training continues to draw the ire of the public and criticism from government officials in the United States of America and abroad. Animal protection and medical ethics organizations, chief among them PETA and PCRM, respectively, have ongoing campaigns aimed at ending the U.S. military's use of nonhuman animals in its medical training programs.

In 2009 and 2011, more than thirty members of U.S. Congress introduced and cosponsored the Battlefield Excellence through Superior Training (BEST) Practices Act, which aims to phase out the Department of Defense's use of nonhuman animals in combat trauma training by 2016 (Filner, 2011, April 8; Lovley, 2010, February 3).

There have also been protests abroad against the U.S. military's use of nonhuman animals in medical training. In 2010, after substantial campaigning from PETA Germany and Ärzte gegen Tierversuche (Doctors Against Animal Experiments Germany), government officials in Germany denied several U.S. Army Europe (USAREUR) applications to conduct live tissue training exercises on nonhuman animals, stating that the procedures would "violate host nation animal protection laws" because "effective alternatives to animals are available" (Vandiver & Kloecker, 2010, August 17, para. 1-2). The German military informed PETA that "the armed forces do no animal tests for training purposes. For training exercises the soldiers learn with really good models and the doctors don't need animal experiments" (German Armed Forces, personal communication, June 18, 2010).

And in records obtained by PETA through FOIA, in 2010, the office of the U.S. Army Europe Command Surgeon (internal memo, 2010) issued an action in response to volcanic activity in Europe that forced the temporary cancellation of a live tissue-based Brigade Combat Team Trauma Training for Army medics in Germany, stating that "we have the resources and experience within USAREUR to conduct a combat trauma training course (no live tissue)," thereby exercising U.S. Army Executive Order 096-09 that allows for the omission of animal use in live tissue training at foreign installations (U.S. Army Medical Department, Office of the Surgeon General, 2009, para. 3B [7][U]). This policy and decision further underscore that the objectives of the medical trauma training can, in fact, be met without the use of nonhuman animals.

Chemical Casualty Training

Although U.S. military animal welfare regulations specifically prohibit the use of nonhuman primates for "[i]nflicting wounds with any type of weapon(s) to conduct training in surgical or other medical treatment procedures" (U.S. Department of the Army, Navy, Air Force, Defense Advanced Research Projects Agency, and Uniformed Services University of the Health Sciences, 2005, p. 3), the U.S. Army Medical Research Institute of Chemical Defense (2005a), until recently, poisoned dozens of vervet monkeys as many as four times each per year for three years in a chemical casualty training laboratory for military medical staff at Aberdeen Proving Ground. During this training exercise, monkeys were injected with a toxic overdose of the drug physostigmine, which was for all intents and purposes being used as a chemical weapon and intended to simulate the symptoms a human would suffer in the case of a nerve agent attack. Monkeys receiving this drug overdose would experience uncontrollable muscle twitching, difficulty breathing, irregular heartbeat, and violent seizures. The monkeys would try to vomit but could only retch incessantly because they had been starved the day before. According to a laboratory exercise worksheet obtained by PETA through FOIA, a U.S. Army medic compared a monkey's apparently agonizing reaction during the exercise to "a chiwawa [sic] shitting razor blades" (U.S. Army Medical Research Institute of Chemical Defense, 2005b).

A U.S. Department of Defense-produced video of this chemical casualty exercise that was released through FOIA and made available online by the Physicians Committee for Responsible Medicine (2009) shows the procedure and the narration details the clinical signs that trainees are instructed to observe and identify. In the video, a vervet monkey with a shaved abdomen and bearing a tattooed number on his chest is tied to a tabletop. That trainees were instructed to note the rigidity of the monkey's tail is only the most glaring example of how lessons learned on a monkey are clearly not relevant to any training focused on human patients. Trainees are further instructed to check for perspiration but in the case of a monkey this must be done by swabbing the animal's paws. Highlighting the sheer uselessness of the laboratory, the students do not do anything except administer an antidote and watch the monkeys' symptoms subside. The whole event is a crude "show and tell" exercise and persisted at Aberdeen even though every other U.S. military training facility in the world already used only non-animal methods like human patient simulators, human actors and computer programs to complete the same training.

In the Fall of 2011, information surfaced indicating that twenty monkeys were being transported from the island of St. Kitts to Aberdeen Proving Ground to replace monkeys whose three years in this training course was expiring. While organizations like PETA and PCRM had been actively campaigning against this laboratory for more than five years, the news of this monkey shipment gave the effort a new sense of urgency. Numerous complaints were filed with the U.S. Department of Defense, an aggressive media campaign was launched and activists flooded army offices with phone calls and held protests at U.S. Army events, officials' homes and recruiting centers across the country (People for the Ethical Treatment of Animals, 2011). Through PETA's Web site alone, more than 100,000 people contacted their congressional representatives and army officials in just a few weeks. Maryland congressman Roscoe Bartlett, himself a former primate experimenter in the military, took up the campaign as a cause célèbre and urged the army to modify its curriculum (Vastag, 2011, October 13).

The effort was successful. After six weeks of intensive campaigning, the U.S. Army confirmed that it would be replacing Aberdeen's chemical casualty training exercises on monkeys with simulators and other non-animal training methods by the end of 2011 (Vastag, 2011, October 13).

Endotracheal Intubation Training

Endotracheal intubation is a vital skill that involves inserting a plastic tube down an injured patient's trachea in hopes of reestablishing an airway and allowing the patient to breathe. It is an emergency procedure that must often be efficiently executed without delay, but using nonhuman animals to teach this skill does not enhance trainees' ability to perform this task. Despite the overwhelming preference for using simulators to teach intubation in civilian pediatric emergency medicine, and the fact that some U.S. military bases and hospitals also do not use animals, other facilities around the country continue to subject nonhuman animals, specifically ferrets, to this painful procedure.

According to military documents, at a number of facilities, ferrets have hard tubes repeatedly forced down their delicate windpipes as many as ten times in a given session with as many as six sessions being held every year. This repeated intubation, especially by unskilled trainees, can cause bleeding and swelling in the animals' tissues of the throat, pain, scarring, collapsed lungs, and even death (Hofmeister, Trim, Kley, & Cornell, 2007, p. 213; Tait, 2010, p. 80). And poor oversight of animal use on intubation training protocols has resulted in nonhuman animal deaths at several U.S. military facilities, leading the director of the Department of Laboratory Animal Medicine at the Naval Medical Center Portsmouth to issue a memorandum stating, "Complacency is currently a big problem during ... the ... intubation training laboratories" (Naval Medical Center Portsmouth, 2009, February 23).

In addition to the cruelty involved, the anatomical differences between ferrets and human patients inherently mar the training process. Attempts to justify the use of nonhuman animals often claim that there is anatomical similarity between species but the fact is that the differences are vast and for decades have been identified as factors that prevent the transfer of skills learned on nonhuman animals to actually treating human babies (Katzman, 1982). An article published in the *Journal of Emergency Nursing* described the anatomical differences that make ferrets poor substitutes for human patients:

> [F]errets have proportionately longer tongues than human infants that are one and a half times the length of their mouth. Further differences include more profuse salivation, dome-shaped arytenoid cartilage, and comparatively larger epiglottises and smaller anterior larynxes...there is no anatomical specificity between the maxillofacial or oropharyngeal features of animals and humans (Tait 2010, p. 78).

Tait (2010) concludes, "The bottom line is that there is no need to traumatize and harm animals to teach [intubation], especially when highly effective non-animal methods are the accepted standard of practice and readily available to instructors" (p. 80).

Indeed, military and civilian research shows that simulators are valid and effective training tools (*cf.* Arnold, Lowmaster, Fiedor-Hamilton, Kloesz, Hofkosh, Kochanek & Clark, 2008; Sawyer, Sierocka-Castaneda, Chan, Berg & Thompson, 2010) and that those trained on simulators demonstrate higher proficiency in pediatric intubation than those trained using an animal laboratory (Adams, Scott, Perkin, & Langga, 2000). Adams et al. (2000) concluded that, "training on mannequins allows for greater concentration by the trainee on technique ... without the urgency to place the tube, which is felt when practicing on animals or humans, the trainee is much more open to suggestions and corrections" (p.7). Participants' discomfort with the use of animals for intubation training has been noted in the medical education literature as well (Waisman, Amir, Mor, & Mimouni, 2005).

There is actually no scientific research indicating that the use of nonhuman animals is an effective form of intubation training, yet the practice persists in U.S. military training programs. Complaints about it are met with form letters that contain unfounded and untruthful claims about the supposed superiority and irreplaceability of animal use for this purpose and which generally illustrate how serious attention and scrutiny has not been given to this issue. In a similarly worded response that has been sent out on the letterheads of the Madigan Healthcare System (personal communication, June 6, 2011), Naval Medical Center Portsmouth (personal communication, March 26, 2010) and the Department of the Air Force (personal communication, July 18, 2011), U.S. military officials carelessly cite a study that reports the poor intubation proficiency of pediatric residents who were trained using animals (Falck, Escobedo, Baillargeon, Villard & Gunkel, 2003) as a reason why the use of nonhuman animals should continue during intubation training.

Perhaps the most compelling evidence that the use of nonhuman animals in the U.S. military's infant airway management training program is unnecessary from a medical perspective is that some military facilities have already replaced it.

The William Beaumont Army Medical Center (personal communication, July 26, 2011) has not used nonhuman animals, specifically ferrets, for intubation training since 2007, and the Uniformed Services University of the Health Sciences (n.d.) also ended its use of ferrets for intubation practice in 2008. In 2011, just months after PETA sent information about the efficacy of simulators for teaching intubation, the Naval Medical Center San Diego (personal communication, April 13, 2011) confirmed that it reviewed the materials and that would end its use of cats for this practice and adopt out the animals who were used for the laboratory. Similarly, in 2012, the Naval Medical Center Portsmouth responded to PETA appeals and wrote that the facility has ended its use of ferrets for training pediatric residents in neonatal intubation (personal communication, March 7, 2012).

Outside of the military, the practice has been all but abandoned throughout the U.S. in favor of specifically designed simulators that replicate human anatomy and physiology, allow trainees to repeat procedures until they are confident and proficient, and have been shown to better prepare care providers to treat their patients.

The Physicians Committee for Responsible Medicine (2011b) conducted a survey that found that more than 90 percent of U.S. pediatric residency programs for physicians use only non-animal methods for intubation training, including Tripler Army Medical Center. Similarly, specialty courses designed to train those providing emergency medical treatment to newborns and infants also recommend only simulation methods to teach intubation skills.

The American Heart Association (2009)—which created and sponsors the widely-offered Pediatric Advanced Life Support (PALS) course—states that it, "does not require or endorse the use of live animals in any of its training courses," and that any facility that continues to use nonhuman animals would be "responsible for responding on behalf of their own business/organization" if targeted by activists for continuing the practice. O'Connor (personal communication, February 3, 2009), who is former chair of the American Heart Association's (AHA) Emergency Cardiovascular Care Committee, elaborated on the AHA's position explaining that, "The use of lifelike training manikins for PALS courses is the standard accepted norm," and that "the AHA recommends that any hands-on intubation training for the AHA PALS course be performed on lifelike human manikins" (American Heart Association, letter to PETA, February 3, 2009). Animal use persists at just a handful of the more than 1500 PALS courses offered across the United States of America.

Like the AHA, the American Academy of Pediatrics (personal communication, August 3, 2005) and the Emergency Nurses Association (personal communication, February 19, 2008) exclusively endorse the use of non-animal pediatric intubation training methods in their sponsored courses.

Perplexingly, a number of U.S. military facilities have acknowledged simulators' viability for infant intubation training yet continue to use ferrets anyway. The U.S. Naval Medical Center Portsmouth (2009b) has written that "the fidelity of intubation manikins has progressed so far in recent years that the use of animals in this [neonatal] intubation training may be unnecessary." The Madigan Army Medical Center (2007) has written that the use of ferrets for teaching how to intubate neonates and infants "will be phased out due to the development of adequate simulation training models" (p. 336). And the Lackland Air Force Base (2011) has written the following:

> [T]here is now a 28 week mannequin that is a reasonable ... substitution for live intubation. Honestly, with the [Defense Base Closure and Realignment Commission] we were looking at terminating both of the animal labs we do (ferrets and rabbits – for chest tubes) and moving to the mannequin anyway. (Lackland Airforce Base, internal communication [obtained through FOIA], April 29, 2011)

However, Madigan Army Medical Center and Lackland Air Force Base, among a few other military facilities, continue to use ferrets in intubation training.

In addition to a number of other groundless defenses for its continued use of nonhuman animals in this area, another facility that still uses animals for intubation training, the David Grant Medical Center at Travis Air Force Base, offers a bewildering explanation in the course of acknowledging the anatomical differences between ferrets and human patients. David Grant Medical Center (2007, January 29) states in its intubation training protocol that the "daunting anatomy" of ferrets actually represents a training advantage because it is "more challenging to the trainee" (p. 7). But anatomy that does not accurately represent future human patients should, in truth, be considered a major drawback and a hindrance to achieving proficiency. Simply making a task more difficult does not alone equate to better training; if it did, then ferret manikins would be preferable to human manikins and trainees would be instructed to practice with one hand behind their back.

And the more one digs, the more it becomes clear that the use of nonhuman animal based training methods isn't determined by the appropriateness of the model for teaching the task at hand, but for political and other reasons that have nothing to do with sound pedagogy.

Lackland Air Force Base (2009, July 27) attempts to justify the selection of ferrets over other nonhuman animals in its intubation protocol by pointing out that a ferret "is not considered a domestic partner animal" (p.7). David Grant Medical Center (2007, January 29) offered a similarly absurd justification for using ferrets in intubation training, stating: "[T]he ferret has replaced the domestic cat as the model of choice ... primarily because the ferret is a species of less political and social sensitivity than is the cat" (p. 7). And in its intubation training protocol, Keesler Air Force Base (2007, July 26) noted that "ferrets were selected for this training because they are not a sensitive species such as companion animals (i.e. dogs and cats)" (p. 9).

This rationale for using ferrets does not address performance outcomes or scientific validity; it is more clearly intended to shield the facilities from public scrutiny and criticism for using nonhuman animals than it is to defend the decision on scientific or pedagogical grounds. Of course, there is no reason why using a less politically sensitive species would result in a better training experience for military personnel.

The U.S. military has also at times advanced other perplexing explanations for using nonhuman animals that are somewhat less tangible to understand. For example, the Naval Medical Center Portsmouth (2008) has defended using ferrets for intubation training because the military claims that it is important that there exists a real risk of injury, stating: "[A]n important difference [between manikins and animal models] is the psychological aspect of knowing that they are dealing with a live being that could possibly be injured if they are not careful" (p. 15). Putting aside the fact that this justification, like others, does not cite performance outcomes or scientific validity of the method being defended, highlighting the vulnerability of the animals being used and the fact that they may be injured should weigh against, not in favor, of using nonhuman animals.

Social Function of Harming and Killing Nonhuman Animals

Non-animal training methods are often well received by medical professionals who—like most people—do not generally want to see harm come to animals particularly when it can be easily avoided. In many cases, the use of nonhuman animals is sufficiently disturbing to learners that their ability to concentrate on the task at hand is compromised and the training session is less productive than it would be otherwise (Kelly, 1985; Paul & Podberscek, 2000). In other cases, learners may even alter their career plans rather than participate in cruel or deadly animal-based training (Capaldo, 2004). In this way, insisting that personnel mutilate and kill nonhuman animals serves the function of a hazing ritual and may filter out candidates who are not capable or willing to overcome inhibitions against cruelty. It is important to the military that soldiers carry out orders without hesitation even when orders seem objectionable. Furthermore, it is unlikely to be a surprise to anyone that the military fosters a hyper-masculine culture and may be openly hostile to expressions of compassion.

A secondary function of live tissue training on nonhuman animals is to elevate the status of those engaged in the exercises as they are given permission to engage in activity that is legally prohibited for members of the general public. They are given this permission because they are thought to be charged with a responsibility so important that it requires they be free from the ordinary rules of society. This elevates the role of soldier from job to profession. It is a mark of a profession to be given privileges not extended to the general public. That not every solder participates in these medical training exercises makes the skills even more specialized and prestigious.

Some have compared the U.S. military's nonhuman animal-based training laboratories to bayonet charges practiced in boot camp (Grossman, 2009). As a military tactic, bayonet charges have been irrelevant for decades; that they continue to be practiced suggests that they serve a purpose other than ensuring that soldiers can competently execute such a maneuver on the battlefield. Marching in step quickly comes to mind as another example. Even at the time of the American Revolution, marching in step was clearly an outdated skill which did not serve British troops well. That said, every military in the world extensively drills its soldiers to march in step. Marching in step builds camaraderie, transforms individuals into a cohesive group, and to be successfully carried out requires that soldiers follow orders instantly without hesitation or second thought.

Finally, nonhuman animal-based training is one of many ways that soldiers are conditioned to become comfortable with killing and death. In *On Killing: The Psychological Cost of Learning to Kill in War and Society*, Grossman (2009) writes that "despite an unbroken tradition of violence and war, man is not by nature a killer" (Introduction to the Revised Edition). This is an obstacle for militaries the world over but obviously not an insurmountable obstacle given the history of the twentieth century. Evidence of a reluctance to kill can be found in the fact that a surprising number of World War II soldiers (from all participating countries) were found to have never fired their weapons in combat. That the percentage of soldiers who have been in war zones without firing their weapons has decreased with each major conflict suggests that military officials are getting better at overcoming this reluctance to kill (Grossman 2009; Marshall 2000). Even modest changes such as firing at a human silhouette instead of at a round target can purportedly mentally prepare soldiers to fire their weapons and kill when ordered to do so.

One of the primary contractors offering live tissue training for the U.S. military, Deployment Medicine International (DMI), has suggested—absent any evidence—that experience treating nonhuman animals who have been shot and blown up, "significantly reduces the effects of Post Traumatic Stress Disorder (PTSD)" suffered by soldiers returning from battle (as cited in Morehouse, n.d., p. 8). They go on to state, "that live tissue training 'pre-conditions' the minds and emotions of Service Members thereby lessening the incidence and impact of post traumatic stress disorder" (Morehouse, n.d., p. 8). DMI clearly means to suggest that exposing soldiers to horrifically mutilated animals is a good thing in that it prepares the soldiers to mentally confront the carnage they'll witness on the battlefield. Similarly, a report on helping soldiers cope with the psychological stress of war by a Master's degree student at the U.S. Army War College stated that having them participate in the "purposeful wounding" of live animals, 'appears to assist in the "shock factor" by exposing Soldiers to the blood and guts prior to combat' (Love, 2011, p. 21).

Yet, research suggests that it is possible that the experience of maiming and killing nonhuman animals could actually cause psychological trauma to course participants, or even lead to PTSD (Capaldo, 2004). And there appears to be little doubt that harming nonhuman animals would desensitize soldiers to the suffering of nonhuman animals, (Arluke & Hafferty, 1996) as well as to the plight of the human victims of war. In surveying physicians' sentiments, Barnard (1986) has described the use of animals in military training as "apt to promote an attitude of callousness to suffering among young doctors" (p.140), with some reporting the experience first-hand and others having observed the effects in their colleagues (pp.140-146). In a military context, these are necessary traits, but in society in general, this cavalier attitude toward pain and violence borders on sociopathy.

Setting a Low Bar for Killing Nonhuman Animals

Military hyperbole included in U.S. Congressional testimony, government reports and media soundbites has insisted that animal-based training laboratories are vitally responsible for improving battlefield medical care and directly saving lives, yet when scientific justifications fail and strange intangible claims do not add up, the military can sometimes be surprisingly forthright about the shortcomings of using nonhuman animals to stand in for human soldiers. In the midst of controversy about the practice, U.S. military medical officials have recently acknowledged that, "there still is no evidence that [live tissue training] saves lives" (Goodrich, 2009, September 15 email).

In general, neither animal experimentation nor animal-based training appears amongst the principal factors for reducing mortality and disability in wartime (Barnard, 1986; Little, 2009, March 29). Unfortunately, in the U.S. military and elsewhere, use of nonhuman animals is frequently treated as a default method for training and experimentation that does not require the same stringent evidence-based justification that simulators and non-animal methods are required to satisfy. The Department of Defense's official 2003 report on the use of live animals in medical training exercises, stated that, "At this time, data are not available to validate either the live animal model or any type of simulation" (p. 7). First, it is simply false that simulators have not been validated for medical skills that the military is teaching, as illustrated extensively in this chapter. Second, one must wonder why if key data were missing on both nonhuman animal use and simulation technology that the former—which presents substantial ethical, educational and economic obstacles—would persist and be given preference. The standard for killing nonhuman animals appears to be considerably lower than for using even state-of-the-art simulation equipment.

The rabbit lesson and the dog lesson make clear that any perceived benefit toward military readiness or a war effort is considered by many to be adequate to justify any cost in nonhuman animal lives or suffering. In some sense, this should not come as a surprise because in war even the lives of other humans are often given little weight provided that those humans are enemy combatants or civilians who are strategically unimportant and can be dismissed as collateral damage.

It is common for the deadly use of nonhuman animals in medical instruction or experiments, be it in civilian or military context, to be described as a "sacrifice" made by the animals for the sake of humans as if it were a consciously made decision on the part of the animal to volunteer for such maltreatment. That this sacrifice is made in a military context is commonly thought to make it even more laudable and certainly is thought to provide a greater degree of justification. The military frames the issue as nonhuman animals who sacrifice their lives for the sake of the war effort just as is required by human soldiers and the nation as a whole. This language projects a sense of fairness. But as one commentator has pointed out:

> [Animals] do not and cannot participate in, let alone benefit from, war's outcome or aftermath. They have no legacy to enhance. Wars to make the world safe for freedom or democracy provide no returns, nor could they, to animals. (Johnston, 2011, p. 6)

Thus, there is almost no limit as to what can be imposed on nonhuman animals and regardless of the results they reap no benefit.

When narrowly understood, the use of nonhuman animals for military medical training purposes makes little sense. Even if one is not strongly motivated by a desire to eliminate the harm done to animals, there are generally better methods available for achieving medical skill proficiency. Ultimately, U.S. regulations—and the public—demand that the military provide scientific evidence that the use of nonhuman animals is unavoidable and educationally superior to non-animal options. In this regard, the U.S. military has utterly failed. But when keeping in mind that mutilating and killing nonhuman animals fulfills a set of often unstated objectives—including desensitizing individuals to the pain and death of others, much like the rabbit and dog lessons—then it becomes easier to understand why these crude practices have persisted in the U.S. military's training program despite the more humane and less violent methods available.

CHAPTER THREE

NONHUMAN ANIMALS AS WEAPONS OF WAR

Ana Paulina Morrón

In the Book of Judges[1], Samson prepares to attack the Philistines by capturing three hundred foxes, igniting their tails, and setting them loose to run through the Philistines' fields, vineyards, and groves. In the end, Samson succeeds in destroying their crops (Judges 15:4-5). In the story, Samson takes advantage of the flammability of fox hair, as well as the natural "flight" response of nonhuman animals placed in dangerous situations. Seeking revenge, the Philistines travel to Judah to capture the man who burned their crops. However, Samson escapes and uses the sharp jawbone of a donkey to murder his enemies. "With the jawbone of a donkey, I have slain a thousand men," he says (Judges 15:16).

Written sometime during the eleventh century BC, the aforementioned story presents two distinct ways that nonhuman animals have been used as weapons of war. Either the behavior of the nonhuman animal is manipulated to achieve a desired outcome, or a fragment of the nonhuman animal's remains is fashioned to create a more traditional kind of weapon. This chapter devotes attention towards understanding the former option, in large part because it is more interesting to learn about the nuances of nonhuman animal behavior, but also because it is the way most nonhuman animals have been used as weapons of war throughout history, subsequent to the discovery and proliferation of non-organic tools.

To study in greater depth the various ways that nonhuman animals have been employed as weapons throughout history is no easy task, for it is limited by many factors, all of which will be described here presently. The first problem has to do with the indefinable nature of war and, by extension, weaponry. Simply stated, what is war, and what makes a weapon a weapon? War is a difficult term to define. In fact, by the end of his book, *A History of Warfare,* military historian John Keegan (1994) hopes that he has challenged the belief that war can be easily understood. Similarly, this project will not limit or restrict itself by assuming to understand war, or by imposing a narrow definition that inevitably excludes millions of lost lives; rather, it intends to include nonhuman animals that have been employed in what some may consider as "traditional wars" (p. 386), as well as alternative forms of violent engagement.

Weaponry is an equally difficult word to define, especially in terms of nonhuman animal warfare. For example, in the aforementioned story, Samson uses foxes to hurt the Philistines economically and psychologically. Whether or not these foxes can be classified as weapons, however, depends entirely upon how the reader interprets the entire story. On the one hand, the foxes are not used to directly kill anyone, at least not in the way that the donkey's jawbone is used later on. Yet, at the same time, the fiery attack is an example of an offensive guerrilla tactic, even if it did not occur in a typical war setting.

Similarly, it can be difficult to ascertain whether or not a nonhuman animal is a weapon when the nonhuman animal is not primarily used as an instrument of attack or defense, but rather as a facilitator of war. For example, the carrier pigeon has consistently helped to provide armies with necessary intelligence. Although the carrier pigeon is not directly engaging in battle, its contribution to war cannot be denied. The point is that the study of nonhuman animals as weapons of war can be extremely subjective at times. Therefore, for the purposes of this project, the term "weapon" will be understood broadly as something which directly or indirectly prevents or inflicts harm or damage.

The study of nonhuman animals as weapons of war is further complicated by the fact that the current understanding of weaponry is rather limited (Brodie & Brodie, 1973). Lost to history are the names of the people who first dreamt up alternative ways to use nonhuman animals, as well as the precise dates that such nonhuman animals were unleashed onto the battlefield. In addition, many of these weapons were not planned, but instead devised out of necessity by soldiers confronted with particular problems, like small infantry units.

Despite these constraints, this chapter will attempt to guide readers through what could easily become an overwhelming intellectual endeavor. After all, a survey of every nonhuman animal ever used for and during war would require countless chapters, and possibly even volumes. Rather than be limited by page constraints, however, this project has intentionally chosen not to discuss every single nonhuman animal weapon ever mentioned in a story related to war. To record every instance in which a nonhuman animal is mentioned would be an impressive but unnecessary undertaking. Since the aim of this project is to examine the different ways that nonhuman animals have been employed as weapons throughout history, the following stories have been selected because they are representative of the time period to which they belong. Some stories are famous, while others are obscure but interesting. Some stories are elaborately detailed, while others amount to no more than a sentence on a page. However, just as Samson set foxes loose to run aimlessly through the Philistines' fields, so should readers be willing to embrace the chaos as they explore this difficult and subjective field of study through five periods of time: Prehistory, Antiquity, Middle Ages, Early Modern, and Modern.

Prehistory, or Pre-Recorded History

A suitable starting point from which to examine the use of nonhuman animals as weapons of war is at the beginning of human evolution, the time when humankind's prehistoric predecessors discovered they could produce tools out of different organic materials. These materials included nonhuman animal remains, such as bone, teeth, and horn. The use of nonhuman animal parts, rather than the living nonhuman animal itself, was the first way in which nonhuman animals were exploited for purposes related to war. This discovery revolutionized hunting practices, as it enabled hunters to advance their knowledge of tool production, and nonhuman animal behavior. This knowledge would prove useful in the entrapment, breeding, and training of wild nonhuman animals. Through the domestication of nonhuman animals, humans discovered a second way to use nonhuman animals as weapons of war.

During the Paleolithic Age, humankind's prehistoric predecessors discovered that tools and, by extension, weapons could be produced using nonhuman animal remains, like bone, teeth, and horn. This discovery likely occurred while humans were out in search of food, shelter, diversion, or a mate. (Dupuy, 1980) Precisely when this discovery occurred is subject to debate, but nevertheless worth mentioning. One theory suggests that it occurred 2 to 3 million years ago when the hominid species *Australopithecus africanus* walked the Earth. In 1925, anthropologist Raymond Dart examined the fossilized skull of what he believed to be a cercopithecid monkey. Soon, Dart realized that the fossil belonged to a hominid of a genus previously unidentified (Dart, 2003/1925). After years of studying the *Australopithecus africanus*, Dart concluded that they created weapons, like daggers, out of the remains of the nonhuman animals that they had killed. Referring to the sharp-edged jaw of a primitive hyena, Dart explained in a BBC interview that "the Australopithecus africanus liked the lower jaws of nonhuman animals that had long canine teeth because these could be used as formidable weapons" (Yale Peabody Museum, permanent exhibit). Such weapons would be used to hunt nonhuman animals and fellow Australopithecines alike.

During the Mesolithic and Neolithic Age, the use of nonhuman animal remains as weapons continued to play significant roles in the inter-species and intra-species conflicts of the time. For example, in prehistoric Egypt, ivory and horn were used to produce a variety of weapons, such as mace heads and compound bows, respectively. The ivory, which was mainly sourced from elephants and hippopotamuses, would be carved and painted by the hunters themselves (Lucas, 1962). It is likely that such weapons were used, not only for hunting, but to inflict harm upon humans as well, especially as competition for power and property began to intensify in the face of a growing population. For example, in Denmark, the fractured skeleton of a thirty-five-year-old man was discovered with a bone arrowhead pierced in his skull, and another in his breastbone. (The National Museum of Denmark, n.d.). The man had been shot from behind and at close range, suggesting that he was the victim of a surprise attack or an execution.

By the Neolithic Age, mankind's prehistoric predecessor began to use nonhuman animals in a different way. With the domestication of nonhuman animals came the realization that they could be used for more than just their bone, teeth, and horn. Nonhuman animals could also have their behavior modified in such a way as to make them useful for reasons related to security and survival. For example, the dog was trained to alert, defend, and attack outsiders encroaching on their masters' environment. Nonhuman animal behaviorists have attempted to reconstruct how wild nonhuman animals were manipulated for such purposes (Lubow, 1977). In terms of the dog, primitive humans may have over time reinforced certain feelings of dependency by providing them with scraps of food and shelter. Only those dogs that overcame their fear, aided in hunting, and identified trespassers were rewarded with leftovers, and consequently interbred among themselves. Such domestication took generations. Ultimately, humans realized that they could minimize their involvement in dangerous situations by employing other species to fulfill their objectives.

Antiquity

Antiquity is marked by an abundance of sacred myths, many of which feature nonhuman animals as major contributors to the formation of human civilization in the world. Much can be learned from these ancient texts. Therefore, included in this section are sacred stories, as well as historical material. The question of whether or not readers should interpret sacred narratives as factual is irrelevant; rather, the purpose is to view them as informative, full of insight to the social and economic practices of the time. Finally, during this time period, people began to take advantage of a more diverse array of species, using them in innovative and deadly ways.

A recurring theme in many sacred myths is that of the cosmic battle between the forces of good and evil. In the biblical story of the flood, found in the Book of Genesis, a grieving God wages war against a violent and sinful earth. Toward the end of the flood, Noah employs the dove as a kind of intelligence weapon, enabling him to find out whether the watery war was over. At first, the dove returns to the ark empty-handed. Eventually, the dove returns with a freshly plucked olive leaf, signaling that the waters had subsided. (Genesis 8) The biblical story of the flood resembles the Babylonian Epic of Gilgamesh in which the character of Utnapishtim releases a dove, a swallow, and a raven in order to learn whether the waters had subsided. In this story, the hero is able to protect himself by invoking the homing instinct of birds (Collins, 2004).

The homing instinct was instrumental in the development of carrier pigeons for war. The fact that birds would return, quickly and consistently, to their nests led people to think about how they could be used to relay information to places too far to reach by foot, or chariot. Evidence suggests that the domestication of birds trained to transmit messages back and forth may have occurred as early as 2,900 BC in Egypt. Skilled pigeons would be released from incoming ships to announce the arrival of important visitors (Fang, 2008). As time went on, people invented different methods and contraptions to attach messages to the birds. Nevertheless, the premise remained the same. The bird, typically a pigeon, would be released to fly long distances back to one or more designated relay posts. During the Gallic Wars of 58 BC to 51 BC, pigeons carried the news of Julius Caesar's conquests all across Europe (Leighton, 1969).

Another nonhuman animal that was typically commonly used was the courageous and loyal guard dog. During the Peloponnesian War of 431 to 404 BC, in which the Greeks fought the Corinthians, fifty guard dogs were stationed by the seashore to protect the city of Corinth. One dark night, the Greeks attempted to infiltrate the coastline. The dogs defended the territory with all their might. All but one died. The one that survived managed to alert the Corinthians just in time (Lubow, 1977). Additionally, guard dogs could be more trustworthy than people. During the siege of Mantinea in 362 BC, King Agesilaus of Sparta discovered that some of his soldiers were betraying him by smuggling goods into the town at night. To end the problem, he surrounded the town with ferocious dogs (Richardson, 1920).

In spite of its talents as a nonhuman guard animal, the dog of Antiquity was just as likely to be used for offensive purposes. Since dogs could easily inflict more damage than the metal weapons that the ancient people had at their disposal, there was a strong expectation that dogs should not only prevent harm, but actively inflict harm as well. For this reason, dogs were trained to fight and kill (Derr, 1997). Dogs would be trained to engage and exhaust the enemy in combat first, before their master could swoop in and finish the job successfully. Sometimes these dogs would be led by slaves, instead of the master, thereby making things safer and more beneficial for the master. The image of the slave and the dog entering the battlefield together calls attention to the inequalities of the time, namely, that these two beings were unluckily considered to be of lesser value than the master waiting safely in the sidelines.

Furthermore, the Romans held mock battles where they would train dogs to respond aggressively to the sight of men armed with swords and shields. Additionally, they would train their dogs, clothed in heavy coats and sharp spikes, to run toward enemy soldiers and their horses, critically wound them, and break their formation. Romans were not the only ones to employ dogs; in fact, other groups used dogs to defend themselves against Roman invasions. Shortly after the Romans defeated the Teutons at the Battle of Versella in 101 BC, for example, they were forced to confront a pack of dogs led by the angry women of Wagenburg (Richardson, 1920). Once trained, dogs could be quite lethal.

The dog of Antiquity was also used for its extraordinary sense of smell. Interestingly, the Greek and Romans believed that dogs could smell the presence of spirits, and the dead. The image of dogs wandering amongst, and possibly consuming, the corpses of warriors is invoked in the beginning lines of the Iliad: "Sing, goddess, the wrath of Peleus's son Achilles ... which sent many brave souls of heroes down to Hades, but left their bodies for dogs and birds" (Felton, 1999). The dog's sense of smell was a valuable asset. In the war against the Thracians, which occurred in 342 BC, Philip II of Macedon relied on dogs to help him and his soldiers safely navigate through the dense forests. The dogs led the way by following their nose, and alerting the soldiers of any incoming danger.

As alert systems, there is one particular instance in which dogs failed to be relied upon. In the Battle of the Allia, which was the first Gallic invasion of Rome and likely fought in 387 BC, the Gauls attempted to invade Rome by climbing up a rocky mountain as silently as possible. Neither the Roman guards nor the dogs heard anything. What ultimately saved Rome was a gaggle of geese that lived in the temple of the sacred goddess Juno. Upon hearing the Gauls, they began to flap their wings and quack as loudly as possible, thereby alerting an army captain of the imminent invasion (Lubow, 1977).

There are countless references to warhorses in the Bible. The armies of the Near East, including those of the Egyptians and the Philistines, relied on horses to carry them into battle. The book of Job devotes several verses toward praising the many qualities of the warhorse (Job 39: 19-25). And, in the book of Revelation, the four horsemen bring wicked things to humanity, such as war and pestilence (Revelation 6: 1-8).

As early as 1800 BC, horses were used to draw chariots on the battlefield. By the ninth century BC, however, chariot technology would be replaced by cavalry technology, which was easier to maintain and more cost-efficient. Invented by the Assyrians, the horse cavalry was unlike its modern counterpart, requiring two people to manage two horses simultaneously. Yet, without the invention of supportive riding structures, like saddles and stirrups, riding horses would be quite difficult and unproductive for most armies. That is, except for the Macedonians for which cavalry was considered as important of an element as the infantry unit. In particular, the cavalry of Alexander the Great consisted of hundreds of riders, each equipped with lances, swords, and armor, whose charge was fast, powerful, and deadly (Gabriel, 2007a).

The horse of Antiquity was also employed as a psychological scare tactic, a means to instill fear in enemy invaders. For example, during the second century AD, the Romans adopted something called the "draco" for their cavalry to carry. The "draco," which looked like a cross between a dragon and a serpent, was fashioned using a metal head and a cloth tube, both of which were later mounted on a pole. As the soldier rode his horse, carrying the "draco," the wind would course through the contraption, making it seem as though it were coming alive. In addition, the wind would cause it to produce a howling noise (Rice et al., 2006). The sight of a "draco" slithering alongside a powerful horse must have been an incredibly intimidating one.

Like the horse, the camel was also used as a mode of transport, as well as resistance. Camels had been used for war since 843 BC, when Gindibu the Arab brought one thousand camel-riding warriors to fight Shalmanezer, the king of Assyria, at the Battle at Karkar (Gabriel, 2007a). Then, in 547 BC, Cyrus the Great used camels as a secret weapon against Croesus' much larger army of soldiers and horses. Although he was seriously outnumbered, Cyrus decided to play on the horse's natural antipathy toward camels, as they supposedly dislike the sounds and smells of these humped nonhuman animals. By deploying the camels that were being used for baggage transport, he managed to frighten the horses enough to win (Mayor, 2003).

In comparison to the previously mentioned nonhuman animals, with its enormous size and ferocious-looking tusks, perhaps the most visually impressive nonhuman war animal was the elephant. A soapstone seal from the Harappan civilization dating back 3.5 to 5,000 years ago illustrates how people would rope an elephant into submission for personal gain. Meanwhile, others would simply take an orphaned calf from the mother they had just killed (Scigliano, 2002).

Then, as early as 1100 BC in the areas of Syria, India and China, people began to take advantage of the size and strength of the elephant for war purposes (Kistler, 2011). Soldiers often rode elephants. Once atop an elephant, a military leader could see for miles, thereby having a better view of the battlefield. Skilled archers would balance themselves on top of the heads of these nonhuman animals so as to shoot from a more advantageous position. The elephants were also trained to fight, and perform labor intensive tasks, such as lifting, hauling, and pushing heavy objects. Specifically, elephants were trained to use their massive trunks to pick up riders and horses, and throw them. In order to inflict even more damage, elephants often had their tusks sawed off and fitted with sharp swords. The apocryphal books of the Maccabbees describe how the armies of Seleucides used enormous elephants from India to strike fear in the opposition, transport soldiers, and stampede over the Jewish rebel forces (3 Maccabbees 5). Indeed, the elephant was a force to be reckoned with.

Although there were benefits to possessing elephants, there were many downsides. Elephants were not the most dependable creatures. If they panicked, which they often did, they would inevitably trample their enemy's army as well as their own. They also disliked the sounds and smells of war. Finally, it could be difficult to transport them across bodies of water, and long stretches of land. Clearly, elephants were not the perfect, indestructible weapons they appeared to be, a reality that helped Alexander the Great defeat King Porus in 326 BC during the battle of the Hydaspes River. As Alexander's troops entered into the Punjab region of India, they encountered a great army unlike anything they had ever seen. Not only did Porus' army outnumber their own, but it was reinforced by two hundred war elephants. According to the Shahnameh, an epic written by the Persian poet Firdausi, Alexander managed to dismantle the war elephants by building a great number of iron horses, lighting them on fire, and sending them off to scare the elephants (Mayor, 2003). Other sources argue that Alexander's triumph was a result of his tactical brilliance, as well as his infantry's undying heroism (Scigliano, 2002). In the end, Alexander won and incorporated the elephants into Hellenistic warfare. Although elephants were far from being ideal weapons, Alexander must have felt it was better to have them than not to, perhaps because elephants were such visually imposing, impressive creatures.

As more and more armies employed elephants as weapons of war, there arose a need for anti-elephant devices. Such devices had to target the elephant's fear and unpredictability, both of which were its weakest characteristics. One such device involved coating pigs in tar, and setting them on fire. During the Pyrrhic War of 280-275 BC, the Romans were victorious in defeating Pyrrhus of Epirus' elephants by sending in squealing, scorching pigs to scare them (Kistler, 2006). The Romans also unleashed chariots, led by armed oxen and rams. These nonhuman animals were not as effective as the pigs, and were quickly killed by Pyrrhus' men.

Finally, it is important to note that even the smallest nonhuman animals could inflict great harm. In the book of Exodus, ten plagues are sent by God onto the Egyptians. These plagues, which revisit the theme of the cosmic battle between good and evil, include nonhuman animals like frogs, and locusts (Exodus 7-10). The people of the Near East were aware of the impact that small nonhuman animals could have, and consequently used mice, insects, and arachnids as biological warfare. In a battle against Roman invaders in 198 AD, the people of Hatra near modern Mosul, Iraq placed scorpions inside a terra-cotta pot. The terra-cotta pot was then thrown at the besiegers, unleashing the deadly scorpion bomb (Mayor, 2003).

Middle Ages

The medieval period is characterized by the decline of Rome and the rise of kingdoms, feudalism, and monotheistic religions. In Western Europe, the strategic and tactical brilliance of the past was superseded by chaos and crudity. In addition, less importance was placed on weapon development and production. Feudalism promoted localized fighting that was waged almost exclusively by armored knights riding on horseback. These knights fought for financial compensation, as well as nonmaterial reasons like chivalry and honor. Interestingly, chivalry comes from the French word cheval, which means horse or horsemanship. Meanwhile, the Crusades and the influence of the Church promoted non-localized fighting in which the propagation of war was not limited by any boundaries. These different elements contributed to the continuing struggles over power and property (Keegan, 1994).

The practice of using birds to carry messages was not limited to Antiquity, but continued throughout the Middle Ages. Carrier pigeons were the fastest way to transmit messages of military import, for they could travel great distances in less than a day. A popular technique, which originated in the Middle East, was to strap capsules with small papyrus sheets to the legs or the back of the pigeon. The pigeon would then travel to its assigned post. These posts were located in many regions, across different continents. In fact, Genghis Khan, emperor of the Mongol Empire, created an elaborate system of pigeon communication posts that occupied one-sixth of the world (Blechman, 2006). Carrier pigeons were frequently used during the Crusades of the eleventh through thirteenth centuries. In one occasion, King Richard I of England and his soldiers intercepted a pigeon carrying an important message to the besieged city of Ptolemais. The message stated that a Muslim relief army was on its way. The message was then deceptively changed to state that no help would be coming. Upon receiving this message, the city ceased all fighting and surrendered (Fang, 2008).

Like the pigeon, the dog continued to assume the same responsibilities it had always been given. Just as the dog of Antiquity was trained to guard and defend its territory, the dog of the medieval period was used to protect its master and his property against enemy forces. Those who owned the fiercest dogs could be certain that their homes, pastures, and livestock would be kept safe. Some of these dogs were so skilled at guardianship that they could easily take down an ill-intentioned outsider riding on horseback. Naturally, this ability translated well to the battlefield. For this reason, numerous leaders, like King Attila of the Huns and Charles V of Spain, employed dogs to guard their military camps (Hausman & Hausman, 1997). Specifically, King Attila the Hun used large Molossian dogs and Talbots, which were the ancestors of Mastiffs and bloodhounds, respectively. Such war dogs would be dressed in armored coats and spiked collars.

Like before, dogs continued to be used for their extraordinary sense of smell. For example, Andronicus, the king of Constantinople, had dogs trained to notice the subtle differences between Christians and Turks. The dogs would then alert the king whenever foreigners entered his royal home (Richardson, 1920). Clearly, dogs were capable of doing impressive things. For this reason, the odds were usually against those armies and communities that owned no dogs.

Another nonhuman animal that was used to preserve order in a feudal society was the horse. Horses were employed to patrol kingdoms and adjacent areas. This was a difficult task, because horses were often forced to engage in plenty of skirmishes, especially during the Hundred Years War of 1337-1453 AD when France and England were overrun by marauders and guerrilla groups (Hyland, 1998).

The warhorse was an integral component of the medieval military system. In particular, the invention of the stirrup dramatically enhanced the effectiveness of cavalry. Invented in Asia around 600 AD, the stirrup increased cavalry efficiency because a rider could now attack without falling down due to the ensuing shock. Other items, like redesigned shields, saddles, and lances, helped too (Brodie & Brodie, 1973). As a result, the horse came to be used more frequently for raids and reconnaissance missions. These nonhuman animals were so important, in fact, that during the Saxon Wars of 772-804 AD, many of Charlemagne's raids would be cancelled if his horses were too sick or tired to work. And, when an equine epidemic killed ninety percent of his horses, Charlemagne's army was left unable to wage a campaign against the Avars in 791 AD (Hyland, 1999).

Finally, the camel was an important nonhuman animal to the early expansion of Islam, and later to the Arab conquests of the seventh and eighth centuries. As a young man, the prophet Muhammad worked as a camel driver, riding to holy cities, like Mecca and Medina. And, during the war against the Koreish, Mohammad captured a camel-rich caravan traveling from Syria in 624 AD. This victory granted him the resources necessary to continue his religious mission. It was a defining moment for him. Some years later, in 630 AD, Muhammad would capture an even greater number of camels in the Battle of Hunayn (Gabriel, 2007b). Camels were clearly valuable assets to possess during Muhammad's time. In addition, nearly all of Muhammad's battles were fought on camel-back (Knapp-Fisher, 1940). Interestingly, in 656 AD, there was even a Battle of the Camel, named after the camel upon which Muhammad's wife A'ishah rode as she led an army into battle.

Early Modern

Although the first half of the early modern period was influenced by religious and superstitious beliefs, the second half would be transformed by a new mode of thinking that combined secular rationalism and industrialism. In terms of warfare, these ideologies rejected the chivalrous and localized engagements of the past, viewing them as irrational, in favor of grander economic and political acquisitions. Unfortunately, war would become more ruthless and casualties far more common. The exploration of the New Worlds incited violent struggles against native peoples, conflicts which pushed them to the margins of their land or, worse, enslaved them. Furthermore, the widespread use of gunpowder affected the way nonhuman animals were used as weapons of war. While some would continue their service, albeit in altered ways, others would be replaced by gunpowder and never again used for war.

The dog of the early modern period accompanied soldiers, explorers, and adventurers as they journeyed through the dangerous and uncharted territory of the New World. A popular breed was the Alaunt, a wolf and mastiff mix that originated in Southern Europe. This dog had a fierce, determined, and loyal nature, which made it quite popular amongst armies, monarchs, and conquistadores. In 1500 AD, Vasco Núñez de Balboa explored the New World with his dog Leoncico. His dog was such a good fighter that it even received payments for its work. Meanwhile, Gonzalo Jiménez de Quesada's dog helped conquer the lands of the Muisca people, located in modern-day Santa Fé de Bogotá, Colombia (Richardson, 1920). However, it was the ferocious dog of Nikolaus Federmann that truly struck fear in the hearts of the Colombian natives. These dogs did so much fighting, in fact, that they needed protective covering to shield them from the barrage of poisoned arrows (Dempewolff, 1943). Ultimately, the dogs were capable of inflicting great physical and psychological harm.

Another popular breed was the bloodhound. Christopher Columbus depended on his bloodhounds to protect him from the dangers he encountered during his voyages. The dogs would use their sense of smell to sniff out natives and prevent potential ambushes. In addition, the breed helped to police the local conflicts of the time. Since most people in the Middle Ages lived in roadless and uncleared land, the only way they could track criminals and desperados was by enlisting the aid of the bloodhound. For this reason, the war dog and the police dog were considered one and the same during this time period (Richardson, 1920).

The arrival of horses to the New World dramatically changed the way the AmerIndians fought wars. Horses were first introduced in North America around 1640 AD to the tribes residing in the southernmost regions of the country. The concept of using horses quickly spread throughout the North and the West. Although horses encouraged trade and communication between tribes, they also increased raids, war and other conflicts. Horses signified wealth and power. And, those who could capture horses were held in high regard. For this reason, AmerIndians would travel long distances to capture or steal horses, as well as other goods. In many cases, this act was considered a rite of passage for young men. As the AmerIndians came into further contact with the Europeans, however, the competition for resources only got progressively worse (McCabe, 2004).

In the beginning of the early modern period, war elephants were used in innovative ways that reflected the changes that had occurred in weapon technology. Visually, these nonhuman animals appeared more impressive than ever. Not only were they adorned with armor, plumes, and poisoned metal tusks, but they were also fitted with large weapons like swivel guns and cannons. These powerful weapons would be mounted in frames on top of their heads (Kistler, 2006). In this sense, the elephant resembled the modern tank.

Although the elephant's ability to annihilate enemies had been enhanced, the same issues that King Porus had encountered nearly two thousand years earlier would arise once again. During the late sixteenth century AD, the Mughal emperor Akbar attempted to extend his empire into Gujarat in Northern India. Although his army was small in number, it carried plenty of artillery. In contrast, the Gujarat army was larger and relied on older technology, like the war elephant. Akbar's army quickly began launching rockets at the elephants, ensuring a stampede as well as the Gujarat's defeat. This battle would mark the end of the elephant's reign as the ultimate weapon of war (Kistler, 2006).

Modern

The modern period witnessed dramatic changes in the field of weaponry, thanks to advances in science, mechanics, and engineering. As tensions increased among nations, political leaders began to acknowledge the importance of weapon testing and experimentation, coordinating large-scale efforts to join hundreds of brilliant scientists together in order to improve upon and/or create new weapons. The goal was to produce, as quickly as possible, weapon technology that was more accurate, more powerful, and more efficient. These efforts led to major developments in air, land, and sea technology. Eventually, science was completely integrated into all aspects of war, from weapon development to strategic and tactical planning. This modern period is also marked by its unique portrayals of fighting nonhuman animals. In other words, there are countless stories in which nonhuman animals are named, personified, and honored as heroes by fellow soldiers, royalty, and society.

Despite having been the world's fastest mode of communication for several centuries, the carrier pigeon would be replaced by the telegraph in the early nineteenth century. Nevertheless, the carrier pigeon continued to be a valuable resource whenever there were technological difficulties. Each time telegraphic service broke down between European cities during the Revolutions of 1848, pigeons would assume the role they had had since Antiquity. Telegraphic service would also break down between France and Germany during the Franco-Prussian War of 1870. By the end of the war, over four hundred pigeons had been used, of which only seventy-three returned safely. The carrier pigeons were then honored with a bronze monument, sculpted by Frédéric Auguste Bartholdi, the artist responsible for designing the Statue of Liberty (Lubow, 1977). Interestingly, during World War I, it was a felony to kill, wound, or molest carrier pigeons under penalty of six months' imprisonment or £100 fine (Gardiner, 2006).

During the twentieth century, the pigeon would be used once as a symbol of peace, and more frequently as a subject for weapon testing. Sometime between 1953 and 1954, during the Korean War's armistice negotiations, representatives of North Korea released hundreds of white pigeons in the capital of Pyongyang. These pigeons had been trained to reach the top of high buildings, a gesture which was supposed to symbolize North Korea's peaceful intentions (Lubow, 1977). Unfortunately, the pigeon would also be used for less harmonious reasons, namely as unwilling test subjects for weapons, like pigeon-guided missiles and ambush detection devices. Pigeons were used because of their excellent vision and mental faculties. They were also a more practical and cost-efficient choice than other nonhuman animals.

The widespread use of firearms, cannons, and, later, mechanized weaponry would replace nonhuman animals that had previously been used to fight enemies, such as the dog. It was simply more effective to rely on advanced technology than a nonhuman animal. Yet, the dog did not disappear from the battlefield altogether. Rather, the dog would be used more for defensive purposes. Both Frederick the Great and Napoleon Bonaparte employed watchdogs in their campaigns (Jager, 1917). One such dog was a black poodle named Moustache. During the Napoleonic Wars of 1800-1815 AD, Moustache alerted troops of the presence of an Austrian spy. Later, in the heat of battle, Moustache managed to retrieve the French flag, and return it to its proper place with the regiment. For these acts of patriotism, Moustache was awarded a medal of honor (Kistler, 2011).

Surprisingly, Moustache was not the only small dog to earn accolades for its bravery. Since it was no longer absolutely necessary to possess larger and more aggressive fighting dogs, smaller dogs were given a more active role in military life. Smaller dogs were not only considered great companions for human soldiers, they were equally as heroic. One particularly heroic dog was a white terrier named Bobbie. Bobbie was adopted as a puppy by Sergeant Peter Kelly of the 66th Regiment of Foot in Malta's capital of Valletta in 1870. In 1880, the regiment was deployed to Afghanistan to fight the Battle of Maiwand. Many died. Bobbie tried to defend the few remaining soldiers. When a relief army arrived six weeks later, they were surprised to spot a small dog limping into their encampment. It was Bobbie. On the morning of August 17th, 1881, the survivors were invited to meet with Queen Victoria and receive military awards. Recognizing Bobbie's heroism, the Queen wrote in her diary that "They had their little dog, a sort of Pomeranian, with them, which had been with them through the campaign and is quite devoted to the men ... Bobby, as he is called, is a great pet and had a velvet coat on embroidered with pearls and two good conduct stripes and other devices and orders tied around his neck. It was wounded in the back but had quite recovered" (p. 30). Today, Bobbie's remains can be found at the Duke of Edinburgh's Royal Regiment Museum (Le Chene, 1994).

Dogs like Moustache and Bobbie had regular duties, including patroling camp sites, warning soldiers of incoming dangers like snakes, quick-sands, and strangers, as well as a few curious others. In the United States of America, where the Civil War of 1861-1865 carried on, both the Northern and the Southern sides employed dogs to fulfill a number of roles, such as that of guards, orderlies, messengers, and even prison wardens. So valuable were these dogs, in fact, that by the end of the nineteenth century, countries would begin to officially implement dog-training programs for service in the army (Le Chene, 1994).

During the twentieth century, the dog would also be employed for its extraordinary sense of smell. During the Vietnam War, there was a desperate need for something that could track guerrilla groups back to their base camps, as well as identify the booby traps that they had hidden in the jungle. The guerrillas would sneak into villages in the middle of the night to raid, pillage, and kidnap (Lubow, 1977). Instead of using advanced technology, American troops relied on Labrador Retrievers to pick up the enemy's trail (Levy, 2004). The guerrillas would also hide booby traps throughout the jungle, such as the Punji pit, in which feces-covered stakes would be placed in a deep, concealed pit. These booby traps were troublesome because they affected the morale of American soldiers, making them feel helpless and anxious all the time (Lubow, 1977). Dogs were trained to sniff out these booby traps, as well as mines, ambushes, and trip wires.

Other nonhuman animals have been used to detect similar kinds of threats. The French used pigs to detect mines during the Phoney War of 1939, while the Israeli army currently trains pigs to do the same (Gardiner, 2006). More recently, African giant-pouched rats have been trained to search through potential minefields, and uncover hidden bombs. Although these rats are fairly large nonhuman animals, thirty inches long to be precise, they are light enough to run through the minefield without setting anything off. Thanks to their sense of smell, as well as intelligence, they can clear land quickly and efficiently (Kristof, 2010, June 16).

There are many wonderful war stories in which the heroes are cats. During World War I, there lived a small, white cat with the courage of a lion named Pitoutchi. The cat had been raised by Lieutenant Lekeux of the 3rd Artillery Regiment, and consequently followed him everywhere. One day, the lieutenant went to spy on the Germans. The cat went too. Once he arrived at his destination, he hid inside a nearby shell-hole and began to sketch all that he saw. Three German soldiers soon felt his presence, and went to investigate. The soldiers were just about to discover the lieutenant's hiding place, when suddenly Pitoutchi jumped out and attacked the soldiers. The Germans laughed at themselves, believing they had mistaken the cat for a human. Meanwhile, the lieutenant finished the sketch and escaped safely (Baker, 1933).

With the exception of Pitoutchi, most cats were not used for fighting. Rather, they were used for more traditional purposes, such as leading troops to food, and chasing and killing rodents. During the Crimean War, a cat named Tom led sick and starving soldiers to a hidden storeroom full of food. Like other nonhuman detection animals, the cat was able to use its nose to find something that ultimately saved everyone. Meanwhile, other cats protected their military family by keeping the rodent population down on ship and base camps. This was an important task, because rodents posed a potential health risk. Specifically, one cat named Simon was awarded the Dickin Medal posthumously for its rat-killing skills while on the naval ship HMS *Amethyst* during the Chinese Civil War (Le Chene, 1994).

By the modern period, infantry and cavalry had been superseded by trench warfare. Fighting no longer consisted of troops moving around by foot or horse. Instead, fighting was much more immobile, consisting of troops hiding in trenches and dugouts, shooting at each other from stable positions. For this reason, during World War I, the horse was mainly used to carry and transport goods and materials, rather than soldiers. Interestingly, military leaders continued to ride horses into battle as a symbol of leadership. The horses that were employed during this time had to be fearless, because trench warfare was dirty, difficult, and dangerous. These nonhuman animals would constantly be in the line of fire. Needless to say, it was important for horses to be comfortable with the sights and sounds of trench warfare (Baker, 1933).

The donkey too was used as a nonhuman transport animal during World War I. Due to the dangers of trench warfare, it could be quite difficult to transport food and ammunition to the troops. Although it was easy getting supplies to the bases, it was impossible to bring it to the trenches. The donkey, it seemed, had a better disposition for the job than other beasts of burden. It was patient, obedient, and resistant to disease. It was also smaller than the horse, which meant it could pass safely through tight spaces without being detected (Baker, 1933).

During World War I, Britain reestablished a Camel Corps that Napoleon had organized years earlier. Comprised of hundreds of camels, it was used to preserve order in the North-West Frontier, and wage guerrilla-type warfare in the Turkish campaigns. Camels would be used for transport, carrying two men each, as well as ammunition, equipment, and food rations. At the same time, however, camels could be excellent nonhuman fighting animals, capable of reacting offensively by charging at enemies (Knapp-Fisher, 1940). A charging camel could be quite dangerous.

Finally, one of the most surprising nonhuman animals to be used as a weapon of war during the modern period is the dolphin. Since the 1950's, American and Russian defense departments have researched different ways to use dolphins as weapons of war. From a war perspective, it makes sense to exploit dolphins. In water, dolphins are capable of doing anything that dogs or other intelligent nonhuman animals can do. Dolphins can retrieve objects, detect intruders, transport devices to fixed locations, and distinguish between different objects. According to a *Newsday* article published in April 1976, the Navy and the CIA had even managed to train a dolphin to extract a fallen nuclear bomb from the bottom of the sea. Another *Newsday* article claimed that the United States government was using dolphins to gather intelligence data on the capabilities of Russian ships (Lubow, 1977). Moreover, the Soviet Navy was supposedly using dolphins as killing machines, training them to stick limpet mines onto ships and exploding devices onto enemy divers, both of which would then be activated remotely (Gardiner, 2006). Other nonhuman marine animals to be used for similar purposes include sea lions and orca whales. Today, research continues to be done on the potentialities of using marine nonhuman animals for war purposes.

Throughout Prehistory, Antiquity, the Middle Ages, Early Modernity, and the Modern Period, nonhuman animals have played significant roles in the preparation and propagation of war. In fact, for as long as humans have possessed the mental capacity to create tools, nonhuman animals have been exploited as weapons of war and conflict. In the context of war, then, nonhuman animals have historically been viewed and treated as nothing more than living, breathing instruments, bred and trained to accomplish specific tasks, with or against the nonhuman animal's will. No nonhuman animal that has ever participated in war was there without a reason, without a purpose. Their very existence depended on their ability to reduce or, worse, increase human casualty and property loss. Essentially, they existed for the benefit of humans, and not for their own sake. Even in the face of heart-wrenching oppression, most people have only thought of the repercussions on their own lives, fearing that a war waged without nonhuman animals would be too costly, too dangerous, and too hopeless. Unfortunately, it has always been preferable to use nonhuman animals than challenge the entire social construction of war. But, war is the real culprit, as it promotes and reinforces a state of thinking that makes it impossible for humans to coexist peacefully, let alone humans and nonhuman animals. War with or without nonhuman animals is too costly, too dangerous, and too hopeless. Instead we need to aim for the kind of positive peace that is inclusive and transformational. Only then will it be possible to discern the problems inherent in war and other manifestations of violence.

Notes

1. Biblical quotations are from Attridge, H. W. & Meeks, W. A. (2006) *The HarperCollins Study Bible: New revised standard version.* New York, NY: HarperCollins.

CHAPTER FOUR

WAR: ANIMALS IN THE AFTERMATH

Julie Andrzejewski

Invisibilization and Empire

The invisibilization of animals is a major aspect of speciesism and empire. While stories of individual animal harm or triumph may receive sensationalistic attention, the systemic effects of human policies and projects on vast numbers of animals are rarely noticed, investigated, or reported in the media, even when animal bodies and lives are drastically impacted. The human activity of war, most often promulgated in the interests of empire and the theft of land, labor, and resources from animals and one another, is no exception. Even definitions of imperialism only identify the theft of resources from other groups of humans, ignoring the claim of animals to any of the resources upon which they have evolved and survived. Indeed, the idea that land is "owned" by the humans who have lived in that place the longest, ignores any recognition that animals have lived on all the earth's surfaces longer than any humans, and yet they are denied any claim to their living spaces while humans dominate the earth.

Thus, in plans, preparation, research, testing, fomentation, cessation, legalities/illegalities, body counts, medical services, migrations, rebuilding, reparations, or truth commissions pertaining to war, the lives and concerns of animals receive little to no consideration whatsoever. They are "collateral damage" in the most invisible sense of that euphemism. Because of the global invisibilization and oppression of animals, especially during and after armed conflicts, it is not easy to research the impacts on animals during or after wars.

The invisibilization is obvious in the language of the sparse documentation to be found. Animals are depicted by using the singular to mean plural. "Wild boar, wild goat, water buffalo, tiger" describe populations, not individuals. Terms like livestock, farm animals, wild animals, wildlife, domestic animals, define animals in terms of their use or relationship to humans. Separating "human" from "animal" creates a false duality since humans *are* animals. While I do not attempt to analyze these aspects of invisibilization throughout this chapter, the language creates unfortunate distance from our emotions and intellect as we consider the immense brutality of the aftermath of war on animals (Dunayer, 2001).

Secrecy and Censorship

Another obstacle to scrutinizing the long-term impacts of war on animals is that governments maintain high levels of secrecy about militarism and war. Citizens of democratic countries are told that such secrecy is necessary for "national security," but as whistleblowers, leaks, and lawsuits reveal, secrecy is often maintained to protect the illicit self-serving activities of policy makers. Hence, many common aspects of militarism such as creating false justifications for war, offering cost-plus no-bid contracts to war profiteers, employing torture and war crimes, and the widespread killing of animals, children, and civilians are hidden or covered up to avoid increasing public opposition to war.

Further, most information about various weapons systems, their uses, their costs, and the environmental, animal, or human impacts of the damage generated by military preparation and mobilization is unavailable to the U.S. and global publics (Sanders, 2009, 23). Weapons information may be censored directly based on claims of national security, or repressed by the corporate-owned media, many of which have direct investments in military contracts. Or, it may be packaged as propaganda through "public relations" campaigns designed to convince the public of the proficiency of weapons as "surgical" or "smart," or the beneficial and humanitarian motivations of military activities. As a prime example, most Americans are completely unaware that the U.S. Department of Defense is the worst polluter on the planet because this information is so heavily censored (Huff, Roff & Project Censored, 2010).

Oppression of Animals

In spite of pervasive secrecy and invisibilization, this chapter explores questions about animals in the aftermath of war through direct evidence about animals where it exists, and by gleaning information from related areas where observations or information about animals may be included. In other instances, it is imperative to delve into some of the most dreadful aspects of war making and use our imaginations to consider the consequences of such weapons and policies on animals where specific evidence is either missing altogether or sketchy.

As part of this exploration, applying the concept of *oppression* to animals can amplify and enrich our understanding of how they are impacted by militarism and war.

By any definition, it can be argued that nonhuman animals are subjected to *oppression*. Under Young's (1990) five faces of oppression, nonhuman animals are *exploited* as their bodies are used for labor, food, clothing, research, education, entertainment, and more "products" than one can imagine, making it almost impossible to avoid their consumption on a daily basis. *Marginalization* takes on new meaning as nonhuman animals have little to no space on earth to exist where their lives are free of the negative effects of human activities and they are regularly and systemically "subjected to severe material deprivation and even extermination" (p. 53). We have learned to identify our species as "the norm" and the mental, emotional, and physical attributes of all other species are measured, categorized, and devalued in relation to that norm (Young calls this *cultural imperialism*). Under extreme domination of the earth by humans and our technologies, other animals are *powerless* to change their conditions and cannot avoid the many forms of *violence* perpetrated against them. (Andrzejewski, Pedersen, & Wicklund, 2009)

What happens to animals in the aftermath of war and all related aspects of war-making can be identified as oppression in every facet of this definition. The harm and devastation of war to animal bodies and psyches, their homes, their families and communities, their losses, and, not uncommonly today, their extinctions must be brought to light. And, given such little consideration by human beings, whether by those promulgating wars or by the victims of war, it is also vital to recognize the capabilities of animals, when possible, to recover from war and live wherever and however they can.

This chapter will investigate the following questions:

- What core aspects of contemporary warfare inflict long-term effects on animals?

- What are the long-term effects of environmental war (chemical, biological, radioactive, explosive, and environmental modification weapons) on animals?

- What are the aftermath effects of war on particular groups of animals?

- What options do animals have in the aftermath of wars and war-making?

- What is the answer: Band-aids vs. root cause solutions?

What Core Aspects of Contemporary Warfare Inflict Long-term Effects on Animals?

A number of key causes and trends related to the long-term effects of warfare and war-making offer an indispensable foundation for grasping the plight of animals affected by this gruesome human endeavor. These include:

- Imperialism exacerbates animal oppression and extinctions through endless wars.

- Human disruptions of nature are increasing global conflicts.

- Wars are concentrated in biodiversity hotspots.

- Environmental warfare leaves a pervasive habitat of death.

- The destructive capabilities of contemporary weapons initiate omnicide.

- Refugees increase the impact of war on animals.

- Wars divert resources from global problems affecting animals.

Imperialism Exacerbates Animal Oppression and Extinctions through Endless Wars

Under global capitalism, maximizing profits inherently conflicts with what is best for animals, humans, and the earth. The well-being of all is sacrificed to extract natural resources, monopolize land and habitat, and exploit labor (animal and human). As the histories of imperialism will confirm, humans seeking riches have organized militaries or sought the collaboration of governments to use aggressive forces to extract profits anywhere and everywhere on earth, or from war-making itself. There is no end to invasions, occupations, and wars as long as money can be made (Parenti, 1995; Shiva, 1995).

Desired resources are commandeered by whatever violence is needed: imprisonment and torture, assassination of individuals or groups, environmental decimation, war and/or extermination. No violence is too great to serve the interests of human greed. While many millions of humans have suffered, died, and been forced to flee their homes in wars, these same events have certainly affected *billions upon billions* of animals, given the extensive number of animal species and the density of their populations over every surface of the earth. In some cases, animals or animal products, like body parts or ivory, are the resource motivating imperialist wars (Enzler, 2006).

While various peoples have fomented imperialist wars over millennia, the United States has been an imperial nation from its inception and has emerged in the twentieth century as the dominant military power. The United States of America expends more on the military than all other nations combined and it is the biggest seller of arms to other nations. Hence, while this investigation is meant to be global, a preponderance of information will be drawn from the activities of the United States.

Human Disruptions of Nature Are Expected to Increase Global Conflicts

With exponential increases in the human population and human encroachment on every part of the earth's surface, the impact of global problems created by humans will increase the incidence of conflicts. As climate change fosters extreme weather, water and food scarcities intensify, the gap between rich and poor increases, and war profiteering continues to be the most lucrative business, wars are expected to multiply (Broder, 2000). Further, as the largest weapons merchant by far, the United States military industrial complex and its related global arms sales create increased tensions and fuels regional arms races, making future conflicts more likely (Berrigan, 2010; Deen, 2010). The displacement, suffering, deaths, and extinctions of animals will intensify with the concomitant upsurge in conflicts.

Wars Are Concentrated in Biodiversity Hotspots

While animals experience short- and long-term terror, injuries, and death from wars everywhere they occur, there is evidence that warfare is now occurring predominantly in biodiversity hotspots, defined as limited regions of great biological richness and extensive loss of habitat. Eighty percent of armed conflicts are concentrated in areas where "three-quarters of the world's threatened mammals, birds, and amphibians occur only in the hotspots" (Hanson et al. 2009, p. 579). While no theories are offered to explain this phenomenon, it is likely that these areas are the last to be completely exploited and there is a rush to profit from any and all "resources," including animals, still to be found in these hotspots.

Environmental Warfare Leaves a Pervasive Habitat of Death

Scorched earth practices have historically been a tool of war, but contemporary environmental warfare has created unparalleled devastation. For example, in the Gulf War, Iraq dumped ten million barrels of crude oil into the Persian Gulf—at that time the largest spill in history—killing tens of thousands of migrating birds and untold numbers of sea animals (Loretz, 1991, p. 3).

Crude oil was also poured directly into the desert, creating oil lakes covering 50 square kilometers, despoiling the fragile ecosystem and eventually percolating into the aquifers (Enzler, 2006). Fleeing Iraqi troops ignited Kuwaiti oil sources, releasing pollutants into the atmosphere. These fires caused smog, acid rain, and toxic fumes. A layer of soot was deposited on the desert, covering all plant life. Then seawater was applied to extinguish the oil fires causing increased salinity. Tanks damaged the delicate desert surface, and particles of depleted uranium mingled with the sand everywhere weapons or tanks were used. In the cities, water treatment plants were targeted, allowing sewage to flow directly into the Tigris and Euphrates rivers. After many years of war in both Iraq and Afghanistan, the environmental damage is pervasive and irreparable. Animals and humans occupying these areas are destined to suffer disease, birth defects, and death.

While the continued suffering on human lives and families is slowly being documented, the impact on the animals who live in these areas, goes mostly unnoted. Occasionally, animals are mentioned as a side comment, such as this observation on the Israeli war on Lebanon in 2006: "The oil spill spread rapidly ... covering over 90 km of the coastline, killing fish and affecting the habitat of the endangered green sea turtle . . . A total of 9,000 acres of forest burned to the ground, and fires threaten tree reserves and bird sanctuaries" (Enzler, 2006, p. 8). Images and stories of the individual animals affected are not circulated, nor are investigations or reports on the immediate status or long-term effects on green sea turtles, fish, or birds available.

The Destructive Capability of Contemporary Weapons Initiate Omnicide

Contemporary weapons are more powerful, more destructive, more contaminating, and have longer lasting effects than ever before. Indeed, most US weapons now contain radioactive depleted uranium with a half-life of 4.7 billion years. The total long-term consequences of such weapons are not known but some, such as Sanders (2009) suggest it is:

> *Omnicide* - the destruction of all life, human and animal and vegetable . . . Human beings are not the only victims of this unspeakable poisoning through exposure to uranium. Plants and animals also absorb the radioactive particles, making uranium a permanent part of the food chain. Once in the soil, a report by the United Nations Environmental Program concludes, depleted uranium pollutes the groundwater by increasing uranium levels one hundred fold. (p. 88)

A brief description of a few of the major bombs built by the United States provides an inkling of the destructive power that may initiate a process of omnicide. The Bunker Buster explodes underground disbursing 1/5 metric tons of depleted uranium. The Daisy Cutter "creates a concussive effect . . . sucking oxygen out of a wide area, killing every living thing through incineration or asphyxiation, or both" (Sanders, 2009, p. 96). The largest of all bombs, MOAB or Mother of All Bombs, called "steel rain" by people who have experienced it, causes lung disease and neurological disorders for drawn out death with ten tons of aluminum powder (Sanders, 2009). The DIME (Dense Inert Metal Explosive) bomb, filled with tungsten alloy, "explodes into billions of pieces of super-heated micro-shrapnel—an incredibly destructive blast in a small area, or what the military calls 'focused lethality'" (p. 113). Also known as the "Cancer Bomb" side effects include almost 100 percent cancer rate (Nichols, 2010).

Considered "conventional" rather than nuclear weapons, these bombs have been tested in the United States of America and deployed in recent wars. Everywhere they have been tested or used, their toxic payload continues to impact the living beings who were not immediately destroyed.

Refugees Increase the Impact of War on Animals

The massive displacement of humans by wars as internally displaced persons or refugees is creating another disaster of epic proportions, destroying undeveloped areas, wildernesses, national parks, forests, and contaminating water. Often titled "uninhabited," these areas are, in fact, inhabited by other animals. Upon arrival, desperate humans destroy animal homes for fuel and shelter, and often kill animals for food (Hanson et al., 4). Water resources are contaminated by the concentration of humans without supportive infrastructure. Further, "farmed" animals may be moved into areas where "wild" animals have been living, causing habitat conflicts. For example, Bedouin refugees fleeing the Gulf war brought 1.6 million sheep, goats, camels, and donkeys into Jordan where the extirpated Arabian Oryx was being reintroduced, making the survival of the Oryx unlikely (Harding, 2007).

Wars Divert Resources from Global Problems Affecting Animals

Military expenditures and the costly privatization of war divert precious and limited resources away from the urgent global problems humans have caused. This aftermath of war has enormous long-term effects on the animals of the world. Global warming continues with a rapidity far exceeding that predicted by scientists (IPCC Report, 2013) and new incidents of the massive death of trees is turning carbon sinks into carbon emissions (Carrington, 2011). But the most significant global problem affecting animals is the sixth mass extinction of species, another story mostly censored by the corporate media (Andrzejewski and Alessio, 2013). Scientists now estimate that three-quarters of the earth's species (amphibians, mammals, plant, fish) may become extinct within 300 years if nothing is done. Nothing *will* be done to tackle any of these urgent problems as long as trillions of dollars fund imperialism, greed, and wars.

What Are the Long-Term Effects of Environmental Warfare on Animals (Chemical, Biological, Radioactive, Explosive, and Environmental Modification Weapons)?

To facilitate even a rudimentary sense of the aftereffects on animals that survive war, we must probe further into the types of weapons being tested and used in wars. Given the destructive consequences of weapons developed over the last century, most aspects of warfare should be considered environmental warfare.

For the purposes of this chapter, environmental warfare includes all war-related short- and long-term environmental destruction that affect life and natural systems. Some analysts differentiate by considering activities occurring directly in war as "active," and those which appear to be tangential to war as "passive" (Jenson, 2005). This differentiation seems arbitrary since both types of activities may have equally devastating impacts on animals and the environment, and none could truly be characterized as "passive." Instead, I will differentiate two types of impacts as *direct environmental warfare* and *environmental warfare through secondary targets and warfare support activities.*

Direct environmental warfare includes the direct deployment of explosive, penetrating, chemical, biological, or radioactive weapons, as well as the use of the environment itself as a tool of war. First I will provide a brief overview of the weapon types and then they will each be examined with regard to their impact on animals, with as much specificity as can be found.

Explosive weapons combine explosives with chemicals, heavy metals, radioactive substances, and/or incendiaries. Only a few of the many bombs were described above. Chemical weapons may entail the use of nerve or mustard gas, chromium, tungsten, and other toxic materials in explosives or in some cases through direct application. Chemical weapons also include the deployment of herbicides, dioxin, white phosphorus, and incendiary weapons like napalm. Biological weapons involve the production and targeted distribution of diseases to debilitate or kill animals, crops, and/or humans. All of these weapons systems involve testing on animals, either purposefully in laboratories, or when the weapons are exploded or disseminated as there is no way or attempt to evacuate animals from the testing areas.

Oil has been used as a weapon by purposefully "spilling" it, lighting it on fire, and using it to pollute water or land surfaces. Other environmental methods of war involve draining swamps, defoliating forests, poisoning water, and placing land mines in agricultural or natural areas. Chillingly, research and testing of environmental modification (ENMOD) or war by weather has progressed in spite of a 1977 Geneva Convention on prohibition (Chossudovsky, 2009).

Environmental warfare through secondary targets and warfare support activities comprise practices such as:

- the massive burning of fossil fuels;

- research and production of weapons;

- testing of sonar, missiles, and bombs;

- dumping spent ammunition, unexploded ordnance, chemicals, or radioactive waste into oceans or "storing" them in places where they leak into the air, ground, and water;

- bombing chemical plants, oil refineries, water treatment, electrical, and other industrial and infrastructure facilities;

- purposefully destroying military and industrial machinery;

- constructing military bases.

Even this extensive list of the destructive environmental activities, direct and secondary, of militarism and war is hardly exhaustive. Yet, as we can imagine even if documentation is not available, their combined effects on animals and nature are resulting in unspeakable short- and long-term consequences—again—*"omnicide"* (Sanders, 2009, p. 88).

Explosives and Bombs

The story of Mosha and Motala, Asian elephants who survived land mine explosions, each losing a large part of one of their legs, has been publicized with a major documentary (Borman, 2010). Unlike many other elephants and animals who die from these explosions, Mosha and Motala were saved by the Friends of the Asian Elephant Hospital. Still, suffering from depression and refusing to socialize, their lives have been unnecessarily curtailed by multiple surgeries and loss of a leg. In these two rare instances, prostheses were created to make their lives better. But, extrapolating from the few numbers available, it is likely that millions of animals have been killed and/or severely injured by land mines. In one of the few articles available, Roberts and Stewart (1998) report:

A study of the social and economic costs of mines in Afghanistan, Bosnia, Cambodia, and Mozambique concluded that more than 54,000 animals were lost to land mine detonations. Mines deployed during World War II eventually killed more than 3,000 animals per year in Libya between 1940 and 1980. (p. 36)

Hundreds of millions of land mines and cluster munitions lay ready to maim and kill innocent victims (animals and civilians) in more than sixty-six countries long after the wars are over (ICBL, 2011). "We often hear of landmines causing death and severe injury to innocent people, but animals are suffering the same fate ... In fact ten or twenty times more animals are killed and maimed from landmines every single day" (Looking-glass, n.d.). In some cases, mines were planted in agricultural areas to prevent humans from growing crops. Sometimes, cows or sheep are purposefully driven through the fields as mine-clearing devices, victims of the aftermath of war:

In western Bosnia there are unconfirmed reports that residents of Sanski Most have developed their own method of demining called "sheep-demining" where they simply let sheep loose into unsecured areas. Sheep were also used to clear minefields during the 1980-1989 Iran-Iraq War. (Roberts &Stewart, 1998, p. 2)

Explosive bombs, small and large, exact a cost that goes far beyond the immediate terror and death of impact. Along with other consequences of war, they affect survival and quality of life for individuals and populations as they contaminate even the most remote environments, as noted here about the mountains of Afghanistan.

> Bombs threaten much of the country's wildlife ... In the mountains many large animals such as leopards found refuge, but much of the habitat is applied as refuge for military forces now. Additionally, refugees capture leopards and other large animals and trade them for safe passage across the border. Pollution from application of explosives entered air, soil and water. (Enzler, 2006, p. 5)

Chemical Agents and Incendiary Weapons

Tested on animals, key chemical weapons like blood, blister, nerve, and choking or pulmonary agents are identified as "lethal to humans." Other chemical agents cause temporary incapacitation (WILPF). Incendiary weapons, such as napalm and white phosphorus, burn and melt upon contact with flesh—any flesh. Other chemicals, like herbicides, defoliate forests, jungles, and coastlines where animals abide so "enemy forces" cannot hide.

While international agreements ban chemical weapons and prohibit or restrict incendiary weapons, they have all, in fact, been used numerous times since their development, most recently by the United States in Fallujah, Iraq, and possibly in Afghanistan (Hambling, 2009). Even though there is little information about the direct impact of these chemicals on animals during and after wars, a few estimates of affected land, waters, and decreases in populations of various animals impart only the most limited sense of the suffering and loss that animals actually experience.

Vietnam, Laos, and Cambodia.

Minimal evaluation of the impact of defoliants (herbicides), bombs, cluster bombs, napalm, and land mines on the forests and wildlife of these Indochinese countries has been conducted. Twenty million gallons of Agent Orange, an herbicide used to defoliate "massive tracts of forest in Vietnam killed, wounded, or evicted many of the animal inhabitants" (Loretz, 1991, 1). One source noted:

> The damage to the plant life of South Vietnam caused by the spraying of Agent Orange is still visible today. The most severe damage occurred in the mangrove forests (tropical trees and shrubs) of coastal areas where spraying left barren, badly eroded coastlines. The number of coastal birds declined dramatically, and with the disappearance of the web of water channels beneath the mangrove trees, fish were deprived of important breeding grounds. It is estimated that full

recovery of the mangrove forests to their former state will take at least 100 years ... As the rich, diverse tropical forests disappeared, so did animal habitats. As a result, the number of bird and mammal species living in the areas that were sprayed declined dramatically. Wild boar, wild goat, water buffalo, tiger, and various species of deer became less common once the cover and food resources of the forest were removed. Domestic animals such as water buffalo, zebus (an Asian ox), pigs, chickens, and ducks are also reported to become ill after the spraying of Agent Orange. (Science Clarified, n.d.)

Agent Blue, an arsenic derivative, was also used to destroy crops. Fifty years later the devastating impact of these weapons on animals is impossible to fully assess, yet the impact on watersheds, vegetation, and the pervasive existence of dioxins is still evident in freshwater animals (King, 2006).

Hawaii and U.S. Coastal Waters, Atlantic and Pacific

From 1944 until 1970, several hundred thousand tons of chemical weapons and radioactive wastes were dumped in approximately thirty sites around the Atlantic and Pacific oceans. In some instances, holes were shot into the containers to make sure they would sink. Bombs containing chemical mustard, lewisite, sarin and tabun have been decomposing under the sea, allowing these substances to leak into the oceans. Only recently has a study of these chemical weapons, the Hawaii Undersea Munitions and Material Assessment, been initiated (Branan, 2009, January 27). No results are available yet.

Gaza

International organizations and human rights groups are investigating potential war crimes by Israel against Gaza in 2009, specifically the illegal use of white phosphorus, and DIME weapons (Dense Inert Metal Explosives) containing tungsten that severs limbs and ruptures internal organs with no sign of an entry point. Tungsten has the long-term effect of being "extremely carcinogenic, and can produce an aggressive form of cancer" (Cunningham, 2009, 3). While there is no mention of animal victims, animals are undoubtedly impacted by these terrible weapons as well. How could it be otherwise?

Philippines and Pacific Islands: Wake Island, Johnston Atoll, Guam and others

Numerous Pacific Islands are profoundly contaminated with chemical and radioactive weapons, as a result of:

- detonating nuclear bombs during atmospheric testing,

- storing chemical weapons and military waste shipped from around the world,

- disposing of contaminated soils and wastes from around military bases,

- disposing of unexploded bombs, and

- incinerating chemical weapons at the Johnston Atoll Chemical Agents Disposal System.

The contamination of these activities ranges from polychlorinated biphenyls (PCBs), Agent Orange (dioxin), phosgene and mustard gas, insecticides and pesticides, to mercury, arsenic, lead, aldrin, dieldrin, toluene, benzene, methyl ethyl ketone, xylene, and trichloroethylene, to high-level radioactive waste including plutonium. All are extremely hazardous and toxic substances (Nautilus Institute for Security and Sustainability, 2005).

These sensitive island habitats host a large variety of animals, birds, and marine life, some of them endangered, yet they continue to be used as disposal sites, polluting the air, soil, marine and freshwater with the most dangerous contaminants created for the uses of warfare. There is no measure of the impact that these wastes, many of which continue to leak, are having on the millions of animals coming in contact with them. Indeed, in attempts to cover up the severity of the devastation, several of these islands have been designated as bird or wildlife sanctuaries.

Mass bird and fish deaths

On New Years Eve 2010, five thousand red wing blackbirds and 83,000 drumfish deaths were reported in Arkansas and 500 bird deaths in Louisiana a few days later (Brean, 2011). The Arkansas Game and Fish Commission stated, "the birds suffered from acute physical trauma leading to internal hemorrhage and death. There was no sign of chronic or infectious disease" (MSNBC, 2011). Months later, no official or plausible explanations of these and other mass deaths have been offered or proven. While evidence is extremely difficult to obtain, given the extensive history of unethical secret weapons programs, questions relating these phenomena to chemical or scalar (weather) weapons cannot be dismissed.

Radioactive weapons and testing

Radioactive weapons were developed by the United States, Britain and Canada during World War II with the first atmospheric test in New Mexico in July 1945, just before the United States dropped two atomic bombs on Japan in August 1945. Little concern has been expressed for the animals affected by the direct use or long-term effects of these weapons on Japan or the over 2000 atmospheric and underground tests between 1945 and 2008 (United Nations, n.d.). Yet, harmful contamination of the air, soil, and water may last for years, decades, millennia or longer. In a separate radioactive weapons initiative, the United States began making and using Depleted Uranium (DU) weapons in 1968 with potential omnicidal effects (Lendman, 2006).

In the absence of long-term investigative research on animals living in particularly contaminated areas, only a glimpse of the effects on animals can be deduced from the evidence available from sources describing the testing and use of radioactive weapons.

Nevada test site (NTS)

The area most used for atmospheric and later for underground testing of nuclear bombs is a desert area northwest of Las Vegas, Nevada. While considered by humans to be barren or desolate, a description of the animals living there *before* the testing presents a different picture:

> the NTS supported over 190 different species of birds, including some waterfowl near the sparse springs and temporary lakes created by run-off from the rains. The area was home to 14 types of lizards, 17 species of snakes, 94 varieties of spiders, 4 types of bats, 42 kinds of terrestrial mammals, and 1 class of tortoise before the nuclear testing began. The great diversity in the plants and animals of the areas demonstrated how much the destruction of the area would affect the miniature ecosystem of the land (Cherrix, 2008, p. 1).

An observer monitoring ground zero from a helicopter noted, "the sand, it would be melted just like glass ... All the weeds and grass, and if there were trees, they were on fire too. Rabbits would run across there and they would be on fire" (Gallagher, 1993, p. 5).

Over 200 atmospheric and 800 underground nuclear tests were conducted at this site. Atmospheric tests were discontinued with the Nuclear Test Ban Treaty in 1963 but underground tests continued until 1992, "after it was known that exposure to large amounts of radiation caused cancer and birth defects in humans, as well as in animals" (Cherrix, 2008, p. 2).

Island test sites

Atmospheric nuclear tests were also conducted on the delicate island ecosystems of Eniwetok and Bikini Atolls (Marshall Islands), Johnston Island, Christmas Island (Kiribati), and three underground tests, including the largest, were conducted at Amchitka Island, Alaska. Although very minimal and unsatisfactory, the impact of this testing on animals may be considered by comparing the animals living in other parts of the Marshall Islands with a 2002 research visit to the Bikini Atoll which only discusses the corals:

> Marshall Islands are the home to diverse species of corals ... 180 species ... on Arno Atoll and 156 species ... on Majuro Atoll ... All five of the world's species of marine turtles have been found in the Marshall Islands ... As many as 27 species of whales, dolphins, and porpoises occur here ... More than 250 species of reef fish ... 70 species of birds ... of which 31 species are seabirds ... 15 species breed here ... The Polynesian rat is the only (mammal) species ... 7 species of lizards and 1 species of blind snake ... numerous species of insects, spiders, and land crabs, coconut crabs are seen here. Endangered species: Blue whale, sperm whale, Micronesian pigeon, leatherback turtle, hawksbill turtle are found here (Maps of World, n.d.).

In a research team visit to Bikini Island, 70 percent of the coral species were found in 2002 dives into the crater left by the Bravo test. However, "the team found no signs of 28 delicate corals that used to live at Bikini" (Dance, 2008, p. 1). The soil and plants remain contaminated.

U.S. Navy war exercises and weapons testing in Pacific Coast waters

In spite of numerous challenges to the environmental impact, the National Oceanic and Atmospheric Association (NOAA) issued a permit in November 2010 for the US Navy to conduct war exercises in the waters off the Pacific coastline. These tests involve missile and sonar testing, underwater training minefields, and the dumping of wastes containing toxic and radioactive substances like depleted uranium, chromium, and cyanide (Hotakainen, 2010, Van Strum, 2010).

In descriptive materials designed for public consumption, the affects on animals are minimized by the use of the euphemism *takes*:

> the Navy anticipates more than 2.3 million takes (significant disruptions in marine mammal foraging, breeding, and other essential behaviors) per year, of 11.7 million takes over the course of a five-year permit ... To "take" is a legal euphemism for to kill or maim. (Van Strum, 2010).

Wildlife and environmental organizations are especially concerned about the effects of sonar on the pod of orcas living in Puget Sound.

Depleted uranium (DU)

DU weapons use a highly radioactive nuclear waste product to produce high-density weapons which can pierce armor. Although not specifically named in any international bans, these weapons are illegal under several international documents for failing four tests of legality:

- Temporal Test: Weapons must not continue to act after the battle is over.

- Environmental Test: Weapons must not be unduly harmful to the environment.

- Territorial Test: Weapons must not act off of the battlefield.

- Humaneness Test: Weapons must not kill or wound inhumanely. (Moret, 2003, p. 3)

DU is now a component of many, if not most, weapons manufactured by the United States (Sanders, 2009) including bombs, missiles, bullets, tanks, antipersonnel shells, and some land mines (International Coalition to Ban Uranium Weapons [ICBUW], n.d.). When DU weapons are deployed, they produce tiny dust particles that contaminate the air, soil, water, as well as entering the food chain. They can be distributed by weather and are virtually impossible to "clean up." Although illegal, DU weapons have been used by Israel in the Yom Kippur war in 1973, and by the United States in the Gulf War in 1991, in Yugoslavia in the 1990s, and in Iraq (and possibly Afghanistan) in the 2000s (Lendman, 2006, p. 5).

While very little research has been done even on the long-term effects on humans, the information available from Gulf War veterans and human victims in the Middle East is grim, including increased cancer rates, extreme birth defects, and an entire host of severe body disorders, most commonly identified in veterans as *Gulf War Syndrome*. DU is a "radiological hazard ... kidney toxin, neurotoxin, immunotoxin, mutagen, carcinogen and teratogen" (ICBUW, p. 4).

While very few US soldiers were injured or killed directly in the first Gulf War, thousands have died since, and hundreds of thousands are now disabled, purportedly as a result of exposure to chemical, biological, and radioactive weapons. There is no reason to believe that animals exposed to DU would experience any less catastrophic health consequences than humans. Yet, only one study could be located that showed serious changes in blood samples taken from camels exposed to DU in Iraq and Algeria in comparison with healthy camels living in uncontaminated areas (Alaboudi). I believe it is safe to assume that animals are similarly suffering, dying, and experiencing serious birth defects in their offspring from one-time and/or continued exposure to depleted uranium in their environment, water, and food.

Biological and Entomological Warfare

Biological warfare is "the deliberate spreading of disease amongst humans, animals, and plants ... for hostile purposes (using) bacteria, rickettsiae, viruses, toxins, and fungi" (Biological and Toxin Weapons Convention, 2008). Most of this secret "research" uses animals and/or insects (entomological warfare). Throughout history many humans (and countries) have practiced this diabolical warfare. While exposés of testing biological weapons on domestic citizens, racist disease research, extreme safety violations, and outbreaks of diseases never before seen in the United States establish a scandalous reputation for U.S. biological weapons experimentation, the long-term consequences for animals appear to be devastating, widespread, and potentially catastrophic for the future. A few examples provide a small sense of the suspected injury and death experienced by animals under the auspices of this dangerous pursuit.

Lyme disease

Although conclusive proof is not available, evidence suggests that the Plum Island Animal Disease Center (PIADC), established in the 1950s, is the likely initiator of Lyme Disease into animal and human populations in the United States (Carroll, 2004).

1975: PIADC begins feeding live viruses to "hard ticks," including the Lone Star tick (never seen outside Texas prior to 1975). The Lone Star tick is a carrier of the *Borelia burghorferi (Bb) bacteria,* the causal agent of Lyme Disease. The first *(human)* cases of the illness are reported in Connecticut, directly across from the facility. Current epidemiological data conclusively demonstrate that the epicenter of all U.S. Lyme Disease cases is Plum Island. (Burghardt, 2009, pp. 4-5)

Since 1975 countless dogs, cats, horses, cows, goats, and other animals have suffered needlessly from heart, kidney, liver, eye and nervous system problems, fever, lameness, listlessness, loss of appetite, swollen joints, poor fertility, abortions, chronic weight loss, temperament changes, and chronic progressive arthritis related to Lyme disease (Miller, n.d.).

West Nile virus

PIADC is also suspected of releasing West Nile Virus into animals and humans in the United States (Carroll, 2004):

> August 1999: The first four human cases of West Nile virus, a mosquito-borne pathogen never diagnosed in North America are diagnosed on Long Island. Horse farms within a five-mile radius of one another, directly opposite Plum Island, report horses dying following violent seizures. An investigation reveals that 25% of the horses in this small, localized area test positive for West Nile. (Burghardt, 2009, p. 5).

Other biological weapons have likely been released upon pigs, sheep, and other animals as a method of harming the human populations who are "farming" them, but evidence for such events to date has not been conclusive.

Environmental Modification Weapons (ENMOD or War by Weather)

Although banned by the Geneva Convention on the Prohibition of Military or Any Other Hostile Use of Environmental Modification Techniques in 1977 with both the United States of America and Soviet Union as signatories, *war by weather* research, testing, and deployment continues unabated in the United States. The High-Frequency Active Auroral Research Program (HAARP) based in Gakona, Alaska, is capable of heating the ionosphere to accomplish a number of nefarious objectives from disrupting electricity and communications to targeting severe weather patterns on unsuspecting areas of the planet (Chossudovsky, 2009).

Dr. Nicholas Begich, coauthor of the book *Angels Don't Play This HAARP* (Begich, 1995), depicts HAARP as "a super-powerful radio wave beaming technology that lifts areas of the ionosphere by focusing a beam on them and then heating them. Electromagnetic waves then bounce back onto earth and penetrate everything—living and dead." HAARP has the potential to jam global communication systems, change weather patterns over large areas, interfere with wildlife migration patterns, and negatively affect human health. It is also capable of potentially triggering targeted floods, droughts, hurricanes and earthquakes. The military report, *Air Force 2025*, asserts, that by 2025 US forces can "own the weather" (Gilbert, 2004, pp. 1-2).

It is clear that ENMOD must be taken into consideration as one of the greatest threats to animals and life on earth, interfering with far more than "wildlife migration patterns." Animals may already be living or dying from the effects or aftereffects of this warfare. Highly secretive, the technology can be used without detection, preventing national or international legal action from pursuing injunctions or accountability.

What Are the Effects of War On Particular Groups of Animals?

In the aftermath of war, certain animal groups may experience particular effects. For instance, animals controlled by humans in various ways may experience distinct problems because of their particular relationship to or "use by" humans. Wildlife or animals not under the direct control of humans may experience problems related to environmental destruction or contamination, poaching, impact on their habitat or food source, etcetera. Endangered species, already living on the brink, may experience local extinctions in biodiversity hotspot war zones, near military bases, or on testing grounds, and thus may become another component of "collateral damage" that goes virtually unnoted until years later. While the effects on some animals have been addressed above as related to specific weapons systems, other significant problems arise for certain groups of animals from the entire war situation.

Animals controlled by humans

Beyond the immediate impacts of war, animals controlled by humans in some way may be injured, mistreated, displaced, lost, stolen, eaten, or killed after a conflict has ended. If animal needs are addressed at all, animals immediately of use to humans like working animals or farmed animals appear to get attention first.

Companion animals

If not killed or injured with their human families, it is not uncommon for companion animals to become lost, displaced, or left behind if family members become refugees. The future for these animals is not optimistic. Forced to "fend for themselves," they often become part of a feral population, living in war-decimated areas or on the edge of tenuous human encampments. In some cases they become the target of cruel and ineffectual eradication efforts. In Iraq, for instance, authorities are trying to control an increasing urban feral dog population by relying upon shooting and poisoning (Dearing, 2010). Not only are these efforts inhumane, they are unsuccessful.

Working animals

The fate of animals forced to work for humans in various capacities changes dramatically for the worse after war. Some animals are required to carry heavy burdens for long-distances as people lose their homes or have to flee. For example, Afghan's used donkeys and horses loaded with household belongings to escape across borders, "Their animals are often terribly thin and have large, untreated blisters or saddle sores where household goods chafed during the journey" (MacDonald, 2002). Under great duress and sometimes with little or no food and water, the likelihood these animals can survive and thrive in the future is greatly diminished, along with their human "owners."

Animals have been forced to work for militaries for centuries. It is not unusual for them to be abandoned or killed after the project or the war ends. For instance, after the fall of the Berlin wall, most of the 7,000 Ovcharka dogs used to guard the wall were purportedly shot because they had been trained to attack escapees and West Berliners were afraid of them (Amiel, 2009). Likewise, most dogs used by the U.S. military in Vietnam were abandoned and left behind. In situations where they are not abandoned, their future is still uncertain. Today, for instance, after "years of war and frequent deployments," some trained military dogs returning to the United States from war zones have been diagnosed with canine PTSD (post-traumatic stress disorder) with symptoms similar to those of veterans (Tan, 2010, p. 1).

Animals imprisoned in zoos

Zoo animals are particularly vulnerable after wars since they are often incarcerated in appalling prisonlike circumstances under "normal" conditions, are completely dependent upon human "keepers" for basic needs, and cannot even escape to "fend for themselves." Zoo personnel may be killed, leave, or not be paid for services. Thus, animals may be neglected, stolen, eaten, or abandoned to starve (Curry, 2003).

Farmed animals

As noted previously, if not killed in the immediate conflict, farmed animals are likely to suffer exaggerated dangers, be eaten by their "owners" or poachers, moved long distances, endure contamination or debilitation from chemical, biological, radioactive, or explosive weapons, or experience disability or death being used for dangerous war-related activities like demining agricultural areas.

Wildlife

In the aftermath of military activities and wars, animals in the "wild" are likely to lose their communities, family members, homes, food, water supplies, life patterns, and lives. Further, years of war creates conditions that give rise to habitat destruction by refugees, poaching for skins, bush meat, and disease from the aftereffects of toxic weapons, purposeful water pollution, and unexploded ordnance. These impacts often have a long-term impact on individual animals, on populations, and on species. Focusing on the lengthy war in Afghanistan, MacDonald (2002) contends:

> Bombing damage to Afghanistan's wild animals and their habitat has not even begun to be assessed, but is likely to be considerable. The country is home to more than 100 mammal species—snow leopards, ibex, bears, wolves, foxes, hyenas and jackals, many of them highly endangered well before the latest conflict (p. 3).

Because of the targeting of mountains in the "War on Terror," the habitat of these animals is disproportionately affected. Indeed, the Afghanistan National Environmental Protection Agency, which listed thirty-three endangered species in 2005, expected the number to grow to over eighty species by the end of 2009 (Frank, 2010).

Bird migrations have been affected dramatically as Enzler (2006, p. 4) documents: "One of the world's important migratory thoroughfare leads through Afghanistan (*sic*). The number of birds now flying this route has dropped by 85 percent." The migration of endangered Siberian Cranes has been disturbed and "entire bird populations have since gone missing across the entire Afghan and Pakistan region" (looking-glass, n.d., p. 3).

In the aftermath of war, government and law enforcement are often corrupted or absent. This lack of structure greatly contributes to the killing of animals and the destruction of habitat. For example:

> The natural resource base of Mozambique was severely affected by recent armed conflicts. Wildlife resources (*sic*), especially large mammal species, were decimated inside and outside of protected areas in many parts of the country, and infrastructure in some of the protected areas was destroyed. The immediate post-war period saw largely uncontrolled (and often illegal) harvesting (*sic*) of wildlife and forestry resources ... (Hatton, Couto, & Oglethorpe, 2001, p. 11)

Sea animals are particularly affected by sunken warships leaking oil, chemical dumping, and underwater nuclear testing, and navy sonar is responsible for whale deaths and strandings. For wars near large bodies of water, fish may be especially targeted. In Somalia, when the International Red Cross encouraged people to eat fish, international fishing protocols were abandoned resulting in massive decimation of the fish populations. When challenged, fishermen began carrying guns to assert "fishing as a property right" (Enzler, 2006, 2). What fish are left off the coast of Somalia still suffer from these practices long after the war ended.

Endangered Animals and Extinctions

The impact of war on the animals cannot be divorced from the knowledge that the earth in rapidly undergoing the sixth mass extinction of species, an extinction crisis caused by human activities (Ulansey, 2010).

Reinforcing the link between economic exploitation and natural resource extraction as primary motivations for war, Shambaugh et al. (2001) identify the vicious cycle that arises once the conflicts take hold:

> Depletion of biodiversity and the natural resource base because of armed conflict can weaken the chances of lasting peace and sustainable livelihoods for a region's long-term residents (read: humans). Although conflicts may start for other reasons, there is a risk that resource depletion and environmental

degradation can drag a region into a vicious circle: poverty, further political instability, more armed conflict, greater environmental degradation, and even greater poverty. (p. 10)

Thus, while global corporations and elites get rich from wars, the desperation of human victims experiencing extreme poverty, inequality, and exploitation contributes to the long-term suffering, and death of individuals (animal and human), the extirpation of populations (animal and human) and extinction of entire species of animals. Further, in the chaos and disorganization following war, refugees, former soldiers, and impoverished populations violate animal lives even more aggressively as a result of their own desperation. A variety of examples offer only a tiny window into the extent and complexity of the problems:

- Rwanda: "Two-thirds of the original area of Akagera National park was removed from protected status, and numerous refugees and their livestock were resettled there. The result was the virtual local extinction of some species of ungulates, including the roan antelope ... and the eland" (Shambaugh, et al., 2001). Further, the endemic birds of Makura forest reserves are now considered "nonviable" (Hanson et al., 2009). However, even though habitat of the eastern mountain gorilla was harmed, the population still increased during the war (Clarke, 2007).

- Sri Lanka: 100,000 acres of war zone jungles, still riddled with land mines, have been designated a wildlife sanctuary, particularly for elephants who have been entering villages for food because their habitat has been destroyed by war and deforestation. Where 10,000-15,000 elephants used to live a century ago, only 3,000 remain (Mallawarachi, 2010).

- Democratic Republic of Congo (DRC): Ten years after the war, Conservation International reported the eastern lowland "gorilla numbers had collapsed by as much as 70 percent" (Clarke, 2007)

- Lebanon: Grave predictions suggested that endangered baby green turtles would experience "high fatalities" and that blue fin tuna would also be harmed by the Lebanon oil spill caused by Israeli planes hitting a power plant (Milstein, 2006). However, updated research on the status of the turtles and tuna are not available. Once the immediate crisis is over, the plight of endangered animals becomes invisible once again.

- Uganda: After three decades of civil war, local extinctions and drastic declines in large animals have undermined genetic diversity, especially for savanna elephants and warthogs, damaging "the ability of species to evolve and adapt to changing environments as a result of genetic erosion" (Muwanika & Nyakaana, 2005, p. 107).

- Mojave desert: Animals are drastically affected by war preparations as well as wars. Even though previous U.S. Army actions moving 600 threatened California desert tortoises resulted in 252 deaths, they propose moving another 1,100 tortoises in 2011-12 to expand their training operations in the Mojave desert (Cart, 2009).

As can be seen from the examples, only the plight of large mammals are usually noticed, and, on rare occasions, birds and larger reptiles. The effects of war on smaller animals, less-recognized birds, fish, sea animals, and particularly insects often go completely unnoticed by humans, yet the consequences of such losses may significantly alter the web of life and the chances of survival of other animals and species in the future.

What Options Do Animals Have in the Aftermath of Wars and Warmaking?

Under the onslaught of modern warfare and its global impact, many animals of the earth have suffered indescribable injury to body, family, community and home from which they cannot recover. Most of this pain and suffering has gone unnoticed and untold—invisibililzed. However, given the slightest chance of recovery, recuperation, and freedom from human domination, oppression, and war, some animals have found ways to forge new lives, however difficult, in spite of their tragedies.

Resilient animals are reclaiming migration patterns, having families, re-establishing communities, and maintaining the web of life even under the most adverse conditions. They eke out existence in devastated, destroyed, or polluted environments. Where land mines lurk and humans fear to tread, animals re-establish their lives without knowing the dangers. Or perhaps some can use their greater sense of smell to detect and avoid unexploded ordnance as demonstrated with dogs used to clear mines in Afghanistan or giant Gambian pouched rats in Mozambique (Lindow, 2008).

Despite the capability of some animals to persevere in the aftermath of human-created military activities and wars, human projects proposed to alleviate the damage done to nature and the earth often expose animals to further dangers or destruction of habitat.

Wildlife Refuges to Protect Animals or Contamination?

At first, I was encouraged to read about so many war zones and military lands being returned to wildlife, but the deeper my investigation went, the motivations became clear. Disingenuously new "wildlife sanctuaries" are being established where the environment has become so contaminated by military activities that humans cannot safely live. The U.S. military bombing range on the island of Vieques in Puerto Rico was successfully challenged by activists in 2003 and quickly turned over to the U.S. Fish and Wildlife Service for a refuge. Extremely contaminated, it was designated as a superfund site by the EPA in 2005. A critical analysis of such "wildlife refuges" explains the self-serving motivations of the military:

> one of the major reasons the US government prefers this kind of development of contaminated lands is that it releases them from much of the financial burden of cleaning up the contamination to the level necessary for human use ... A second type of criticism of the FWS centers on what is seen as the hypocrisy of turning over the land to an agency in charge of environmental protection when the US government, through the Navy, is seen as the culprit behind the contamination of the island ... there is a majority local perception that what is being "preserved" on Vieques by the US federal government is not nature as much as it is the contamination (Davis, Hayes-Conroy, & Jones, 2007).

Scores of sites contaminated by the U.S. military have been turned into "national wildlife refuges," such as Alaska Maritime, Aroostock, Great Bay, Hanford Reach, Oxbow, Rocky Mountain Arsenal, Salt Plains, Teltin, and the list goes on.

The dangerous Demilitarized Zone (DMZ) in Korea, varying from three to twelve miles wide area along 155 mile border, is recognized as one of the most successful areas for animal protection and resurgence, a wildlife preserve in all but name. Azios describes the animals living there:

> Perhaps one-third of all red-crowned cranes, the world's rarest, depend on the DMZ's wetlands and nearby agricultural fields while migrating. The spotted seal, Chinese water deer, and lynx are just a few of its resident mammals. Up to 67 percent of all plant and animal species found in Korea live in and around the DMZ. Several species are found only there (2008).

Yet, human encroachment, urban sprawl, extensive deforestation, nearby industrialization, and pressure to "develop" the area threaten to remove even this land-mined reconstituted wilderness area from the animals. With over a million visitors to the area each year, tourism is being touted as a good reason to make it a "nature preserve" (Azios, 2008).

National Parks for Animals or Tourism?

Where enough large animals remain to attract tourism for human economic exploitation, national parks or "game" reserves are created or reconstructed. During the twenty-year civil war in Sudan, "the more agile creatures—white-eared kob, gazelles, and other species—fled in massive numbers to Uganda, Ethiopia, Kenya, and northern Sudan" (McCrummen, 2009, p. 2). With "important populations of wildlife and vast intact habitats after 22 years of war," according to Paul Elkan, director of Sudan Wildlife Conservation Society, a national park and "game reserve" are planned. But will animals be the main beneficiaries of such ventures? In this case, human economic interests are the underlying motivation as documented by Benham, "South Sudan appealed for investors to plough $140 million into its war-hit wildlife parks, seeking to kick-start a tourism industry" (2011, p. 1).

In other instances, the plans appear to have serious goals for animal protection, including a community-government partnership, wildlife corridors, seeking designation as a UNESCO World Heritage Site, and modeling for other community managed protected areas (Wildlife Conservation Society, 2009). While such proposals sound good, significant questions remain regarding: funding, government corruption, and control of the area or further military interventions by hostile forces.

Similarly, trans-boundary peace parks being proposed between countries with conflicts or civil wars, seem promising. Sierra Leone and Liberia created the Trans-boundary Rainforest Park in 2009 to protect what's left of the Upper Guinea Forest Ecosystem where 25 threatened bird species and 50 mammal species live. But the list of funders, like the European Union, the World Bank, and USAID among others raise concerns about likely conflicts with financial goals. Some troubling statements reinforce these concerns, such as, "the Peace Park will provide the potential to raise tens of millions of dollars over forthcoming decades, ensuring sustained funding for protected area management and community development" (*Wildlife Extra News*, 2009, May).

While tourism may be used to entice countries and impoverished local populations to protect wildlife in the short run, it does not seem to provide lasting protection as evidenced by the predicted extinction of lions and other large animals living in "protected" national parks.

What Is the Answer: Band-aids v. Root Cause Solutions?

Conservationists, environmentalists, animal rights activists, and other dedicated people and organizations all work passionately and diligently to save individual animals, to engage communities in protecting populations, and to create policies to safeguard endangered species. As wishful as I would like to be about the results of these efforts, none seem to address the root causes of the massive destruction that humans, and in particular, human greed, imperialism, militarism, and war have created.

Based on my lifelong investigation and activism for social justice, peace, environment, and animals, and based on my specific research for this chapter, I conclude that immediate activism must focus on the root causes of the global devastation to animals and the earth, as follows:

- Legal Rights of Nature:

- Human Overpopulation: Now approaching 7 billion, immediate efforts to educate about and provide resources to prevent more human births.

- Speciesism: The immediate need to challenge the myth of human superiority and dominion and extensive education about animals and the web of life, with corresponding specific major shifts to living a low-impact life.

- Overconsumption: Educate and provide resources and incentives for an immediate shift to a low consumption life, including moving rapidly toward a plant-based diet.

- Imperialism: Immediate shift from support of predatory capitalism and imperialist extraction of natural resources to a recognition of the fragility of the earth's natural systems under the continued assault of human domination.

- Militarism and War: Immediate and concerted activist focus to defund militaries in general and the United States military in particular, decommission all bases, re-educate soldiers and civilians for peace, stop all production and sale of weapons, create and shift funding to a Department of Peace, begin to dismantle and decontaminate military sites.

- Redistribute resources: Place a cap on wealth and income, tax harmful activities, re-create and strengthen government regulations of all economic activities.

- Fair Elections: Immediate prevention of corporate and wealth intervention into elections and government decisions everywhere; careful regulation and prevention of conflicts of interest by government officials and representatives.

- Conservation and Renewable Energy: Oil is a major motivation for imperialism. Nuclear power plants create tritium and plutonium for nuclear weapons. These sources of energy must be replaced with extreme conservation measures and renewable, non-harmful energy sources.

- Shifting Resources: Resources currently wasted on militarism, war, extraction, overconsumption, fossil and nuclear fuels, and other harmful activities should be shifted to education, meeting basic life needs, birth control availability,

- Shifting Scientific Priorities: Scientific research and related industries should be shifted away from weapons production and other dangerous technologies like nuclear power, genetic modification, nano-technologies, etcetera, to enforcement of the precautionary principle, to respect for indigenous knowledge, and for the natural processes of the earth.

While addressing these root causes may seem extremely difficult, if not impossible, given current political and economic power structures, focusing on the root causes can help us maximize the impact of our energies to have the greatest impact, wherever we live in the world, joining collectively with others wherever possible to make major changes as quickly as possible. The lives of the earth's animals and our own lives are at stake.

CHAPTER FIVE

ANIMALS AT WAR

Rajmohan Ramanathapillai

Humans have complicated relationships with nonhuman animals and wildlife. Accounts from various cultures demonstrate caring as well as fearful relationships with nonhuman animals that led humans to worship them respectfully. On the other hand, humans also have appalling accounts of exploitation and cruelty toward nonhuman animals. Human chauvinism and anthropocentric attitudes have led humans to treat them as a means to their ends. This chapter defines five different stages of human and nonhuman relationships in which domesticated nonhuman animals and wildlife were devalued from sacred status to exploited lives. Exploitation of nonhuman animals and the destruction of wildlife habitat for military advantages by military and guerrilla fighters is the most troubling history of modern warfare. Nonhuman animals became a means to an end in human wars. This utilitarian calculation opened the floodgates of using nonhuman beings on the battlefield—a widespread practice in the military around the world. The rights and moral standing of nonhuman animals are disregarded and our moral obligations to them are knowingly neglected. Modern warfare introduced by Napoleon and the modern guerrilla warfare deployed since the Chinese Revolution have had a dreadful impact on nonhuman animals, wildlife and the environment. By demonstrating the historical exploitation of nonhuman animals, wildlife and the environment, this chapter will conclude that the use of these beings is not only unethical and inhuman but that the military industrial complex and methods of warfare are detrimental to nonhuman animals, other wildlife and their habitats.

Animals Are More Than Equal

Forests are often associated with a feeling of anxiety toward the unknown or danger, which develops a sense of fear and respect for the forest. At this *first stage*, great civilizations emerged beside the banks of the Indus, Tigress, Yellow, Yangtze and Nile rivers, and enjoyed the richness of wildlife; yet they suffered floods, an uncontrollable aspect of nature, which made humans reach out to higher powers for protection (Adler & Pouwels, 2008). In the Vedic period, seers living near the Indus River praised the powers of nature; they elevated nature and its inhabitants to the status of divine and sought protection from them (Radhakrishnan & Moore, 1989). Artifacts and other relics found in ancient Egypt, Greece, China, India and South America demonstrate the human craving for the superior powers of nonhuman animals (Sanua,1983). Images of gods and goddesses controlling wild creatures are widespread in many cultures and are an expression of the superior powers of the divine. On the other hand, the emblems of powerful nonhuman animals and birds represent the power of earthly kingdoms, and demonstrate the limits of human beings (Daly, 1979). Some nonhuman animals are seen as superior because they are believed to be only able to be tamed by gods and goddesses. For instance, in Hinduism the image of Kali sitting on top of a lion and Siva taming the demonic elephant, Gajan, demonstrate that gods and some nonhuman animals are above humans.

Some Indian subcultures still today see nonhuman animals as equal and divine. These cultures dedicate a day to celebrate domesticated nonhuman animals for providing milk and helping them in paddy fields and at harvest. Amazonian chiefs held the title of Jaguar because they believed their ancestors were the jaguars of South America. Their mythology presents half-human, half-animal images, a hybrid superior being. The union of jaguar and human is represented in Olmec artwork (Saunders, 2004). Similar mythologies can be found in many cultures, for instance, the union between a lion king and a princess is claimed as the ancestry of the Sinhala race in the South Asian island of Sri Lanka. Mythical creatures such as the centaur, chiron, pegagus, minotaur, phoenix, namtar, pangu, nuwa, fuxi, and gonggong are found in Greek, Egyptian and Chinese mythologies (Sanua, 1983). The custom of praying to gods and goddesses through vehicles such as bulls, eagles, peacocks, snakes, elephants, tigers and lions are found in Indian tradition. All these stories demonstrate the unusual powers of nonhuman animals.

This recognition brought respect for nonhuman animals in ancient traditions and elevated their status beyond the human realm. Ancient warriors' desires to have the strength and power of fierce nonhuman animals, and to use them to obliterate their enemies, resonates with the mythologies of many cultures (Schaefer, 1967). "Glorious" fights of gladiators with a ferocious nonhuman animal in a coliseum pit in front of a fanatic crowd in Rome are a manifestation of this human yearning. Confronting nonhuman animals with superior physical strength brought glory, status and recognition to the warriors of India, Rome, and Africa along with status and recognition.

Domestication: The Evolution of the New Status of Animals

While humans were constantly in confrontation with powerful wildlife, they also began to domesticate them for food, work, and transportation. At this *second stage*, small communities were sustained by domesticated cattle, buffalo, goats, sheep, pigs, chickens, llamas, camels, donkeys, mules, oxen and horses (Majumdar, Raychaudhuri & Datta, 1950; Saunders, 2004; Schaefer, 1967). Possessing these nonhuman animals created affluent communities, which brought new challenges, namely the issue of security. Raiding the livestock or grazing pastures of others became an acceptable norm and it was celebrated as a form of heroism and bravery, which indicated the beginning of larger scale conflict (Schaefer, 1967). Tools and weapons made out of stone and by other sophisticated techniques found at the banks of the Indus and Nile rivers, demonstrate organized warfare (Langley, 2005). Preservation of domesticated animals and grazing pasture was seen as a form of self-preservation since small communities relied heavily upon them. As a result, defending or raiding grazing pastures and domesticated animals led to wars between groups. Conceptualization of defensive and offensive war became an outcome of such conflicts. The idea of self-preservation became a thread of moral reasoning that was tied to the defense of grazing land and domesticated nonhuman animals. A group eager to secure livestock or to expand their grazing pastures went to war with others, while the attacked saw them as aggressors. For example, in the *Republic,* Plato argues that dispute over pasture and the need for annexing others' pastures becomes the source of war (Plato, 2004/*circa* 380 BC).

Animals at War

Involvement of kingdoms in defensive and offensive warfare demanded the establishment of mobile standing armies. This *third stage* use of nonhuman animals began to prove a great advantage in military expeditions. The advantages gained from nonhuman animals' capabilities forced them into human warfare. For instance, Kautilya, the author of the political and military treatise of *Arthasasta,* describes Indian kings building forts with three moats filled with crocodiles (as cited in Singh, 2008). The use of elephants, horses, camels, donkey, mules, pigeons, falcons, crocodiles, monitor lizards, and poisonous snakes became an integral part of military operations in Indian, Greek, Egyptian, and Roman warfare.

Elephants in Warfare

Elephants, horses, dogs, and pigeons are the most used nonhuman animals in human warfare. Elephants are a significant part of Indian war history. It was the elephant regiment that confronted the army of Alexander the Great at the gate of India (Basham, 1968). *Arthasastra,* which was written in this period, describes the rules on catching, training and maintaining war elephants. Though *Arthasastra* warns against catching young and pregnant elephants, the process of catching and taming an elephant in India are not humane. In ancient times, mahouts (the elephant handlers) caught elephants in hidden pits that they built along the elephant paths in the jungle. Elephants in the pit naturally expressed their violent resistance; and mahouts starved and dehydrated them for days to subdue them. Once the will of an elephant was broken, mahouts brought other tame elephants to pull the weakened elephant out of the pit. Mahouts believed it was the fear of punishment that made elephants to obey their orders. During training, mahouts used an ankus (a long stick with a sharp hook) against the animal to force them to obey their commands. Mahouts rewarded elephants with food, water and a bath if they learned the command quickly, while elephants that resisted received severe injuries. Since elephants live nearly sixty years, a trained elephant was generally handed over to a younger man so he would grow old with his elephant. Often the young mahout and the elephant eventually developed affection for each other. Despite the mahout capturing and training the elephant, it became and remained the property of the state or the king. Preparedness of healthy elephants for war was an absolute duty of the king. He allocated forests to feed the elephants; and cutting trees in protected jungles is severely punished.

The history of war elephants and the heroism of warriors is filled with gruesome images. The Cankam poetry of the first and second century of South India, describes the essential characteristics of a fearless warrior as *maram,* which includes the qualities of valor, bravery, anger [righteousness], wrath, enmity, hatred [of his enemy], strength, power, victory, war, killing, and murder (Kailasapathy). Poetry provides vivid details of the acts of heroism, gruesome wars, and the generosity of kings. Male elephants go through a period of musth: a time where the male produces high levels of testosterone, which advertises his healthiness and readiness to fight with other males to get a mate. Tamed male elephants in musth do not obey the commands of their mahouts and at times kill them. The violent instinct and the explosive power of musth elephants, continuously mesmerized kings and their bards. The combative abilities of his elephants and the devastating blows they could inflict on enemies, defined the supremacy of a king (Hardt & Heifetz, 1995). In the passage to adulthood, a young prince desires to confront an uncontainable elephant (Hardt & Heifetz, p. 354). The masculine construction of a hero in the Cankam period interlinks with his fearlessness and the ability to confront a massive elephant with rutt. A daring hero according to these poems is invariably a ferocious warrior who never surrenders or retreats from battle; like a victorious elephant in musth, he is enraged by his love for battle. Battling a ferocious elephant was the ultimate test; there was no escape for a hero from such a formidable challenge. Such a warrior was always under pressure to prove his reputation for fearlessness and to demonstrate his utter disdain for death (Kailasapathy, 1968). A warrior doing otherwise would be shamed; he would lose his fame as well as his dignity in this and the other world. In a battle with a maddened elephant with rutt, the victorious or fallen king secures the eternal fame of confronting the uncontrollable, which only the divine possess. Witnessing such heroic battle in the war the poets elevate him to the status of divine, in which the heroic kings were worshipped. Thus, heroes preferred such a death over worldly possessions (Hardt & Heifetz, p. 333) and the immortal status evoked worship in society (Hardt & Heifetz, pp. 312-3).

> One of your ancestors mastered the movement of the wind
>
> When his ships sailed on the dark and enormous ocean!
>
> Karikal Valavan, you who master rutting elephants!
>
> You did march off and you did win the victory and you displayed
>
> Your power, since you were the one who triumphed in combat but yet
>
> On the battlefield of wealthy Venni didn't he surpass you,
>
> Gaining great fame across the world when ashamed
>
> At the wound in the back, he sat turned northward and starved himself
>
> To death. (Hardt, 1999 [trans.], p. 51)

The strength of a king and his elephants brought victory, wealth and new fertile land to the kingdom. Wars in this period were defensive: recovering stolen cattle herds, protecting daughters, and defending the land (Hardt & Heifetz, pp. 314). Only later were defensive as well as offensive wars fought for the political survival and expansion of a kingdom. New victories resulted in expanded territory and wealth and reinforced the security of a country (Hardt & Heifetz, pp. 226-228). The malevolent powers of elephants were efficiently used to eliminate the land of the enemy. Fleets of elephants trampled paddy fields and soldiers commanded elephants to destroy water tanks, an act which would ultimately kill the enemy (Hardt & Heifetz, pp. 39-44). Captured agricultural land, gold and enemy elephants made the victor more powerful and provided the king with a larger military (Hardt & Heifetz, pp. 248 -250).

However, all the glamor, wealth and power came at a cost to elephants. Cutting off the tusks and trunks of countless elephants transformed a fighter into a hero. But for the modern observer, the details of such brutalities are horrifying; scenes of confused elephants fleeing from the battle are shocking (Hardt & Heifetz, pp. 410-411). Fleeing elephants trampled the bodies of wounded soldiers stuck in the blood-soaked mud fields. A number of questions can be raised here. Did warrior elephants "enjoy" their bloody fights? Did poets really respect them as heroes? Elephants have no interest in human battles for fame; nor do they enjoy death by arrow or sword. It is most likely that elephants in battle were terrified as they fled from the cannons when European soldiers used them in the battles in Sri Lanka. Battles with elephants expanded beyond India into many parts of South East Asia such as Thailand, Burma, Laos and Cambodia and continued until the seventeenth century (Bock, 1985; Shaw, 1993).

Elephant warfare became obsolete when Europeans used cannon in their colonial conquests in Asia. The progress of history has caused the elephant to not only lose its socially constructed superior status but also to become an undesirable pest that has to be eliminated. Though hundreds of elephants were deployed in wars at different times in South and South East Asian history, these wars were limited and war elephants were used only within these regions (Bock 1985; Geiger, 2003; Shaw, 1993).

Fate of the Horse

Horses are an integral part of human warfare, which began around BC 5000-3500 in some parts of the world. Horses gave enormous advantages to military maneuvers and helped to expand kingdoms and create empires. Xenophon provides vivid details of choosing and handling warhorses. Though it is not natural "leaping ditches, scrambling over walls, scaling up, springing off high banks, galloping up and down steep pitches and sharp inclines and along the slaps," this must be considered basic standards for selection and training of warhorses (Xenaphon, 2008, p. 9). In ancient China, the name of Lord Szu-ma Niu was associated with nonhuman animals. Szu-ma meant, "Master of the Horse" and Niu meant "Ox" (Schaefer, 1967). Later the introduction of the game of Polo evolved as a part of military exercise with Mongolian ponies and Iranian horses in China. Though horses were originally used to pull light chariots in ancient wars, the creation of cavalry gave maximum speed and flexibility for military expeditions. Records of the Greeks, Romans, Chinese, Arabs and Mongolians clearly demonstrate the advantage of speed in their military exploits, thus helping to successfully expand their empires. (Bakhit, 2000, p. 74; Gianoli & Monti, 1969).

At the *fourth stage* large-scale deployment of horses was involved in empire building. Modern warfare began in Napoleon era, and involved massive size of the drafted armies and the powerful artillery forces, which were heavily dependent upon a massive number of horses. The newly introduced artillery warfare devastated the traditionally held thin boundaries between battlefield, civilian space and forest thus exposing civilians and wildlife to even more unintended devastation than ever. With colossal military preparation, Napoleon marched into Russia with over 600,000 soldiers (Duiker & Spielvogel, 2010). Beside his trained cavalry, his military depended on large numbers of horses for transportation of food, equipment, weapons and artillery. Within a few months of his long march, Napoleon's army lost 10,000-40,000 horses due to lack of grazing land. Horses were often kept with their gear on without rest; they were exhausted by the restless march and starvation. They were also susceptible to infection from the crupper: a leather loop under the horse's tail designed to keep the saddle balanced. Large numbers of horses succumbed to infections and untreated wounds, since the military kept the saddle on the horses for days without removing it, even when they were not on the march or fighting. Untreated wounds and constant marching brought devastation upon Napoleon who lost 200,000 trained horses at the end of the war with Russia (Sutherland, 2003). Even after this tremendous tragedy the suffering of horses continued. Mortar vehicles, trains and ships greatly improved military transportation in World War I and efficiently delivered supplies to the frontlines. Yet, nearly 16 million horses were also used for cavalry, ambulances, and for transportation. According to Elizabeth Schafer, nearly half of them died due to "wounds, exhaustion and exposure" (Schafer, 2005, p. 103).

The First World War also became a time for experimenting with other nonhuman animals and birds. For instance, Australian troops brought canaries, cockatoos, ducks, emus, ostriches, owls, parrots, pigeons, and swamp hens onto the battlefield. Some of these birds were used as pets and companions. Others were used as messengers and some were used to test the air for gas attacks. Donkeys were deployed as ambulances, and as carriers to supply water and ammunition to Australian troops at the battle of Gallipoli in 1916 (Department of Veterans Affairs, 2009). The success story of 100,000 private communications with the help of pigeons at the Siege of Paris convinced Germans to take thousands of Belgian pigeons away during World War I (Lubow, 1977, p. 28). At the Egyptian front, mules, oxen and donkeys were mobilized along with 40,000 camels (Tucker, 2008). Unfortunately, World War I was also the time in history that chemical warfare was intensely used, in particular, mustard and nerve gas: 113,000 tons of chemical weapons were used killing 90,000 people and injuring 1.3 million people (Bullock, Haddow, Coppola, & Yeletaysi, 2009). Deaths and cases of temporarily blinded soldiers were widely reported, but few reports on the effects of chemicals on nonhuman animals exist. The idea of shell shock is only described in terms of human suffering but its effects on nonhumans on the battlefield were not observed. Yet, there are many records of starved soldiers and civilians eating dead nonhuman animals, especially horses during the First and Second World Wars.

The use of horses and pigeons became less frequent during World War II. However, the potential use of nonhuman animals for new military projects was always seen as an essential part of military research, and some of these projects push the boundaries of our imagination. For instance, Harvard professor Dr. Louis F. Fisher was associated with a unique military project that developed the idea of attaching tiny incendiary bombs onto the backs of bats and then dropping them in thousands of Japanese cities. Behavioral scientist Skinner, on the other hand, explored the possibility of developing Pigeon-Guided Missiles, "a control system for the hoist with head movements sending the appropriate motors into action, which in turn affected the hoist's position" (Lubow, 1977, p. 36). Russians manipulated dogs to be suicide bombers. They trained the dogs to eat under battle tanks. Later they starved the dogs and then released the dogs with high explosives towards German tanks. When the hungry dogs ran underneath the German tanks, it then detonated the bombs (Biggs, 2008). These examples demonstrate how militaries had no moral qualms at times and disregarded nonhuman animals when under pressure or desperate.

The use of dogs increased during WWII and they were used for patroling, passing messages and carrying light weapons. German Shepherds, a breed developed in the late 1800s, became well known war dogs, who possessed the intelligence, strength and the ability to learn and follow orders. It is estimated that 75,000 dogs were used during WWI, including for transportation. For example, Canadian and Alaskan dogs were used for crossing the snow with loaded sledges efficiently, which other animals could not do (Schafer, 2005). The German military used 30,000 dogs and did not show any compassion to the dogs in occupied territories. During the demobilization of France they killed 26,000 French civilian dogs to deny any military use of dogs (Schafer, 2005). During the first and the second world wars, dogs were recruited from civilians and then returned after the war, if they survived. Since then militaries have begun to breed their own dogs so the military owns the nonhuman animals. However it then reserves its right to dispose of war dogs. In the 1960s, the Americans took nearly 4000 dogs to Vietnam to face the guerrilla/conventional warfare conducted by the North Vietnamese army. The military desperately depended on the dogs' ability to smell and differentiate odors from a distance so they could locate fighters in the forest waiting in ambush. The dogs were trained to pinpoint snipers and to alert American soldiers on patrol. There were many cases where dogs successfully located trip wires and saved many lives. Yet at the end of the war there were only 200 returned. Many were killed in the war but the rest were euthanized or given to South Vietnamese army, who lost resources and interest in maintaining such a unit. The military categorized them as military equipment and disposed of them after the war, an act which outraged the handlers (Bennett, 1999).

Military research on dolphins increased in the United States and Russia at the beginning of the Cold War. Their intelligence, quick learning, and ability to perform tasks became a great attraction to the U.S. Navy. Dolphins' capacity to adapt to new environments convinced the navy and the government to invest millions of dollars in dolphin programs. Dolphins displayed an eagerness to learn new tasks, and to especially assist marines who lived in underwater stations in the deep sea. They can dive quickly in deep water to over 200 feet, where this would present a human diver with a great risk. Dolphins are able to deliver equipment and are trained to rescue divers who can be easily lost in murky waters. Dolphins also picked up parts of tested missiles from deep water after tests were conducted.

Dolphins can differentiate between coral rocks and man-made debris in murky shallow water. The military quickly learned that the sonar ability of dolphins could be put to use to detect metals in the sea, especially sea mines. This gave weight to a moral and humanitarian argument against the use of dolphins. Whitlow Au, who studies Marine Bioacoustics at the University of Hawaii's Marine Mammal Research Program in Kailua argues that the only technological sonar possessed by the navy that can find buried mines are dolphins. When dolphins were deployed during the Iraq War, Major General Victor Renuart from the port of UUM Qasr, stated that the mission of using dolphins was to clear the way for ships so humanitarian aid could reach Southern Iraq (Associated Press, 2003).

The total number of mines in WWI was 235,000 and allied forces used nearly 600,000 in WWII, The US Navy deployed sixty-five bottlenose dolphins and fifteen sea lions to detect mines, find combat divers and locate lost equipment (Fuentes, 2001). Russia trained dolphins and beluga whales to attack ships and conduct "suicide" missions. However, the collapse of the U.S.S.R. ended the mammal program. Recently, according to BBC News (2000), twenty-seven starving nonhuman animals, including walruses, sea lions, seals, and a white beluga whale were sold to Iran.

The United States of America began its program with a small number of wild dolphins and they used the program for twenty to twenty-five years. A few dolphins were used during the Vietnam War to guard the ports where the ammunition was unloaded and stored (Big House Productions, 2002). Like elephants, dolphins are social animals and one of the challenges faced was what to do with them after their "retirement."

White (2007) states that dolphins are "self conscious-beings with the ability to reflect on the contents of their consciousness" (p.152). He points out that the brain architecture of dolphins demonstrates that they have deeper emotional attachments than humans; and they have the capacity to reflect their emotions to others, which gives them the ability to act appropriately in a situation. He states, "the fact the sensory and motor regions interlock with each other (cortical adjacency) may give more interrogative perception of reality than us" (p. 152). Because of these capacities, the social and emotional lives of dolphins suffer greatly in captivity. In the early seventies, 20 percent of military dolphins died in the British dolphin program and the average dolphin lived in this program for only two years. Many of them got bored in the sterile tanks and through not eating or cooperating with trainers, the neurotic dolphins committed suicide (Hussain, 1973). Domesticated dolphins, after a long time in captivity, can be released back to the ocean. But the main challenges to the military were: first, captive dolphins can be vulnerable to larger predators; second, they cannot survive without their own social group; and finally there is the possibility of capture by other militaries. To resolve this dilemma the U.S. Navy developed a breeding program, similar to the military dogs program, so that there would be no need to either recruit wild dolphins or release them into the open ocean when they are of no further use.

If capacity to reason and ability to choose between right and wrong, qualify as moral standing for humans, the same qualities must also qualify as moral standing for elephants and dolphins. The complicated social and emotional lives of these nonhuman animals bring more awareness to our limited understanding of them. Only this inadequate understanding allows their involuntary use by us as a means to our military ends.

Guerrilla Warfare and Wildlife

Modern guerrilla warfare rose out of the Chinese Revolution and became an influential method of many wars that involved revolution, liberation and independence fights since WWII. This chapter has already established how conventional warfare can inflict great harm on animals, yet the duration of large-scale conventional war between standing armies lasts a relatively short time. On the other hand, guerrilla warfare, which is used against conventional military to bring revolution, lasts longer in many countries. At this *fifth stage*, forests are exploited by guerrilla fighters and military and this exploitation puts wildlife and their habitat at a greater risk. Hiding and training in the forest with weapons not only exposes wildlife to the danger of being shot but also disrupts their daily life. Young guerrilla fighters and newly recruited child soldiers are not well informed about the fragile nature of terrain and the significant role wildlife play in the landscape. Human-centeredness and politically driven goals make it impossible for them to see the need and values in protecting the forest and wildlife.

Guerrilla warfare aims to bring down an oppressive and unjust government with the help of revolutionaries and liberation fighters, who intend to build a new government according to their ideologies. Fighting the occupied Japanese army, the Chinese revolutionary Chairman, Mao Tse Tung, called guerrilla warfare a "weapon that a nation of inferiority in arms and military equipment may employ against a more powerful aggressor nation" (as quoted in Griffith, 2000, p. 42). Using the method of guerrilla warfare, Mao secured the Chinese Revolution and established a communist nation. Che Guevara, a South American revolutionary and a potent symbol of rebellion around the world, defined guerrilla warfare as "the weapon of the poor" (as quoted in Dijk, 2008, p. 39). Che fought alongside Fidel Castro to begin a revolution in Cuba during the late 1950s and went to other Latin American and African nations to spread his message and method of guerrilla warfare. Both Mao and Che viewed guerrilla warfare as a weapon for the weak to use against overwhelming powers with well-trained conventional armies. The methods of hit and run in guerrilla wars bleeds and exhausts conventional armies; and war is prolonged for decades without conclusion.

Inspired by the Chinese and Cuban revolutions, rebels in countries such as Vietnam, Cambodia, Burma, El Salvador, Guatemala, Nicaragua, Mexico, Sri Lanka, Kashmir, Chechnya, Zaire, Afghanistan, Pakistan, Liberia, Angola, Uganda and Rwanda base their military training camps in forests, where they coordinate military exercises and operations (Ramanathapillai, 2008). Militaries and guerrillas intentionally wrap themselves with the colors of their environments so they can hide themselves from the eyes of the enemy. Camouflage uniforms, military vehicles, and equipment represent an intricate relationship between military enterprises and nature. The symbolic aesthetic connection between war and nature creates a micro- and macrocosmic continuum of their relationship. Even on a symbolic level, nature becomes that which is defended, targeted and attacked during war. Unnecessary harm to nature by warfare is a routine occurrence that demonstrates the military's disregard for the intrinsic value of individuals and ecosystems. War zones are understood as dangerous places for humans, but it must be recognized that all living beings who reside in war zones are also put in danger.

In his book *The Land Ethic: In a Sand County Almanac*, Leopold (1966) points out, "we can be ethical only in relation to something we can see, feel, understand, love, or otherwise have faith in" (p. 230). Our ethical relationship to land and wildlife comes from our deeper connection with them. Notably, revolutionaries are often city born and their recruits come from different parts of a country or from other countries. Due to this reason, they may never have any ancestral connection to the forest they camp, train and conduct warfare in, nor do they consider the efforts of locals to preserve the land. Unlike a conventional army, the guerrillas tend to rely greatly upon forests, and regard nature only as a means for their own purposes, that is, either as a means of defense or offense.

This use directly brings forests into the midst of conflict between warring parties that care only for their military advantages and victories. When guerrilla fighters depend on people in the villages, members of the villages become "legitimate targets" of the army. Farmers are devastated when forests are destroyed and wildlife disappears from their lands. For instance, the Sri Lankan army destroyed numerous Tamil villages when guerrilla fighters used those villages as their support system (Chelvadurai, 1987).

In guerrilla warfare, rebels rely extensively on the forest for cover and ambush. The occupation of the forest by such rebels has two drastic impacts on ecosystems, particularly ecologically sensitive rain forests and wildlife. First, rebels exploit the forest for their cover, food, and fuel supply. They clear the land for their camps and military exercises, and hunt animals for target practice, food, illegal trade, and other purposes. In Angola, for example, the warring parties killed rhinos and elephants for tusks and horns so that they could buy uniforms and weapons. In Uganda and Tanzania, the hippopotamus population was wiped out in target practice, and other animals were killed for meat and ivory (Thomas, 1995). During the civil war in Congo, rebels occupied the Garamba National Park and massacred many animals. As a direct result, the white rhinoceros is currently on the verge of extinction (Stockholm International Peace Research Institute [SIPRI], 1980). Throughout the 1990s, the Rwandan Civil War gravely threatened chimpanzee populations, as the Gishwati Forest was destroyed during the resettlement of refugees. Refugees hiding in the forest tend to rely upon wild animals for food (Brauer, 2009). At the same time, rebels also depend on deer and wild pigs for food sources in Asian and African countries. Losing these animals would produce a domino effect, harming their prey as well. Prey animals in these regions are already under stress for space and food as forests continue to be cleared for cultivation. Having armed men, especially child soldiers who are too young to comprehend the importance of preserving wildlife, shoot nonhuman animals for adventure is not only unethical but also devastating (Brauer, pp. 199-499). For example, in 1987 young Tamil militants in the Northern part of Sri Lanka killed three parent elephants to capture the baby to exhibit it at a temple festival. Such thoughtless activities further disrupt the lives of herds that already had become smaller due to lack of feeding space (personal observation).

The most lethal impact on the forest occurs when government troops target the land to destroy rebels. Since forests can be a tool for revolutionary purposes, they can also be a major obstacle to the success of government military operations (Thomas, 1995). This problem makes the forest a primary military target. In order to defeat the rebels, government troops or their allies use "scorched earth" tactics to destroy their enemies by making the forest unsuitable for sustaining life or military operations. This is a general practice of militaries to clear thousands of acres of rain and tropical forest on both sides of main roads so they can protect themselves from the rebel ambushes. At the same time, troops also target rebels in the forest by using artillery and shells that decimate wildlife and the ecosystem. As an example, elephants living in war zone forests are terrified by random air and artillery attacks or land mines.

Further, loud blasts force them to leave the forest to move to areas closer to villages and cultivation. This movement creates conflict between farmers and elephants, as famers often shoot crop-raiding elephants to save their cultivation. Many elephants were shot in Sri Lanka, and over a hundred of them were captured or injured during this conflict. At least one elephant at the Pinnewela Elephant Orphan Centre was injured by a land mine and is now living with three legs. Elephants living along the Burma and Thailand border have also been exposed to land mines planted deep in the forest (Guardian, 2011).

Using nature only as a means to military ends has great moral and practical consequences. Fragile ecosystems often become unstable and unsustainable because of military operations. Developing technology and methods for destroying the plant cover for military advantage, has accelerated ever since guerrilla warfare became the prevalent method of combat (Westing, 1973). This upswing has occurred because guerrilla warfare intentionally exploits nature for its defensive and offensive purposes and therefore invites enemies to resort to environmental warfare. Mao urged his fighters to "move with the fluidity of water and the ease of the blowing wind. Their tactics must deceive, tempt and confuse the enemy" (Griffith, 2000, p. 103). When guerrillas mingled with civilians or blended into nature with fluidity, often using water to swim like fish without being detected, the enemy would "intelligently" drain the water to capture the guerrillas.

In Vietnam, the Vietcong used forests and villagers in the South for their guerrilla warfare and engaged in discrete "hit and run" warfare to frustrate the American military. In effect, soldiers rarely saw their elusive enemy except when hit by mines, snipers, surprise ambush or in rare conventional battles. In retaliation, the U.S. government adopted the military, political and diplomatic strategy of waging massive air raids, applying huge amounts of Agent Orange, and dropping tons of napalm to wipe out villages and forests. In village raids, shooting the water pots, and poisoning and burning the rice stock in the villages, were deemed necessary military tactics (Ramanathapillai, 2008). The overwhelming firepower of the United States and smart, the dreadful, guerrilla warfare inflicted an enormous environmental impact on Vietnam, Laos and Cambodia.

Westing (1975) breaks down the estimate as: 11 million x 214 kg bombs and 217 million x 13kg artillery shells A bomb, nicknamed the Daisy Cutter, was designed during the Vietnam War for the purpose of clearing large areas of dense rain forest (Westing, 1973b). Another tactic the U.S. military used at this time was bulldozing the forest, destroying 1,000 acres a day and wiping out at least 750,000 acres altogether (Westing, 1973a). This included the destruction of forests, rubber and fruit plantations and other agricultural land. Without plant cover, the soil was exposed directly to rain and flood erosion, causing the loss of minerals so that the land could support only grasses and no longer maintain its former biological diversity. In response to this ecological warfare, the Viet Cong created the infamous Ho Chi Minh trails through the forests to keep paths open to troops and have a supply lifeline for the Southern Vietnam front. To avoid further attacks on the trail, the Viet Cong expanded the trail to the south through neighboring countries, Laos and Cambodia, which were regarded as parts of Indochina. In the long march to the south, the Viet Cong also used elephants to carry weapons and food from the north to the battlegrounds in the south. In retaliation, the United States expanded its war to Cambodia and Laos and ordered pilots to shoot any elephants on sight in the jungles and to expand their environmental war tactics to Laos and Cambodia. War against villages and jungles resulted in nearly a million of refugees. The dynamic of elusive guerrilla warfare and the inability of the conventional military to weed out guerrillas, placed enormous stress on the forests of Indochina. This military assault against human beings and nature has not only resulted in massive ecological damage but also affected wildlife for decades. For example, war elephants were rarely found in the forest and still the Vietnamese government is struggling to reintroduce the elephant population back to the forest. A second effect of the environmental war was that it created a massive refugee problem. Large numbers of displaced people were forced to hide in the forest, causing enormous damage to land and wildlife as those displaced needed food and shelter from the forest.

Conclusion

The human relationship with nonhuman animals and other wildlife is rich and complicated. This complex relationship with nonhuman animals has gone through five stages. In the first stage, humans felt vulnerable before dominant animals and birds, while at the same time they admired them because they were powerful. This relationship of both vulnerability and respect later caused humans to elevate wildlife and nature to the status of divine in many cultures. At this stage, some animals, birds and reptiles even enjoyed a status of superiority over humans. In the second stage, societies learned to domesticate animals and birds to enrich their social and agricultural life. This brought humans and animals into a much closer relationship. Though nonhumans were treated with respect at this stage and some cultures celebrated them with a day of recognition for helping in paddy fields and at harvest, nonhuman animals become subordinated to humans. In the third stage, human conflicts and their dependence on nonhuman animals persuaded humans to explore the ways in which nonhuman animals can be used in warfare. At this stage, the sacred or respectful relationship to nonhuman animals slowly began to diminish, and humans increasingly used them as a means to an end, which was winning in war. However, the exploitation of nonhuman animals in wars in this period occurred at a low level since the scale of warfare was small. The large-scale modern war, which began with Napoleon and continued through WWII, crystallizes the fourth stage, in which nonhuman animals are forced into situations of unprecedented cruelty and abuse. In a war, nonhuman animals and birds not only suffered injury and death by explosion, but were also exposed to chemical and biological warfare. Starvation was the greatest cause of death for millions of nonhuman animals. In the fifth stage, modern guerrilla warfare, and the scorched earth methods used in counter-guerrilla warfare by governments, puts nonhuman animals, wildlife and its habitats to maximum stress. The use of Agent Orange and other methods of destroying thousands of acres of plant cover to deny guerrilla warfare annihilated wild habitats in many parts of Indo-China. Conventional and guerrilla warfare in our time pose the greatest threats to nonhuman animals, wildlife and its habitats. Therefore, humans must use nonviolent methods to deal with conflicts with others. Nonviolent methods not only defend the well-being of life forms, in all their diversity, but also provide genuine protection for the habitats in which they live.

CHAPTER SIX

THE FUTURE OF WAR AND ANIMALS

Bill Hamilton and Elliot M. Katz

Animals exploited by scientists to perform anthropomorphic tasks, whether mundane or dangerous, have been the subject of fiction for over a century. H.G. Wells wrote his famous novel, *The Island of Dr. Moreau*, in 1896 as an indictment of vivisection. In it the eponymous scientist performs horrific experiments on animals to convert them into human-animal hybrids. True to his theme, Wells has all his human protagonists come to an unhappy end, while the human-animal hybrids eventually revert to their normal animal state. Hollywood produced movie versions of the novel in 1932, 1977 and 1996. Today, military experimenters are exploring ways to modify animals either organically, through genetic engineering, or discretely, through the fusion or attachment of robotic parts or tools of remote control by humans. The military scientists' purpose may be to create "animal soldiers," to keep humans out of harm's way, to divert the adversary's attention, to gather intelligence, to discover possible defenses against weaponary or to test the practicality of human-robot hybrids. Modern scientists have replaced Dr. Moreau's inhumane methods with genetic engineering to produce genetically modified organisms (GMOs). This type of work will undoubtedly continue, whether or not such experiments are deemed worthwhile by the military scientists involved.

As described in the introduction of this book the pervasive cultural trait of human chauvinism has allowed scientists, researchers and their assistants and staff, whether military or civilian, to view subject animals as mere tools in their experiments, of no more value or importance than their lab equipment. Since this ingrained attitude is unlikely to change, particularly when huge sums of money are at stake, the only hope for animals caught up in this industry is for such experiments to repeatedly fail. This has often been the case.

The previous chapters of this book describe how military leaders and scientists have exploited animals for centuries, up to the present day. This chapter identifies possible new directions that animal experiments for military applications could take in the future. Because of the high level of secrecy of military projects, hidden under the veil of "national security," we can only surmise the exploitative projects and inventions to come.

Much of our inspiration for the ideas presented in this chapter comes from current publicly revealed research in the civilian sector, military research abroad, science fiction in all media, the video gaming industry and other forms of popular entertainment, rather than from strictly peer-reviewed studies and scholarly publications. Since the U.S. military branches, like any civilian researchers, have easy access to the Internet, news releases and clipping services, and since they use popular entertainment media to attract recruits, they have their toes in many streams of creativity, whatever their source. Thus, Hollywood or Silicon Valley may unwittingly inspire the next animal bioweapon.

The U.S. Department of Defense has published a database of its own biomedical research from 1998 to 2007, the DoD Biomedical Research Database, though its latest Animal Care and Use Reports only go up to 2005 (U.S. Department of Defense, 2009, para. 20). Most research with animal subjects relates to trauma experiments, in which animals were crushed, blown up, poisoned, suffocated or tasered to extrapolate treatment methodologies for human soldiers. Putting animals on the battlefield or in combat roles is not a mainstream military strategy, and the few clues available do not indicate a future change in that direction. Military researchers are not about to reveal cutting-edge research or the weaponization of animals in an easily accessible public database. This chapter examines any clues about such research and conjectures about what the military-animal industrial complex may have up its epauletted sleeve.

Putting the Pieces Together

It is possible for civilian researchers to examine the disparate threads of public studies involving nonhuman animal subjects and to forecast potential military applications that may include that research. Although the various branches of the U.S. Defense Department have conducted their own research they have also contracted with nonmilitary research facilities in both universities and private sector corporations. Since each military contract examines only a piece of a project, and since results may not be published in peer-reviewed journals, such outside contractors and researchers may be kept in the dark about the component nature of their research. Only the military project manager can integrate the pieces of research, maintain the secrecy of the project and eventually, in the final stages of the project, develop a viable weapon or other military application that incorporates the most successful results of individual experiments.

Thus, even research with no immediate or apparent military application may slide under the radar of public scrutiny. For instance, Canadian scientific consultant Bob Holmes of *New Scientist Magazine* reports that progress in the genetic modification of animals has led to the development of a "zinc finger," an enzyme that "allow[s] engineers to cut a cell's DNA at a preselected spot":

> This will revolutionize genetic engineering of animals," says Bruce Whitelaw, a geneticist at the Roslin Institute in Edinburgh, UK. "You can design your zinc finger to cut at a specific site in the genome, and it doesn't matter what that genome is. It could be pig, sheep, dog, rat—it doesn't matter. (Holmes, 2010, para. 10)

Although the article does not mention military applications, a military scientist reading about such research might want to investigate and, if possible, appropriate such a tool.

The military can develop nonmilitary research for military applications, even adapting nonhuman animal behaviors. For instance, CNN reported that a Dutch organization has trained giant African rats to detect land mines in Mozabique (McLaughlin, 2010, para. 8). Likewise, engineers at the University of Moratuwa in Sri Lanka have guided a dwarf mongoose to detect land mines while tied to a remote-controlled robot (New Scientist, 2008, no page number). Military ordnance engineers could be devising future mines undetectable by animals or, conversely, mines that animals can be trained to arm or trigger, rather than detect.

The most active research on and development of "transgenic" or genetically modified organisms in the United States of America has been in the field of agriculture, specifically in crop seed and livestock production. The chemical companies Monsanto and Dupont have patented and licensed herbicide-proof crop seeds like soy and corn around the world and cattle that produce milk with proteins of benefit to humans (Margawati, 2003, para. 6). Most genetic manipulation of animals has been to increase the size, reproduction rate and resistance to disease of farm animals, all for an (argued) increased and safer (to humans) food production (Margawati, 2003, paras. 27-29). Military experts could easily access the research of private-sector corporations in an eminent domain tactic, claiming national security interests, particularly if federal grants or tax dollars funded any of that research. Thus, animals in the United States of America or its allies could be genetically fortified against bioweapons, like anthrax, swine flu and foot-and-mouth disease, and staple crops could be protected against wheat blast and rice blast.

Even student dissertations, widely available on the Internet, can inspire military researchers to investigate lines of research they might not have otherwise considered. For instance, Benjamin Resner's thesis for a Master of Science degree at MIT created "a method to allow dogs and humans to interact over the Internet," and he extrapolates his research to cats and parrots (Resner, 2001, pp. 2, 80-81). The dog control device "consists of a computer-controlled treat dispenser to reward the dog, a webcam for visually monitoring the dog, and a speaker for the dog to hear clicks and the owner's voice" (Resner, 2001, p. 9).

A canine training program initiated in person could thus continue remotely. Future applications could consist of wireless earphones or other forms of remote communication for dogs or other trainable animals on the battlefield. The trainer's transmitted voice or other nonverbal cues, such as a clicker sound that consistently triggers a trained behavior, could even be simulated by a computer, so that the trainer, or indeed any human, need not be present once a desired set of behavior triggers is programmed.

Another public source of transgenic research available to the military establishment is biotechnology conferences. For instance, the Biotechnology Industry Organization (BIO) produced its first national industry conference on GE animal technologies, the Livestock Biotech Summit, in September 2010. To quote from the Summit's marketing material:

> The lineup of GE animals to be represented at the Livestock Biotech Summit will include:
>
> Pigs that have been genetically engineered to produce human compatible donor tissues, cells and organs;
>
> Cattle that have been genetically engineered to produce human antibodies that can help prevent and/or treat a wide variety of human health conditions and diseases;
>
> Cattle that have been genetically engineered to be "prion-free" and therefore resistant to bovine spongiform encephalopathy (BSE, or "mad cow disease"); and
>
> Goats that have been genetically engineered to produce a spider silk fiber in its milk. With its strength and elasticity, the spider silk has a variety of applications such as providing artificial ligaments and tendons, eye sutures, and for jaw repair. The silk could also have industrial applications in bulletproof vests and improved automobile airbags.
>
> These healthy animals will make an appearance at the Summit, and future applications of genetically engineered animals will be discussed.
>
> The Livestock Biotech Summit will provide participants three days of cross-cutting discussions among industry, academic and government leaders on the care and use of animals in research and the many possibilities in the realm of GE animal research, regulation, and funding within the biotechnology industry (Biotechnology Industry Organization, 2010, paras. 1-8).

If you were a military researcher looking for advances in fiber technology for protective vests or underwater security nets or parachute cords you would certainly notice the chimeric application of spider silk in goat's milk. If you were a military physician you would want more information on the xenotransplantation of pig organs to wounded G.I.s or Marines and antibody-bearing beef in soldiers' meals. The condition and fate of the animals corralled into such anthropocentric research would likely be of minimal concern.

As the marketing materials for this Summit states, "BIO represents more than 1,200 biotechnology companies, academic institutions, state biotechnology centers and related organizations across the United States and in more than 30 other nations" (Biotechnology Industry Organization, 2010, para. 26). Not only are seven other international biotech conferences listed, but we can assume that many of the other 1,200 BIO member organizations, as well as organizations that are not BIO members, hold their own conferences, to which military researchers can gain admission. The grist for future applications in the deployment or exploitation of militarized animals is virtually unlimited.

At another conference produced by the Association of Computing Machinery in Canada in 2006, three scientists from Singapore—Teh, Lee and Cheok—presented a paper on the "haptic," remote control of animals (also discussed under *Direct Military Research* below):

> This system has a tangible interface encompassing both visual and tactile modes of communication. It allows humans to interact remotely with pets anytime, anywhere. The pet owner views the real time movement of the pet in the form of a pet doll sitting on a mechanical positioning system. Meanwhile, the real pet wears a special jacket, which is able to reproduce the touching sensation. The pet owner can tangibly touch the pet doll, sending touch signals to the pet far away. Also, the pet owner receives a haptic feedback from the movement of the pet. (Teh, Lee & Cheok, 2006, para. 1)

This technology has obvious military implications, particularly for animals trained to act aggressively toward pre-established targets when triggered by remote tactile commands.

Popular science media, particularly magazines and websites, can provide an easily accessible resource to military investigators. As far back as 2002 the BBC News site described cyborg research on rats conducted by a research team at the State University of New York: "Electrodes were implanted into areas of the rats' brains, [and] commands and rewards were transmitted by radio from a laptop computer to a backpack receiver strapped to each rodent. The scientists were able to make the rats run, turn, jump and climb where they wanted" (Whitehouse, 2002, para. 5). The public's interest in such tabloid fare makes the job of military researchers combing popular media for potential cutting-edge applications relatively easy.

Direct Military Research

Military research agencies have been examining the uses of cyborgs, in this case, animals or insects implanted with nonanimal parts that direct the animal to surveil enemy installations while responding to remote stimuli. For instance, the Defense Advanced Research Projects Agency (DARPA), a division of the Department of Defense, has implanted sensors in insect pupae so that when they reach their adult flying stage they can transmit data about enemy ordnance and movements. At the same time, researchers can control the flight of these same insects outfitted with tiny electro-mechanical devices. The demonstration of a flying cyborg beetle under human control, developed by DARPA in 2009, has inspired plans for similar future cyborg experiments with other insects, fish, mammals and birds, including bees, sharks, rats and pigeons (Guizzo, 2009, para. 2).

At yet another technology conference, the 2009 Institute of Electrical and Electronics Engineers Micro-Electronic Mechanical Systems (MEMS) Conference in Italy, engineers from the University of California, Berkeley, under contract from DARPA, demonstrated a wireless flying insect cyborg:

> With the mind of a machine and the nimble body of an insect, this bug-bot may be the perfect scout: inexpensive, expendable, and capable of surreptitious reconnaissance … beetles are strong enough to carry useful payloads, such as a miniature camera.
>
> DARPA … is also sponsoring research on ways to implant insects with machinery during early stages of their lives. Butterflies can fly thousands of miles without feeding; a cyborg version would be a good candidate for long-range missions. Perhaps caterpillars could be modified to grow into adults that look like regular butterflies but have embedded wires and electrodes, allowing humans to control their flight. Dragonflies, which can reach 45 miles per hour, might take on high-speed missions. And with a wingspan of almost 10 inches, the moth Thysania agrippa has caught DARPA's attention as a miniature cargo ship (Ornes, 2010, paras. 2-3).

A DARPA researcher, Dr. Jack Judy, explains one of the primary goals of this ongoing and future research: "HI-MEMS [hybrid insect micro-electronic mechanical systems] derived technologies will enable many robotic capabilities at low cost, impacting the development of future autonomous defense systems" (Judy, 2010, para. 3).

Noninvasive tactile devices have been used to control animals remotely, for example, haptic technology. Similar to operating a Nintendo Wii home video game, researchers "clothe" animals in confining devices that translate a human operator's forces, vibrations, and/or motions to an animal (Robles De-La-Torre, 2010, all paras.). A primitive version of this technology has been used, as referenced above, to guide a land-mine-detecting mongoose. Current and future research is expanding into computer gaming, mobile telecommunications, surgery, robotics, manufacturing, the arts and other industries. Though few specific animal control applications are found in public literature the leap to remote control of animals by military haptic specialists is a logical if not inevitable development.

Other sources of research with potential military animal applications in the United States of America are the military departments of governments worldwide. For instance, Lousky (2007) tracked the use of animals in military experiments in Israel from 2000 to 2004:

> [I]n a 5 year average, the MSS [the Israeli Military and Security Sector] is responsible for using 58% of the guinea pigs, 31% of the pigs, 16% of the dogs and a staggering 75.7% of the primates used in Israel. On average, the MSS uses four times more primates than the other sectors combined, despite the fact it is far smaller than either the industrial or academic sectors ... [Furthermore, Israel's] animal experiments act ... excludes the MSS from normal legal regulation, [and] experiments which are considered less ethical are more easily authorized in the MSS. (Lousky, 2007, p. 263)

Accessing and possibly implementing the research of foreign governments, particularly allies of the United States of America, avoids oversight by the Animal and Plant Health Inspection Service of the U.S. Department of Agriculture, as mandated by the Animal Welfare Act of 1966 and amended in 1985. In fact, military-to-military sharing of animal research is likely to advance faster than indigenous research because of this lack of oversight. Although Lousky (2007) does not specify the types of experiments Israeli military scientists performed on animals, the sheer numbers of animals harmed and killed suggest that at least some of that research would be of interest to the nation's largest foreign benefactor, the United States. Again, because of the secretive nature of military research in both Israel and the United States of America we can only conjecture both the symbiotic international scientific relationship and its exploitative outcome.

In fact, the United States of America has many other allies, particularly those whose defense departments the United States of America funds with military aid, whose laws and cultures hold different regard for nonhuman animals, including companion animals and other species afforded status and consideration by U.S. residents. We can only assume that such an attitude overseas sustains a fertile environment in which U.S. military scientists can "outsource" research on animal subjects for military projects totally hidden from both public scrutiny and the oversight of animal welfare laws. In a 1992 Supreme Court case, *Lujan v. Defenders of Wildlife*, the Court ruled that U.S.

citizens do not have the right (or standing) to sue foreign nationals or governments that kill or harm their own endangered species (Hamilton, 2008, pp. 8-9). We can assume that such a restraint would apply to animal subjects in foreign military tests as well.

Richard Cochrane, in a far-fetched scenario that sounds like it was inspired by a Sea World act or an animated film, the U.S. Navy planned to train dolphins in 2010 to detect underwater intruders and bump them from behind to knock a tracking device off the dolphin's nose near the diver. Trained sea lions then "carry cuffs in their mouths that clasp shut around a diver's leg when bumped by the sea lion. Cuffs are attached to a tether, so military personnel can haul in the intruder after he is cuffed" (Cochrane, 2009, paras. 1-12). It is not clear if the navy followed through on this idea for dolphin-sea lion "strike teams" or if it is still on the drawing board, and Cochrane does not reveal his source. The U.S. Navy previously used dolphins in 2003 to detect underwater mines in Iraqi ports.

Besides those military projects designed to attack adversaries, military researchers expend considerable resources on defensive and prophylactic projects. The soldiers routinely vaccinated against anthrax today undoubtedly owe the safety of the procedure to research using countless animals infected with the deadly and painful pathogen. Extending that policy into likely scenarios in the future, we can assume military scientists or their surrogates will massacre animals with sophisticated but insidious weapons using radiation, viruses, lasers, biotoxins and other deadly agents and then perform autopsies on the animal corpses to determine appropriate survival regimens and shielding, if any, for combat troops.

Inspiration from Popular Media and Entertainment

The military development of animal hybrids for combat is grist for active imaginations. The concept has been exploited by Hollywood to ludicrous extremes, such as the made-for-TV movie *Sharktopus*, about a genetically engineered giant species hybrid (half shark/half octopus) developed as a weapon for, and remotely controlled by, the U.S. Navy (Stuart, 2010, paras. 1-4). Unfortunately, what appears ludicrous at first glance may seriously be considered and explored by military decision makers.

Another major form of animal militarization, robotics, is still in an early conceptual stage. One artist's idea of such a hybrid is the avatar or cartoon character, "War Wolf," created by Abel Padilla, who uses the nom de blog "Sphinx Magoo." Padilla's avatar is a werewolf like armored soldier, vicious, deadly and ready for combat (Padilla, 2009, para. 1). A Special Forces contingent of such creatures would likely garner public support, since most military researchers would not consider the lives of such animals comparable in value to the lives of human soldiers. Again, creative imaginations may generate ideas that appear outrageous to the person on the street but which may inspire military minds.

According to physicist Aaron Saenz, senior editor at the popular science site Singularity Hub, the concepts and designs of the future, as imagined by artists and other creative types, are based on hybrid concepts of current technologies:

> Scientists really are making cyborg beetles and robotic hummingbirds, why not an android anaconda or a missile-toting toad? Picking which of these concepts might actually make it from Photoshop to the engineering bench isn't easy.... our concepts of the future are usually just mash-ups of the things around us today. Accelerating technologies mess with our abilities to accurately predict what is possible ... I see ideas that someone, someday, is going to want to make a reality (Saenz, 2010, para. 3).

Saenz also theorizes that fully mimetic robots, based on animal movements and skills, will be easier to realize than partially roboticized animals or insects. Referring to the previously referenced experiment funded by DARPA, "reliably powering electronics on [an insect-size] scale may require enough effort that creating robotic bugs will be a better choice than making cyborg ones" (Saenz, 2009, para. 5). Thus, the seemingly arbitrary or ambivalent self-empowered movements of insects and animals may work in their favor. The military may be inclined to discard such highly variable and labor-intensive (and thus expensive) experiments. It may be easier and more cost-effective for military scientists to create robots that imitate these creatures than to try to remotely control their behavior for intelligence and other military purposes, particularly when human lives depend on the accuracy of such interventions.

Conclusion

We have examined the many obvious, opaque and potential abuses and inhumane experiments that the military may be considering, conducting, or on the verge of conducting with animal subjects.

We find many sources of free or nonproprietary research and groundwork available to military investigators, including private research facilities, research universities and private sector corporations with and without military contracts. Military minds may be inspired to repurpose animals trained or forced to demine battlefields, so that the creatures arm the mines instead of disarming them. The controversial field of genetic engineering has produced many "unnatural" plants and animals for human consumption. Military scientists could build on this research to produce animals for human destruction. Graduate and postgraduate theses and dissertations, technology and biotechnology conferences, and even popular media could provide grist for the military weaponization of animals.

DARPA has, in fact, contracted with research universities to produce insect cyborgs, with the idea of extending cyborg technology to "higher" phyla-like mammals and birds. The military is also directly and openly involved in remote, haptic control of animals for combat duty. The third area of direct military research is the training of dolphins and sea lions for counterterrorism missions, presumably using positive reinforcement/behavior modification techniques. We do not know if the military has stopped such programs. In fact, military researchers may very well be refining and expanding them. They are also most likely letting foreign governments perform much of the "dirty work" of inhumane animal research for them and appropriating whatever appears promising. At the same time, the military will undoubtedly counterbalance its development of animal-based and animal-enhanced weapons with defensive research that destroys animals in the hope of discovering methods of protecting soldiers. Even with past research as a guide we can barely imagine the weapons of annihilation that military scientists will dream up as they attempt to keep one step ahead of the enemy.

Finally, we have examined the potential inspiration to military research from popular media, including novels, films, blogs, and online contests for artists. Though often appearing merely as whimsical "eye candy" or mindless entertainment, such concepts may be subverted for military purposes.

Because of the confidential and secretive nature of such research we have had to surmise the many public sources of inspiration for such research that the military could conceivably appropriate or extrapolate. Future monitoring by journalists and whistleblowers may be the only means of confirmation of these hypotheses. Those not involved in the use of animals for military purposes must be on guard for such unnecessary and inhumane exploitation. That said, the very sentience of sentient beings makes them less than ideal subjects for the precise and absolute control needed in military conflict and intelligence gathering operations. Nonhuman animals are by nature not as reliable and predictable as human soldiers, even with military "enhancements" and human manipulation. At least one prominent animal expert, Temple Grandin, has even posited that animals are naturally autistic (Grandin & Johnson, 2005, pp. 67-68), a liability that would quickly disqualify human registrants for military service. Such characteristics may save animals from extensive weaponization and related military research in the future. Thus, the innate inappropriateness of animals in combat may eventually lead at least some military scientists, researchers, contractors and soldiers to a *de facto* total liberation from chauvinistic and speciesist biases. Such an attitude and strategic change would help those nations enmeshed in military research (and those contracting universities dependent on it) to exceed negative peace, or the absence of war, and to achieve positive peace, a more diverse, liberated and humane future for a peaceful world.

A CRITICAL ANIMAL AND PEACE STUDIES ARGUMENT TO ENDING ALL WARS

Anthony J. Nocella II

The greatness of a nation and its moral progress can be judged by the way its animals are treated.
— Mahatma Gandhi

In exploring the abolition of war, there is no field of study that examines it more thoroughly than the interdisciplinary field of peace studies. Similarly, the intersectional field of critical animal studies is vital for exploring the abolition of nonhuman animal oppression. However, there are many shortcomings in both fields. First, they are reformist because they exist in higher education, an oppressive system, and are dominated by white, European, able-bodied academics. Further, peace studies, more than critical animal studies, is dominated by liberal, Christian, heterosexual males. I am editor of the *Peace Studies Journal* and former organizer of the Central New York Peace Studies Consortium, so I have observed firsthand that most of the people involved in peace studies are white, heterosexual, able-bodied, Christian men with very little experience in community organizing and activism, aside from reading about it.

Peace studies was begun in the 1960s and 1970s by antiwar activists who wanted more education and conversation on social justice and peace at their colleges and universities. But today the professors involved have very little or no activist experience. Today, there are more than 300 programs, centers and departments with one, all, or a combination of an undergraduate minor, major, concentration graduate degree and certificate in the field. I did not have the ability to get an undergraduate degree in peace studies; but I did assist in creating the Social Justice minor at the University of St. Thomas in Houston, Texas. After obtaining my bachelor's degree in political science, I went to Fresno Pacific University where I received a Master's degree in Peacemaking and Conflict Studies, finally ending up at Syracuse University, where I was a graduate assistant in the Program for Advancement of Research on Conflict and Collaboration (PARCC). At Syracuse, I managed the annual Peace Studies

Conferences and graduated with a doctorate in Social Science. Both my master's and doctorate focused on critical animal studies and peace studies. I attempted to make them complement one another, rather than ignore or oppose each other's field's mission and theory.

Even Mohandas Gandhi, the most well-known and respected peacemaker in modern history, who was inspired to become vegetarian by Henry Salt's *A Plea for Vegetarianism* (1886), could not influence those in the field of peace studies or the peace movement to adopt vegetarianism or care for nonhuman animals in a deliberate, political way. Gandhi, a member of the London Vegetarian Society and advocate for animal rights, states:

> To my mind the life of a lamb is no less precious than that of a human being. I should be unwilling to take the life of a lamb for the sake of the human body. I hold that, the more helpless a creature, the more entitled it is to protection by man from the cruelty of man. But he who has not qualified himself for such service is unable to afford to it any protection. I must go through more self-purification and sacrifice before I can hope to save these lambs from this unholy sacrifice. Today I think I must die pining for this self-purification and sacrifice. It is my constant prayer that there may be born on earth some great spirit, man or woman, fired with divine pity, who will deliver us from this heinous sin, save the lives of the innocent creatures, and purify the temple. (1993, pp. 235-236)

Gandhi, world-renowned peacemaker, made the connection between ending violence amongst humans and ending the violence of humans against nonhuman animals. However, U.S. peace activists who protest against war focus on ending the military-industrial complex and needless spending, rarely looking past those blatant obstacles to peace, thereby ignoring nonhuman animals and environmental destruction. Why this disconnect? Because it is easy to protest injustices in far off countries one can barely pronounce. Further, sole focus on wars in foreign lands means less or no self-reflection by a liberal mainstream, who will not consider the ways in which they personally need to change, in order to foster peace in their own countries. Often, liberal mainstream antiwar activists do not de-invest in war-profiting companies or adopt alternative means of transportation other than cars, although they may buy hybrids thinking that they've "done enough" to help the environment. Too often, these activists are actually working for corporations that are profiting from the exploitation and domination of others. For these reasons, I must stress that if anything is going to change for the better, it must start at home—and with individuals making more ethical decisions from the foods that we eat to the shoes on our feet and the shirts on our backs.

The Wars on Nonhuman Animals

Nonhuman animals are casualties of war in two ways. Obviously, they die in wars amongst humans, but they are also the casualties of an unspoken and unseen war that humans wage, and are winning, against nonhuman animals. In *Animal Liberation—By "Whatever Means Necessary"* Robin Webb (2004) writes,

> Animal liberation is not a campaign, not just a hobby to put aside when it becomes tiresome or a new interest catches your eye. It's a war. A long, hard, bloody war in which all the countless millions of its victims have, so far, been on one side only, have been defenseless and innocent whose tragedy was being born nonhuman. (p. 80)

The acknowledgment of a "war against animals," however, should not be proffered lightly. Rather, to make the idea true, "war" needs to be explained, rather than compared, as is often done when activists casually analogize nonhuman oppression to the Holocaust, genocide, and slavery, which are unique human experiences and not the same as the "war against animals."

The title of Steve Best's chapter in *Terrorists or Freedom Fighters? Reflections on the Liberation of Animals* (Best & Nocella, 2004) was inspired by Webb's passage quoted above. In "It's War! The Escalating Battle Between Activists and the Corporate-State Industry" (2004), Best defines war as:

> the intensification of the conflicts inherent in politics, and politics is the waging of war through nonmilitary means such as class warfare of economic politics that are as devastating to people as dropping bombs (as the World Bank and International Monetary Fund wreck havoc on underdeveloped countries by enforcing harsh austerity policies, or as the US blockade of Iraq before 2003 war killed over one million people, half of them infants and small children). (p. 301)

War is a strategic political act of violence of one group against another, often, but not always, for financial gain, but also for reasons of supposed religious or ethnic superiority. Thus, the Holocaust, slavery and genocides throughout history have been more than mere violence; they have been wars against the oppressed, although the oppressed had little means of fighting back. One of the leading scholars of the field of peace studies, Colman McCarthy (who wrote this book's foreword), is also vegan and an animal rights scholar-activist. He states in *All of One Peace: Essays on Nonviolence* (1999),

> Most of us feel helpless to act meaningfully against the world's war on conflicts. They are too distant, too entrenched. Students in my classes repeat

this refrain every semester, and every time—because teaching is repeating—I suggest that there is a war they can take action to end: the war on animals.

> Nonviolence to animals means signing a peace treaty in the war that rages against them. Few of us see the battle zones—the kill floors of slaughterhouses, to take the largest zone—so such numbers as seven hundred thousand animals slain an hour for food have little if any impact. In my classes on nonviolence, few students are unmoved after they examine the thinking of [Albert] Schweitzer and they learn the facts about the war on animals. (p. 159)

McCarthy eloquently and correctly argues that there is a war on nonhuman animals, but *this* book is more about how human wars affect nonhuman animals, as opposed to the larger war against and on nonhuman animals by humans. J. William Gibson, in his recent article "The New War on Wolves" (2011) in the *Los Angeles Times*, covers the violent methods of managing the roaming and population growth of wolves in Montana:

> In early November, Sen. Max Baucus, a Montana Democrat, made his own political contribution. Thrilled at the testing of a drone aircraft manufactured in Montana, Baucus declared: "Our troops rely on this type of technology every day, and there is an enormous future potential in border security, agriculture and wildlife and predator management." A manufacturer's representative claimed his company's drone "can tell the difference between a wolf and a coyote." Pilotless drone aircraft used by the CIA and the Air Force to target and kill alleged terrorists now appear to be real options to track and kill "enemy" wolves. (para. 1)

Gibson provides yet another example of how war affects and impacts nonhuman animals. Weapons designed to fight off terrorist attacks, illegal border crossing, and to invade foreign enemies are now being used on nonhuman animals. These weapons are both tested on nonhuman animals and employed to attack nonhumans who are a threat to ranchers involved in the agriculture-industrial complex that raises cows slaughtered for profit.

Wars Amongst Humans Affect All

While nonhumans are tortured in diverse ways by human military forces, the editors of this book discovered six main methods through which nonhumans are directly exploited in human-on-human wars. Those six methods include: (1) nonhuman animals as vehicles, (2) nonhuman animals as test subjects, (3) nonhuman animals as weapons, (4) nonhuman animals as casualties during war, (5) nonhuman animals after war having disabilities and illnesses, and (6) plans for the future of nonhuman animal exploitation during war times. These methods of exploitation are articulated thoroughly through each of the chapters in this book. Moreover, this book, which examines a woefully under analyzed topic, argues for seven overall action points. They include:

- To expand the intersectionality within social justice fields and movements

- To challenge the human-centricism within the field of peace studies

- To expand human rights and peace activism within the field of critical animal studies

- To abolish the military-animal industrial complex and all wars

- To build a total global justice movement inclusive of all plants, animals, and elements

- To abolish all systems of domination and oppression

- Finally, to strive for a holistic inclusive community of peace for all plants, animals, and elements

As an intersectional peace activist and an animal advocate, I always strive to make sure I am not labeled by either movement. Rather, I want to build bridges between the two.

When I became involved in activism at eighteen, I was living in Houston, Texas, and protesting against the death penalty, working with the *Green Party*, being a member of *Earth First!*, *Sierra Club*, *Texas Peace Action*, *Pax Christi*, *Amnesty International*, *Radical Education Community*, *Houston Peace and Justice Center* and the *Houston Animal Rights Team*, the last of which I was president. Despite the variety of areas in which I worked, I became known as an animal rights activist. Consequently, my intersectional work was ignored and I was stigmatized within the broader social justice movement. So in March 2003, right before the War in Iraq officially began, another activist and I took over a bridge by rappelling off of it, and dropping a banner that said, "No War in Our Name." This action closed down the I-10 highway for a few hours, which led to our arrests.

It was that final action, which I did in the name of an organization we created the day before, *Students for Peace*, that led others to see me as an *activist*, not only an animal rights activist. That action told me one thing about alliance politics, multi-movement politics, and intersectionality: if you are truly to build solidarity with other struggles and movements, you must be willing to take risks and act more for others outside of the movements you are entrenched in. You only become a multi-movement global justice activist when you risk your freedom, life, and privileges (such as having a job and attending college), more for others than for yourself. Moreover, when you become a multi-movement activist, you begin to understand the larger connections of oppression, by challenging all systems of domination, rather than reforming these systems in hopes of mass change.

War is a multibillion dollar industry through which banks, weapon and aircraft manufacturers, clothing and apparel designers, grocery stores, Internet providers, cell phones and computer companies and many other corporations and businesses profit. Returning soldiers are often mentally and/or physically wounded, not able to relate to friends and family, without jobs, and often not able to successfully complete a degree in higher education because of other external conflicts. Further, the government does not give soldiers enough financial assistance and services to manage their disabilities; as a result, many soldiers that return to the United States of America find themselves homeless. It is, therefore, critical that if someone is against war, he or she must also be against capitalism and other exploitative economic systems that promote classism. Along with being against classism, peace activists and animal advocates must also be against racism, which fuels many wars so the wealthy white establishment can profit by investing in military actions.

Moreover, children and women are seriously affected by war, often the victims of rape, torture and murder during wartime. Since its establishment, military-based war has been a patriarchal institution that perpetuates the domestication of women and the objectification of women who are used in exploitative industries to entertain male troops. Chandra Talpade Mohanty, Minnie Bruce Pratt, and Robin L. Riley note the following in *Feminism and War: Confronting U.S. Imperialism* (2008),

> Given the centrality of US imperial wars in the world today, it is impossible to understand "feminism and war" on a global scale without understanding the specificities of the racist, heterosexist, and masculinized practices and ideologies mobilized by a USA in pursuit of economic and political hegemony. (p. 2)

One of the oldest forms of destroying other cultures, traditions, and nations is to rape the conquered country's women so the men of that culture would either not have sex with them because they are "tainted" or that their children would be soiled by mixed heritage. Mohanty, Pratt, and Riley (2008) argue that feminism needs to become a global movement against war, the military-industrial complex, and U.S. imperialism. Starhawk, in the anthology, *Stop the Next War Now: Effective Responses to Violence and Terrorism* (Benjamin & Evans, 2005), argues that feminists are not against war because they are inherently kinder or gentler than men; if that was the case, the "Margaret Thatchers and Condoleezza Rices of the world would soon prove us wrong" (p. 85). Women are against war because they "need voices for peace to declare that those who truly care about life and freedom will work to support, not conquer, those women in every culture who are struggling for liberation and social justice" (Starhawk, 2005, p. 86). Further, Starhawk challenges common conceptions of strength and weakness by declaring that "compassion is not weakness, and brutality is not strength" (p. 86).

To truly be against war, one must also be actively against White supremacy, patriarchy, capitalism and similar exploitative economic systems, normalcy, and speciesism. The best way of becoming a total global justice activist is to: (1) read about other struggles/movements, (2) introduce intersectional oppressions into single-issue movements, (3) continuously participate in critical self-reflection and an accountability and responsibility process with others, and (4) be willing to risk more and conduct more extreme actions than those that are oppressed.

To end war, oppression and domination, we must reconsider how we do business, interact with others, and teach our youth. We must resist arguing for reform and focus on a massive transformation, including that of every socially-constructed institution, from schools to hospitals. It is only when *all* institutions change into inclusive, respectful, nonviolent entities that we will have peace for all. While peace studies and critical animal studies are important to education and provide space and place to discuss and critically reflect on how, why, when and where to organize, this strategy has limitations. Animal advocates, to end the oppression of animals. need to follow the lead of intersectional organizations such as Codepink (n.d.). Codepink is an international grassroots movement mostly comprised of women, but open to men, "to end U.S. funded wars and occupations, to challenge militarism globally, and to redirect our resources into health care, education, green jobs and other life-affirming activities" (para. 1). As to nonhuman animals, we must support a diet that is local, unprocessed, organic, and vegan. To do otherwise is to support violence toward nonhuman animals and ecological destruction because of the waste that is produced by dairy farms, fur farms, vivisection laboratories, and slaughterhouses.

The War on Eco-Terrorism

The current post-9/11 U.S. political climate is saturated by the government, media, and corporate community with fear and rhetoric about terrorism and security (Blum, 2004; Brasch, 2005; Chang, 2002; Chomsky, 2003; 2005). This climate filled with propaganda about the fear of terrorism "provides a false sense of fulfillment by telling people what they want to hear. We all want to feel good about ourselves, we all want to believe in what we are doing and we all want to feel proud of our country, culture and government. Propagandists know this and thus use language that fulfills our unmet desires" (Del Gandio, 2008, p. 120). With trillions of dollars backing this agenda of fighting the "war on terrorism," society has fallen prey to total techno-panopticization in which, no matter where one is, sh/e is constantly under surveillance by satellite cameras, identification cards, computers, and other forms of technology (Ball & Webster, 2003; Parenti, 2003).

And so the questions arise: Who and what are "terrorists"? And, conversely, who and what are "freedom fighters"? What is "violence," and who are the main perpetuators of it? It is imperative for analysts (and citizens) to resist corporate, state, and mass media definitions and propaganda in order to distinguish between nonviolent civil disobedience and "domestic terrorism," or between ethically justified destruction of property and wanton violence toward life (Chang, 2007; Chomsky, 2005). Douglas Long (2004) writes, "The FBI categorizes ELF/ALF attacks as acts of 'ecoterrorism,' which it defines as 'the use or threatened use of violence of a criminal nature against innocent victims or property by an environmentally oriented, subnational group for environmental-political reasons, or aimed at an audience beyond the target, often of a symbolic nature" (p. 3-4). I argue the greatest reason the Earth Liberation Front (ELF) and Animal Liberation Front (ALF) are identified not as criminals, but rather as ecoterrorists and top domestic threats, is because of their ideological differences (Del Gandio, 2008), which challenge capitalism by conducting economic sabotage against individuals and corporations. The acts they commit are crimes, but they are nonviolent crimes that physically harm no one. Their crimes are trespassing, vandalism, and arson. With hate groups throughout America wanting to harm people, the question asked over and over again by critical animal studies scholars is: how is it possible that these right-wing hate groups are not more of a national threat? The answer for many in the animal advocacy movement is that these right wing hate groups are conservative and not trying to create change (in fact, they want to revert back to a less progressive society). In contrast, the ELF and ALF are left-wing groups demanding revolutionary social change. Even more than posing economic threats, the ELF, ALF and similar groups offer what some see as a more insidious agenda—a challenge to the American way; indeed, to the human way. As Potter (2011) opines,

> At their core, they challenge fundamental beliefs that have guided humanity for thousands of years, and that have for the most part remained unquestioned by prior social justice movements: that human beings are the center of the universe and our interests are intrinsically superior to those of other species and the natural world. (p. 245)

The ELF and ALF want changes that would affect the nation and the world because they want to end all exploitation of nonhuman animals and nature. Currently, this means the obliteration of almost every industry and company that exists. It means the destruction of capitalism.

Corporations are increasingly concerned about the critics of their destructive and exploitive practices to the environment and nonhuman animals, while the FBI is ratcheting up its strategic policing of activists who defend the rights of nature. [1] This is not a coincidence, but a strategic attempt to silence voices that speak truth to power, with the state doing the bidding of petroleum, gas, timber, dairy, cattle, and vivisection industries. What is beginning to unfold is a mass political-repressive environment whereby the state is targeting Earth and animal liberationists (Best & Nocella, 2006; Lovitz, 2010). Similar to the *Red Scare* of the 1950s, in which the U.S. government attacked communists, anarchists, and other political activists, there is currently a Green Scare, characterized by similar state tactics against those defending animals and nature from attack (Potter, 2011). History is repeating itself, such that one ideological scare is replaced by another, and they are all political fronts to protect capitalism from its critics and challengers.

It cannot be stressed enough that the Green Scare is being led not only by law enforcement agencies such as the FBI, but by corporations such as Huntingdon Life Sciences, Bristol-Myers Squibb, Proctor & Gamble, Johnson & Johnson, and Clorox to name a few that, to date, test on nonhuman animals (People for the Ethical Treatment of Animals, 2012) and have been protested by activists. These corporations are fearful of what activists will convey to the public about their destruction and torture on the Earth and nonhuman animals because it will damage the public image of the company, thereby jeopardizing customer trust. Consequently, consumers will find alternatives and the company will lose profits. The Earth and animal liberationists are not targeting people or the government; rather, their target is the new super-power: global corporations. They are conducting legal protests and illegal economic sabotage (the most dangerous but successful tactic against global giants such as Proctor & Gamble and ExxonMobil), engaging in tactics ranging from boycotting the GAP to breaking windows of McDonald's franchises. It is here that the FBI is carrying out the job assigned to them by the U.S. Congress, which has been strongly lobbied by corporations.

Despite these facts, the *Animal Enterprise Terrorism Act* (AETA)—signed by George W. Bush on November 27, 2006, revamped from the *Animal Enterprise Protection Act* (AEPA) of 1992—makes certain types of animal advocacy illegal and labeled ecoterrorism (Best, 2007; Goodman, 2008; Lovitz, 2007; McCoy, 2008; Moore, 2005). It is not just ALF activities that are targeted by the AETA, but more traditional forms of dissent such as protesting in front of a fur store or organizing a letter writing campaign to the CEO of a grocery store. In *Making a Killing: The Political Economy of Animal Rights* (2007), Bob Torres notes:

In particular, two US laws, the *Animal Enterprises Protection Act* (AEPA) and the *Animal Enterprises Act* (AETA) are telling indicators of the way the capitalist state will support the interests of property holders exploiting their animal property unjustly. They also help to illustrate how the dynamics of exploitation are institutionalized in society. (pp. 72-73)

If anyone ever doubted that the U.S. government defended the animal-industrial complex (Noske, 1989) the AETA and AEPA made it publicly clear that the government has the goal of protecting corporations in the business of nonhuman animal exploitation. The Center for Constitutional Rights states that "the AETA covers many First Amendment activities, such as picketing, boycotts and undercover investigations if they 'interfere' with an animal enterprise by causing a loss of profits. So in effect, the AETA silences the peaceful and lawful protest activities of animal and environmental advocates" (n.d., para. 3).

The AETA, a tool for political repression targeting animal advocates and environmentalists, has been challenged by hundreds of organizations, including the American Civil Liberties Union, National Lawyers Guild, and American Legal Defense Fund (Equal Justice Alliance, n.d.). If the AEPA established the criminalization of First Amendment activities, the AETA made way for the terrorization of those same activities of civil disobedience, and it affords nonviolent activists less protection under the law. It must be stressed that the AETA was lobbied into law by wealthy biomedical and agri-business industry groups such as the *Animal Enterprise Protection Coalition* (AEPC), the *American Legislative Exchange Council* (ALEC), and the *Center for Consumer Freedom* (CCF), with bipartisan support from legislators like Senator Dianne Feinstein and Representative James Sensenbrenner (Center for Constitutional Rights, n.d., para. 1).

The AETA, with its broad definition of "animal enterprise" and what constitutes "criminal activity" that interferes with such enterprises, can easily end all social movements if augmented by crafty lobbyists and their government cohorts. Almost every social cause relates in some manner to nonhuman animal enterprises. For instance, the prison abolition movement also would affect companies that have contracts with prisons. Another example is college and university tuition hike protests. Universities contract out to companies for food and clothes, which use nonhuman animals. Hence, there is not a movement that indirectly or directly does not challenge an animal enterprise, because almost every company depends in some way upon the exploitation and murder of animals—including grocery stores, car dealerships, oil companies, shoe and clothing companies, and computer companies.

Of course, law enforcement agencies, from their perspective, need to label groups engaged in criminal activities as criminals. The government must explain the difference between a criminal and a terrorist and define both, which has been a difficult and subjective endeavor. Yet, the government and police need not vilify political activists as terrorists. Instead, they should attempt to understand the motivations and arguments of people advocating radical social change (i.e., animal activists). While officials argue that eco-terrorists are those that destroy a McDonald's or free nonhuman animals from places of exploitation, *green criminologists* (Beirne & South, 2007) argue that corporations as legal individuals are the real criminals and terrorists when they clear-cut forests, slaughter nonhuman animals for Big Macs, and pollute the water, air, and land. (See the following section for more on green criminology.)

Stigmatization of activists as terrorists is an act of political repression in the animal advocacy movement. In *Muzzling a Movement: The Effects of Anti-Terrorism Law, Money, & Politics on Animal Activism* (2010), Dara Lovitz writes, "Although not one death or serious personal injury has been attributed to eco-terrorism, the FBI has labeled so-called eco-terror groups the number-one domestic threat in the United States" (p. 106). Today, primarily due to the terrorist attack on the United States of America on September 11, 2001, "terrorist" is the label attributed to anyone seen as a threat by the U.S. government. For hundreds of years, the general public, when discrediting someone in a so-called joking manner, would demean them by referring to them with a classic disability label such as crazy, moron, idiot, mad, or retarded. Today, while people still utilize these ableist terms, the word 'terrorist' is added to that list as a way to discredit a person's ideology or a movement's tactics.

Lovitz further writes, "Whether one labels another a *terrorist* typically depends on whether one sympathizes with or opposes the cause that the other champions" (2010, p. 106). Activists and social movements, because of their desire for social and political change, are by nature controversial; therefore, they are vulnerable to being victims of stigmatization. "Stigma means an impaired collective identity, where connection with the group is a source of discredit and devaluation because that is how the group as a whole is viewed, whether or not anyone makes an issue of it through name-calling or other forms of ridicule" (Linden & Klandermans, 2006, p. 214). The purpose of stigmatization as a tactic of political repression is to devalue and discredit a person and/or group as socially and/or politically flawed. Thus, when the government stigmatizes a movement, that stigma can trickle down to the public, making said movement a cultural joke and/or a dangerous threat.

From the perspective of critical criminology, the "war on terrorism" (established by the Bush administration to attack those who conducted terrorist acts on 9/11) more accurately describes the war against those perceived as threatening the interests of transnational corporations and the neo-con global military-industrial domination (Fernandez, 2008). After 9/11, the "war on terrorism" provided the perfect cover for *a war on democracy* in the form of government, corporate, and law enforcement attacks on civil liberties, free speech, and domestic dissent of virtually all kinds (Chomsky, 2005). Clearly, terrorism is not just a word; it is a weapon. The definition is politically motivated by the user in order to target certain individuals or groups.

As state and local U.S. law enforcement become militarized with a heightened level of attention on domestic terrorism and an increase in high power weaponry, the local vandal, robber, murderer, and even dissenter, assuming that individual has a political agenda, is constructed into a terrorist. *Terrorization*, rooted in the concept of criminalization, stigmatizes through labeling one's adversaries as terrorists to malign their cause/goal, and it demonizes and portrays the dissenter as deviant, thereby legitimizing and securing the stigmatizer's cause. As previously suggested, this tactic is similar to stigmatizing people with disabilities as retarded, lame, crippled, blind, fool, idiot, and moron, which establish people with disabilities as abnormal, while those with power positions in science, medicine, government and education set the bar for "normalcy."

Terrorization is a form of political repression and social control that has existed for as long as dissent. As the militarization of U.S. law enforcement becomes a reality, so does the terrorization of dissent. Terrorization, a new concept within label theory, falls within two bodies of literature: social control and political repression. Although such labeling has long existed in the United States of America, the scope and magnitude of its use greatly expanded after September 11, 2001.

Historically, the act of dissent has been labeled and demonized as "deviant behavior," and often thought to be a mental illness, or even evil, rather than a rational and emotional response to repressive political and economic forces, especially in the context of social change. It was thought that individuals who could not conform to social change became deviants, mentally ill, or insane (Pfohl, 1994). Today, law enforcement, with the assistance of psychologists, psychiatrists, political scientists, and sociologists, still believe that individuals who conduct certain acts in the name of social justice can be profiled based on *motivation* alone, suggesting that people who carry out acts of social justice do so based on emotions rather than intellectual understanding, and, therefore, can be demonized and categorized as mentally insane. This binary of rational versus irrational, based in patriarchal philosophical traditions, serves as an analytical construct to diminish the legitimacy of dissent. It is another means of terrorization.

A Green Criminology Perspective on Eco-Terrorism

While officials argue that those who destroy McDonald's or free nonhuman animals from places of exploitation are terrorists, I argue that green criminology and the emerging field of green security studies must also open up the possibility that corporations and governments as legal individuals can, by definition, also be identified as terrorists for actions such as clear-cutting forests, slaughtering nonhuman animals, and polluting the water, air, and land. Stressing that the term "terrorism" has no clear definition, the FBI writes:

> There is no single, universally accepted, definition of terrorism. Terrorism is defined in the Code of Federal Regulations as "the unlawful use of force and violence against persons or property to intimidate or coerce a government, the civilian population, or any segment thereof, in furtherance of political or social objectives" (28 C.F.R. Section 0.85). (Federal Bureau of Investigation, 2005, p. iv)

The debate between green criminologists and the law has a central focus: definition of the term "unlawful." Of course, animal advocates and some environmentalists disagree that the land or its nonhuman inhabitants should be identified as property. However, current norms do identify them as such; thus, any act that uses "force or violence" to save a tree from falling or an animal from slaughter is ripe to be labeled terrorism. Further, if green criminologists and critical animal studies scholars argue that nonhuman animals, land, air, and water are *not* property, then they fall under the FBI's categorization as "persons" or "any segment thereof" (Federal Bureau of Investigation, 2005, p. iv), meaning that their destruction, fueled by corporate interests, is terrorism. And these terrorist acts are used "in furtherance of political or social objectives." Vivisection, factory farming, animals in entertainment, clear-cutting a forest for a mall or university, or dumping toxins in to a lake are done for the purpose of creating social and political change. For example, when the owner of a mall destroys a forest, which is a complex ecosystem (ecological social habitat) with many species of plants and animals, to make way for economic growth in a particular community, they have been influenced by "social or political objectives," which are the political and community investors in the new material enterprise.

The first green criminologist to argue the government as terrorists was Nigel South. In "Corporate and State Crimes Against the Environment," South (1998) writes:

> States condemn "terrorism," but of course have always been perfectly capable of resorting to terrorist-type methods when in conflict with oppositional groups. A notorious example is the 1985 sinking of the Greenpeace flagship, Rainbow Warrior, in Auckland Harbour, New Zealand. This was a crime of terrorist violence carried out by Commandos from the French Secret Service.

In his book *Eco-Wars*, Day (1991) charts a variety of state-sponsored acts of violence and intimidation against environmental activists or groups. His comments on these and the Rainbow Warrior affairs are highly relevant to the idea of criminology which takes environmental issues and politics seriously (1998, p. 447).

In the context of green criminology, terrorism committed by corporations is eco-terrorism. Currently, eco-terrorism is the label attached to environmental and animal advocates whose activities cause economic loss to governments, individuals, and corporations (Arnold, 1997; Liddick, 2006; Long, 2004; Miller & Miller, 2000); this has been defined by U.S. law in the AETA. The term terrorism is problematic because it is used as a tool for political repression; hence, the term is malleable and can easily be reshaped to fit governmental or corporate agendas. In other words, one's person's terrorist is another person's freedom fighter.

The potential for shifting definitions of powerful terms such as "terrorism" and "terrorist" is problematic. Thus, I suggest that in the political discourse between animal advocates and environmentalists with governments and corporations, there, in fact, exists two types of eco-terrorists: (1) terrorists that cause economic loss, such as the Earth Liberation Front and Animal Liberation Front and (2) the other that causes ecological destruction such as factory farms and petroleum and gas corporation. To wit, Del Gandio (2008) writes,

Anyone tagged with the terrorist label is automatically deemed evil. It is becoming common, for instance, to label (and legally charge) radical environmentalists as eco-terrorists. This is quite puzzling since over-consumption, fossil fuels and corporate polluters are the ones actually terrorizing the environment (p. 119).

Therefore, rather than the acts nonviolent direct action activists take to protect the environment and nonhuman animals, I define eco-terrorism as the 'systematic or premeditated killing, torturing, kidnapping, or threatening destruction of the environment and nonhuman animals for social, political and economic purposes.' Examples of ecological terrorism/eco-terrorism include clear cutting over half the Earth's forests, removing primates from the wild to use in painful vivisection experiments, polluting drinking water by factory farm runoff, chemical dumping, systematically killing over 10 billion nonhuman animals a year, or any other of the hundreds of terrifying corporate sponsored violent acts to the environment and nonhuman animals. Therefore, corporations who destroy the environment and to gain profit or power are not only criminals, which has already been argued by green criminologists, but eco-terrorists as well (White, 2008).

Transformation and the End of War[2]

As activists demand the end of war and full transformation of society and its institutions, as do the authors in this book, we must define transformation just as I did with war. Transformation is larger than two individuals, stressing that all are connected in a complex relationship of oppressors and oppressed, only able to become free if we address and challenge all systems of domination and violations toward the individual. Transformation is not about destroying and building anew and a win-lose resolution such as a revolution (Skocpol, 1994; Tilly, 1978), but demands everyone in the world—including institutional systems and structures—change as well.

It is through the work of Morris (2000), Lederach (1995), and hooks (1994) that my ideological perspectives and interest in the fields of justice, peace and conflict studies, and education come together under the umbrella of transformation. Within criminology, Morris (2000) promotes transformative justice; within peace and conflict studies, Lederach (1995) promotes conflict transformation; and within education, hooks (1994) fosters transformative pedagogy; together they inform and are interdependent on one another to make social transformation possible. Lederach (1995) writes:

> I have found it useful to step back and look at the big picture related to Freire's pedagogical framework. In *Pedagogy of the Oppressed* (1970) he uses literacy, learning to read and write, which seems to be a uniquely individual and personal agenda, as a tool for exploring and promoting social change. He [Freire] refers to this as *conscientization,* awareness of self in context, a concept that simultaneously promotes personal and social transformation. (p. 19)

In the late 1990s, Ruth Morris, a Quaker in Canada, challenged restorative justice because it did not address issues of oppression, injustices, and social inequities within conflicts. Coker (2002) notes that the terms 'transformative' and "restorative" justice have erroneously been seen as interchangeable. However, Morris argues that while restorative justice challenges the retributive justice system and brings people together, it fails to recognize the sociopolitical and economic issues addressed by transformative justice (Coker, 2002).

For instance, if a fourteen-year-old boy who is queer and from a poor neighborhood robbed a store when it was closed at 2:00 a.m., transformative justice would not only look at the crime of burglary, but why the boy did it. Was the boy kicked out of his home by a father who was homophobic? Did the boy need money for food, clothes, and shelter? While restorative justice only addresses the specific conflict between the victim and offender, transformative justice strives to use the conflict as an opportunity to address larger sociopolitical injustices.

Further, 'restorative justice processes threaten to create a deeply privatized criminal justice process' (Coker, 2002, p. 129) by constructing a victim vs. offender relationship which makes absent the issue of social oppression. It is for this reason that many prison abolitionists and feminists working with domestic violence issues critique restorative justice for its limitation in addressing oppression (Coker). Because society oppresses those who are poor and queer, there are (at least) two victims; therefore, the conflict must be addressed using larger community-based approaches rather than interpersonal mediation.

Transformative justice challenges all aspects of authoritarianism, domination, and control within society. For this reason, transformative justice is more than an alternative to a criminal justice system, but a social justice philosophy for peace with tools to achieve such goals. Further, it is a non-dogmatic, process-based philosophy that allows for creative approaches in transforming conflict and addressing issues of brutality, racism, sexism, homophobia, classism, speciesism, assault, abuse, accountability, responsibility, loss and, most importantly, healing.

I have identified common principles among organizations such as the *Alternatives to Violence Project* (AVP), *Save the Kids*, and *Generation Five* to emphasize what may be thought of as the core philosophy of transformative justice (TJ):

- TJ is against violence and punishment, institutionalization and imprisonment.

- Crime is a form of community-based conflict, where society and the government are also involved as possible offenders.

- TJ brings issues of identity back into the realm of justice by addressing sociopolitical injustices toward women, people of color, those in the gay, lesbian, bisexual, transgender, queer, intersex and asexual (GLBTQIA) community, the poor, immigrants, people with disabilities, and other marginalized groups.

- TJ believes in the value of mediation, negotiation, and community circles to transform conflicts.

When fighting along with the oppressed, social justice activists will often identify the oppressor as the enemy. Transformative justice, while addressing oppression and the role that groups, institutions, and agencies have in creating and maintaining oppression, does not view anyone as an enemy, but rather argues that everyone needs to be involved in a voluntary, safe, constructive, critical dialogue where people take accountability, responsibility, and the initiative to heal. It means that law enforcement, judges, lawyers, prisoners, community members, teachers, politicians, spiritual leaders, and activists, among others, come together.

War is the result of injustice and unhealthy conflicts; therefore, we must also change how we handle conflicts and injustices. In resolving interpersonal or group conflicts, conflict transformation, similar to transformative justice, addresses issues of inequities, injustices, oppression, and domination. Conflict transformation, unlike conflict resolution, requires larger sociopolitical concerns to be addressed, while conflict resolution is only about addressing the specific incident. John Paul Lederach, the founder of conflict transformation, began using the term after his work in Central America. In *The Little Book of Conflict Transformation* (2003, p. 3), Lederach writes:

> I soon found, though, that my Latin colleagues had questions, even suspicions, about what was meant by such concepts ["conflict resolution" and "conflict management"]. For them, *resolution* carried with it a danger of co-optation, an attempt to get rid of the conflict when people were raising important and legitimate issues. It was not clear that *resolution* left room for advocacy. In their experience, quick solutions to deep social-political problems usually meant lots of good words but no real change. "Conflicts happen for a reason," they would say. "Is this *resolution* idea just another way to cover up the changes that are really needed?" (p. 3)

Conflict transformation is about addressing all types of conflicts, including war and interpersonal conflicts which influence sociopolitical and economic change, while also bringing sociopolitical and economic change to the dialogue of the specific interpersonal conflict. Conflict transformation is not meant only for social movement interventions or international disputes, but for all conflicts, including the war against nonhuman animals and wars between humans. Therefore, it is critical to realize that a mass transformation must occur and that reform and working with or within any current system of domination for total social justice is not realistic. Total global social justice will only be possible when all systems of domination are destroyed and replaced with inclusive respectful diverse communities, for this is mass social transformation.

In this chapter, I have identified three specific types of war in relation to nonhuman animals. The first, which this book covers in-depth, are wars by two or more opposing human military forces that unknowingly and indifferently affect the lives of nonhumans. The second, as McCarthy discusses, is the war against nonhuman animals by humans, underpinned by the social construction of speciesism. Finally, the third is the war against animal advocates, the first strategy of which is to stigmatize them as "terrorists." Thus, to end all wars on this planet, we must end wars among people, violence toward the Earth and nonhuman animals, and the marginalization of the so-called other through hegemonic conceptions of "normalcy."

Notes

1. This paragraph is reprinted from: Best, Steven, and Anthony J. Nocella II. "Clear Cutting Green Activists: The FBI Escalated the War on Dissent." *Impact*, Spring 2006 (accessed February 19, 2013).

2. This section is reprinted from: Nocella, A. J. II. "An Overview of the History and Theory of Transformative Justice," *Peace and Conflict Review*, 6, no. 1 (2011).

http://www.review.upeace.org/index.cfm?opcion=0&ejemplar=23&entrada=124 (accessed February 19, 2013).

BIBLIOGRAPHY

Aboud, E. T., Krisht, A. F., O'Keefe, T., Nader, R., Hassan, M., Stevens, C. M. Alif., & Luchette, F. A. "Novel Simulation for Training Trauma Surgeons." *The Journal of Trauma,* 71, no. 6. (2011): 1484-1490.

Adams, Carol J. "'Mad Cow' Disease and the Animal Industrial Complex." *Organization and Environment,* 10, no. 1 (1997): 26-51.

Adams, Carol. J. *The Sexual Politics of Meat: A Feminist-Vegetarian Critical Theory.* New York: Continuum Publishing, 1997.

Adams, Kathleen, Randy Scott, Ronald M. Perkin, and Leo Langga. "Comparison of Intubation Skills Between Interfacility Transport Team Members." *Pediatric Emergency Care,* 16, no. 1. (2000): 5-8.

Adler, Philip J., and Randall L. Pouwels. *World Civilizations.* Belmont, CA: 2005.

Aegerter, Gil, and Jeff Black. "Coast Guard Defends Medical Training on Live Animals After PETA Posts Gory Video." *US News,* April 19, 2012. http://usnews.nbcnews.com/_news/2012/04/19/11286441-coast-guard-defends-medical-training-on-live-animals-after-peta-posts-gory-video?lite (accessed February 18, 2013).

Alaboudi, Abdul K. "Depleted Uranium and Its Impact on Animals and Environment in Iraq and Algeria." n.d. www.uraniumweaponsconference.de/speakers/khadum_du.pdf

Allen, Larry. "AFSOC Training Programs: Briefing to USAF APBI and NTSA." 2010. www.ndia.org/Resources/OnlineProceedings?Documents/01A0/1540-AFSOC.pdf (accessed January 31, 2013).

Allen, Scott and Nathanial Raymond. *Experiments in Torture: Evidence of Human Subject Research and Experimentation in the "Enhanced" Interrogation Program.* Physicians for Human Rights. http://physiciansforhumanrights.org/library/reports/experiments-in-torture-2010.html (accessed November 9, 2013).

American Heart Association. "Message from AHA ECC Programs: PETA Inquiries re: Use of Live Animals in PALS Courses." 2009. www.peta.org/issues/Animals-Used-for-Experimentation/endotracheal-intubation-training-maiming-and-killing-animals.aspx (accessed January 31. 2013).

Amiel, Barbara. "Dogs Are Victims in a Scary War." *Macleans,* November 23, 2009. http://www2.macleans.ca/2009/11/19/dogs-are-victims-in-a-scary-war/ (accessed January 31, 2013).

Andrzejewski, Julie and John Alessio. "The Sixth Mass Extinction." In *Censored 2014: Fearless Speech in Fateful Times*, edited by Mickey Huff, and Andy Lee Roth, 365-385. New York: Seven Stories Press, 2013.

Andrzejewski, Julie, Helena Pedersen, and Freeman Wicklund. "Interspecies Education for Humans, Animals, and the Earth. In *Social Justice, Peace, and Environmental Education: Transformative Standards*, edited by Julie Andrzejewski, Marta Baltadano and Linda Symcox. Routledge, 2009, 136-153.

Arluke, Arnold, and Frederic Hafferty. "From Apprehension to Fascination with 'Dog Lab': The Use of Absolutions by Medical Students. *Journal of Contemporary Ethnography,* 25, no. 2 (1996): 201-225.

Arnold, Jennifer, Becky Lowmaster, Melinda Fiedor-Hamilton, Jennifer Kloesz, Dena Hofkosh, Patrick Kochanek, and Robert Clark. "Evaluation of High Fidelity Neonatal Stimulation as a Method to Teach Pediatric Residents Neonatal Airway Management Skills. Report presented at the 2008 International Meeting on Simulation in Healthcare, Santa, Fe, NM, May 2008. www.dtic.mil/dtic/tr/fulltext/u2/a479674.pdf (accessed January 31, 2013).

Arnold, Ron. *Eco-Terror: The Violent Agenda to Save Nature, the World of the Unabomber.* Bellvue, WA: Free Enterprise Press, 1997.

Associated Press. "Reprieve from Wound Tests Is Ended for Pigs and Goats." *New York Times, January 24, 1984.* http://query.nytimes.com/gst/fullpage.html?sec=health&res=9506EED81F38 F937A15752COA962948260 (accessed October 21, 2012).

Associated Press. "Dolphins Help Spot Mines in Iraq War." 2003. www.apnewsarchive.com/2003/Dolphins-Help-Spot-Mines-in-Iraq-War/id-c615ba06b3622465118e98dfe4dccd9f (accessed October 21, 2013).

Attridge, Harold W., and Wayne A. Meeks. *The Harper Collins Study Bible: New Revised Standard Version.* New York: HarperCollins, 2006.

Aung, Thet Wine. "White Elephants Stabbed by Junta." *Irawaddy.* May 8, 2010. www.irrawaddy.org/article.php?art_id=18428 (accessed October 21, 2012).

Australian Light Horse Association. "The Mounted Horses of Australia." n.d. http://www.lighthorse.org.au/resources/history-of-the-australian-light-horse/the-mounted-soldiers-of-australia www.lighthorse.org.au/resources/history-of-the-australian-light-horse/the-mounted-soldiers-of-australia (accessed February 20, 2013).

Australian War Memorial. n.d. http://www.awm.gov.au/visit/ (accessed February 21, 2013).

Azios, Tony. "Korean Demilitarized Zone Now a Wildlife Haven. *Christian Science Monitor,* November 21, 2008. www.csmonitor.com/Environment/Wildlife/2008/1121/Korean-demilitarized-zone-now-a-wildlife-haven/ (accessed January 31, 2013).

Baillie, Duncan J. "The Breeding of Horses for Military Purposes." *Royal United Services Journal* (1872): 735-748.

Baker, Peter S. *Animal War Heroes*. London, UK: A & C Black, 1933.

Bakhit, Mohammed A. *History of Humanity*. New York: Routledge, 2000.

Balcombe, Jonathan. *Second Nature: The Inner Lives of Animals*. New York: Palgrave MacMillan, 2010.

Ball, Kirstie and Frank Webster. (2003). "The Intensification of Surveillance." In *The Intensification of Surveillance*, edited by Kiristie Ball and Frank Webster, 1-15. London, UK: Pluto Press, 2003.

Barash, David P. *Approaches to Peace: A Reader in Peace Studies*. New York: Oxford University Press, 2010.

Barnard, Neal D. *Animals in Military Wound Research and Training*. Washington, DC: Physicians Committee for Responsible Medicine, 1986.

Basham, Arthur L. *The Wonder That Was India*. New York: Grove Press, 1968.

Battersby, Eilee. "Eight Million Dead in a Single Conflict: 5,000 Years of War Horses." *Irish Times*. January 14, 2012. http://www.irishtimes.com/culture/film/eight-million-dead-in-a-single-conflict-5-000-years-of-war-horses-1.444971

BBC News. "Home Town Party for War Hero Bird." 2009. www.news.bbc.co.uk/2/hi/middle_east/670551.stm (accessed October 21, 2012).

BBC News. "Dickin Medal Awarded to Bomb Sniffing Dog Treo." 2010. 6.http://news.bbc.co.uk/2/hi/uk_news/8502127.stm (accessed October 21, 2012).

Begich, Nick. *Angels Don't Play This HAARP: Advances in Tesla Technology*. Anchorage, AK: Earthpulse, 1995.

Begley, Charle. *A Report on the Elephant Situation in Burma*. October. Bedfordshire: EleAid, 2006. http://www.eleaid.com/wp-content/uploads/2013/10/A-Report-on-the-Elephant-Situation-in-Burma.pdf

Behnam, Sadeq. "Birds Disappear from Afghanistan, Leaving Pests to Flourish." November 19, 2010. http://iwpr.net/report-news/birdlife-disappears-afghan-landscape (accessed January 31. 2013).

Beirne, Piers, and Nigel South. *Issues in Green Criminology: Confronting Harms Against Environments, Humanity, and Other Animals*. (2007): Portland, OR: Willian.

Bekoff, Marc, and Jessica Pierce. *Wild Justice*. (2010): Chicago, IL: University of Chicago Press.

Belloni, Robert. "The Tragedy of Darfur and the Limits of the 'Responsibility to Protect'." *Ethnopolitics*. 5, no. 4 (2006):327-346.

Benham, Jason "Sudan Seeks Millions for War-Hit Wildlife." *Standard for Fairness and Justice,* January 18, 2011.
http://uk.reuters.com/article/2011/01/18/us-sudan-south-wildlife-idUKTRE70H1S120110118
(accessed February 4, 2013).

Behnam, Sadiq. "Birds Disappear From Afghanistan, Leaving Pests to Flourish." *Institute for War and Peace Reporting.* November 19, 2010.
http://iwpr.net/report-news/birdlife-disappears-afghan-landscape
(accessed November 9, 2013)

Benedictus, Leo. "Bounding into action with the dogs of war." *The Guardian.* May 15, 2011. http://www.theguardian.com/world/2011/may/15/dogs-war-osama-bin-laden

Benjamin, Mar. "'War on Terror' Psychologist Gets Giant No-Bid Contract." Salon.com. October 14, 2010.
http://www.salon.com/2010/10/14/army_contract_seligman/

Benjamin, Medea, and Jodie Evans. *Stop the Next War: Effective Responses to Violence and Terrorism.* Maui, HI: Inner Ocean, 2005.

Bennett, Jeffrey P. *War Dogs: America's Forgoten Heroes.* Produced by Jeffrey P. Bennett. 1999. Sherman Oaks, CA: GRB Entertainment. DVD.

Berrigan, Frida. "America's Global Weapons Monopoly." *TomDispatch.* February 17, 2010. www.commondreams.org/print/52891
(accessed October 21, 2012).

Best, Steven. "The Animal Enterprise Terrorism Act: New, Improved, and ACLU-Approved." *Journal for Critical Animal Studies,* III, no. 3 (2007).

Best, Steven, and Anthony J. Nocella II. *Terrorists or Freedom Fighters? Reflections on the Liberation of Animals.* New York: Lantern Books, 2004.

Best, Steven, and Anthony J. Nocella II. *Igniting a Revolution: Voices in Defense of the Earth.* Oakland, CA: AK Press, 2006.

Best, Steven, and Anthony J. Nocella II. "Clear Cutting Green Activists: The FBI Escalated the War on Dissent." *Impact,* Spring 2006.

Bethune, Sir Edward C. "The Uses of Cavalry and Mounted Infantry in Modern Warfare." *Royal United Services Institution Journal,* 50, no. 3 (1906): 619-636.

Biggs, Barton. *Wealth, War, and Wisdom.* Hoboken, NJ: Wiley, 2008.

Big House Productions. *"Animals in Action Volume 4: Underwater Warriors.* Written and produced by Big House Productions. (2002). New York: Big House Productions. DVD.

Biological and Toxin Weapons Convention. "Meeting of Experts." August 18-22, 1975. www.acronym.org.uk/bwd/indes.htm (accessed August 25, 2010).

Biotechnology Industry Organization. "GE Animals to Exhibit at Livestock Biotech Summit." August 25, 2010. http://www.bio.org/media/press-release/ge-animals-exhibit-livestock-biotech-summit
(accessed February 6, 2013).

Blechman Andrew D. *Pigeons: The Fascinating Saga of the World's Most Revered and Reviled Bird.* New York: Grove Press, 2006.

Block, Ernest F. J., Lawrence Lottenberg, Lewis Flint, Joelle Jakobsen, and Dianna Liebnitzky. "Use of a Human Patient Simulator for the Advanced Trauma Life Support Course." *The American Surgeon,* 68, no. 7 (2002): 648-651.

Blum, William. *Killing Hope: U.S. Military and the C.I.A. Interventions Since World War II.* Monroe, ME: Black Rose Books, 2000.

Bock Carl. *Temples and Elephants: The Narrative of a Journey of Exploration Through Upper Siam and Lao,* White Orchid Press: Bangkok 1985.

Boggs, Carl. *Imperial Delusions: American Militarism and Endless War.* Lanham, MD: Rowman & Littlefield, 2005.

Boggs, Carl. "Corporate Power, Ecological Crisis, and Animal Rights." In *Critical Theory and Animal Liberation,* Edited by John Sanbonmatsu, 71-96. Lanham, MD: Rowman & Littlefield, 2011.

Bolivian Army. "Memorandum of Understanding Concerning the Activation, Organization, and Training of the 2nd Battalion." April 28, 1967. www.gwu.edu/~nsarchiv/NSAEBB/NSAEBB5/che14_1.htm (accessed October 21, 2012).

Borman, Windy (2012) *The Eyes of Thailand.* Directed by Windy Borman. 2012. DVA Productions in association with Indiewood Pictures.

Bowyer, Mark, Alan V. Liu, and James P. Bonar. "A Simulator for Diagnostic Peritoneal Lavage Training." *Studies in Health Technologies and Informatics,* 11 (2005): 64-67.

Branan, Nicole. "Danger in the Deep: Chemical Weapons Lie Off Our Coasts." *Earth Magazine,* January 27, 2009. http://www.earthmagazine.org/article/danger-deep-chemical-weapons-lie-our-coasts (accessed January 31, 2013).

Brasch, Walter M. *America's Unpatriotic Acts: The Federal Government's Violation of Constitutional and Civil Rights.* New York: Peter Lang, 2005.

Brauer, Jurgen. *War and Nature: The Environmental Consequences of War in a Globalized World,* AltaMira Press: Maryland, 2009.

Brean, Joseph. "Loud Noises May Have Caused Arkansas Bird Deaths. *National Post,* January 1, 2011. news.national post.com/2011/01/03/mass-bird-deaths-puzzle-arkansas-town/ (accessed October 21, 2012).

Broder, John M. "Climate Change Seen as Threat to U.S. Security." *New York Times,* August 9, 2000. http://www.nytimes.com/2009/08/09/science/earth/09climate.html (accessed February 1, 2013).

Brodie, Bernard, and Fawn M. Brodie. *From Crossbow to H-Bomb.* Bloomington: Indiana University Press, 1973.

Broome, Richard. *Aboriginal Australians: Black Responses to White Dominance, 1788-1994.* St Leonards, NSW: Allen & Unwin, 1994.

Bullock, Jane, George Haddow, Damon P. Coppola, and Sarp Yeletaysi. *Introduction to Homeland Security: Principles of All-Hazards Risk Management.* Burlington, MA: Butterworth Heinemann, 2008.

Burghardt, Tom. "Biological Warfare and the National Security State: A Chronology." *Global Research,* August 9, 2009. http://www.globalresearch.ca/biological-warfare-and-the-national-security-state (accessed October 14, 2012).

Burstein, Stanley M. "Elephants for Ptolemy II: Ptolemaic Policy in Nubia in the Third Century BC." In *Ptolemy II: Philadelphus and His World,* edited by Paul McKechnie and Phillipe Guilleme, 135-147. Leiden, NL: Brill, 2008.

Burt, Jonathan. "Review: The Animals' War Exhibition." *History Today,* October 1, 2006.

Butler, Frank K. "Tactical Management of Urban Warfare Casualties in Special Operations." *Military Medicine,* 165, no. 4 supplement (2000): 1-48.

Capaldo, Theodora. "The Psychological Effects of Using Animals in Ways That They See as Ethically, Morally, or Religiously Wrong." *Alternatives to Laboratory Animals, 32,* supplement no. 1 (2004): 525-531.

Carrington, Damian. "Mass Tree Deaths Prompt Fears of Amazon 'Climate Tipping Point'." *The Guardian/UK,* February 4, 2011. www.commondreams.org/headline/2011/02/04-0 (accessed October 14, 2012).

Carroll, Michael Christopher. *Lab 257.* New York: William Morrow, 2004

Cart, Julie. "Army Seeks to Move More Than 1,100 Desert Tortoises." *Los Angeles Times,* August 5, 2009. latimesblogs.latimes.com/greenspace/2009/08/desert-tortoise-endangered-species-army-training-html (accessed February 2, 2013).

Casey-Maslen, Stuart. 'Introductory Note', *Convention on the Prohibition of the Use, Stockpiling, Production and Transfer of Anti-Personnel Mines and on their Destruction,* Oslo, 18 September 1997. http://legal.un.org/avl/ha/cpusptam/cpusptam.html (accessed November 5, 2013)

Casson, L "Ptolemy II and the Hunting of African Elephants." *Transactions of the American Psychological Association,* 123 (1993): 247-260.

Center for Constitutional Rights. "The Animal Enterprise Terrorism Act (AETA). n.d. ccrjustice.org/learn-more/faqs/factsheet%3A-animal-enterprise-terrorism-act-%28aeta%29 (accessed October 14, 2012).

Chang, Nancy. *Silencing Political Dissent.* New York: Seven Stories Press, 2002.

Charles, Michael B. "African Forest Elephants and Turrets in the Ancient World." *Phoenix,* 62, no. 3/4 (2008): 338-362.

Chayer, Amelie. "United Kingdom Under Fire from Treaty Allies for Failure to Clear Landmines." Geneva, CH: International Coalition to Ban Landmines. November 26, 2008. http://www.icbl.org/index.php//Treaty/MBT/Annual-Meetings/9MSP/Media/pressreleases/pr26nov08 (accessed February 2, 2013).

Chelvadurai, Manogaran. *Ethnic Conflict and Reconciliation in Sri Lanka.* Manoa, HI: University of Hawaii Press, 1987.

Cherrix, Kira. "Test Site Profile: Nevada Test Site." 2008. mason.gmu.edu/~kcherrix/nts.html (accessed October 12, 2012).

Cherry, Robert A. and Jameel Ali. "Current Concepts in Simulation-Based Trauma Education." *The Journal of Trauma,* 65, no. 5 (2008): 1186-1193.

Chivers, C "Tending a Fallen Marine, with Skill, Prayer and Fury." *New York Times,* November 2, 2006.

Chomsky, Noam. *Knowledge of Language: Its Nature, Origin, and Use.* New York: Seven Stories Press, 1987.

Chomsky, Noam. *Power and Terror: Post-9/11 Talks and Interviews.* New York: Seven Stories Press, 2003.

Chomsky, Noam. *Imperial Ambitions: Conversations on the Post-9-11 World.* New York: Metropolitan Books, 2005.

Chossudovsky, Michel. "Excluded from the Copenhagen Agenda: Environmental Modification Techniques (ENMOD) and Climate Change." *Global Research,* December 5, 2009. http://www.globalresearch.ca/environmental-modification-techniques-enmod-and-climate-change (accessed October 14, 2012).

Clarke, Hamish. "The Nature of War." *Cosmos,* May 9, 2007. www.cosmosmagazine.com/features/online/1289/the-nature-war (accessed October 21, 2012).

Clifton, Wolf. "Animal Cruelty and Dehumanization in Human Rights Violations." *The Greanville Post,* November 10, 2009. http://www.greanvillepost.com/2009/11/10/animal-cruelty-and-dehumanization-in-human-rights-violations/ (accessed February 2, 2013).

CNN.com. "UK Honors Glow Worm Heroes." November 24, 2004. http://edition.cnn.com/2004/WORLD/europe/11/24/uk.newwaranimals/index.html (accessed October 14, 2012).

Cochrane, Richard. "Marine Animals Set to Guard U.S. Submarine Base." *Hypocrisy Reigns Supreme,* December 17, 2009. hypocrisy.com/2009/12/17/marine-mammals-set-to-guard-us-submarine-base (accessed February 2, 2013).

Codepink. "What Is Codepink?" n.d. www.codepink4peace.org/article.php?list=type&type=3 (accessed October 14, 2012).

Coker, Donna. "Transformative Justice: Anti-Subordination Processes in Cases of Domestic Violence." In *Restorative Justice and Family Violence,* edited by Heather Strang and John Braithwaite, 128-152. Cambridge, UK: Cambridge University Press, 2002.

Collins, John J. *Introduction to Hebrew Bible.* Minneapolis, MN: Fortress Press, 2004.

Costs of War. n.d. http://costsofwar.org/article/environmental-costs (accessed February 21, 2013).

Crawford, Angus. "UK Misses Falklands Mine Deadline." *BBC News,* November 24, 2008. http://news.bbc.co.uk/2/hi/uk_news/politics/7742661.stm (accessed October 14, 2012).

Creel, Herrlee G. "The Role of the Horse in Chinese History." *American Historical Review.* LXX (1965):647-672

Cunningham, Erin. "In Gaza, Alarm Spreads Over Use of Lethal New Weapons. *Antiwar,* January 23, 2009. http://www.antiwar.com/ips/cunningham.php (accessed February 2, 2013).

Curry, Ajaye. "Animals: The Hidden Victims of War." *Animal Aid,* 2003. www.animalaid.org.uk/images/pdf/waranimals.pdf (accessed February 2, 2013).

Daily Mail. "Forgotten Heroes: A million horses were sent to fight in the Great War - only 62,000 came back." November 9, 2007. http://www.dailymail.co.uk/columnists/article-492582/Forgotten-Heroes-A-million-horses-sent-fight-Great-War--62-000-came-back.html#ixzz2k5AMKSGc

Daily Mail "Black Labrador Treo Becomes 23rd Animal to Receive the Dickin Medal After Serving in Afghanistan." February 24, 2010. www.dailymail.co.uk/news/article-1253312/Black-Labrador-Treo-23rd-animal-receive-Dickin-Medal (accessed October 12, 2012).

Daily Mail. "Huge Rise in Vivisection as 3.7m Experiments on Animals Are Carried Out in a Year." July 14, 2011 www.dailymail.co.uk/sciencetech/article-2014279/Huge-rise-vivisection-3-7m-experiments-animals-carried-yuear.html#ixzz1idSWDlkz (accessed October 12, 2012).

Daly, Peter M. *Literature in the Light of the Emblem.* Toronto, Canada: University of Toronto Press, 1979.

Dance, Amber. "50 Years After the Blast: Recovery in Bikini Atoll's Coral Reef." May 27, 2008. print.news.mongabay.com/2008/0526-dance_bikini.html?print (accessed February 2, 2013).

Dao, James. "After Duty, Dogs Suffer Like Soldiers." *New York Times,* December 1, 2011. www.nytimes.com/2011/12/02/us/more-military-dogs-show-signs-of-combat-stress.html (accessed February 2, 2013).

Dart, Raymond A. "Australopithecus Africanus: The Man-Ape of South
Africa." In *A Century of Nature: Twenty-One Discoveries That Changed
Science and the World,* edited by Laura Garwin and Tim Lincoln, 10-20.
Chicago, IL: University of Chicago Press, 1925.

David Grant Medical Center. "Protocol #FDG20050030A: Neonatal
Resuscitation Training in the Laboratory Animal."
www.travis.af.il/units/dgmc/ (accessed October 14, 2012).

Davis, Jeffrey S., Jessica Hayes-Conroy, and Victoria M. Jones. "Military
Pollution and Natural Purity: Seeing Nature and Knowing Contamination in
Vieques, Puerto Rico." *Geojournal,* 69, no, 3 (2007): 165-179.

Dearing, Stephanie. "Dogs of War: Iraq's Feral Dog Population on the Rise."
Digital Journal, January 18, 2010.
www.digitaljournal.com/print/article/285913 (accessed October 14, 2012).

Deen, Thalif. "Despite Recession, Global Arms Race Spirals." *Inter Press
Service News Agency,* March 16, 2010.
http://www.ipsnews.net/2010/03/disarmament-despite-recession-global-
arms-race-spirals/ (accessed February 2, 2013).

Del Gandio, Jason. *Rhetoric for Radicals: A Handbook for Twenty-First Century
Activists.* San Francisco, CA: New Society Publishers, 2008.

Dempewolff, Richard E. *Animal Reveille.* New York: Doubleday, Doran &
Company, 1943.

Department of the Air Force. "Freedom of Information Act (FOIA) 08-0051-HS,
C-STARS Courses." August 28, 2008. Private Resource.

Department of Defense. "Animal Care and Use Programs Fiscal Year 2002-
2003." 2003. zoearth.org/tag/pigs (accessed October 12, 2012).

Department of Veterans Affairs. "M is for Mates. Animals in Wartimes Ajax to
Zep." Canberra, AUS: Department of Veteran Publication in Association
with the Australian War Memorial, 2009.

Derr, Mark. *Dogs Best Friend: Annals of the Dog-Human Relationship.* New
York: H. Holt and Company, 1997.

Derry, Margaret E. *Horses in Society.* Toronto, Canada: University of Toronto
Press, 2006.

Diamond, Jared. *Guns, Germs and Steel: The Fates of Human Societies.* New
York: W. W. Norton and Company, 1997.

Dijk, Ruud V., ed. *Encyclopedia of the Cold War (Volume One).* Agingdon, UK:
Routledge, 2008.

Doctors Against Animal Experiments Germany. *Military Experiments on Living
Animals Prohibited.* August 11, 2010.
www.aerzte-gegen-tierversuche.de/en/component/content/article/55-
resourses/262-military-esperiments-on-living-animals-prohibited
(accessed October 14, 2012).

Drury, Ian. "Their Last Journey: Tragic Bomb Dog Theo in Line for an 'Animal VC' as He and His Master's Body are Flown Home Together." *Daily Mail,* March 5, 2011. www.dailymail.co.uk/news/article-1362837/Bomb-sniffing-Army-dog-master-repatriated-Wootton-Bassett.html (accessed February 2, 2013).

Dube, Mathieu. "Strathconas Celebrate the Battle of Moreuil Wood. Lord Strathcona's Horse (Royal Canadians)." www.strathconas.ca/strathconas-celebrate-the-battle-of-moreuil-wood?id=835 (accessed October 12, 2012).

Duiker, William J., and Jackson J. Speilvogel. *World History* (6th ed.). Boston, MA: Wadsworth, 2010.

Dunayer Joan. *Animal Equality: Language and Liberation.* Derwood, MD: Ryce, 2001.

Dupuy, Trevor N. *The Evolution of Weapons and Warfare.* New York: Bobbs-Merrill, 1980.

Ellul, Jacques. *The Technological Bluff.* Grand Rapids, MI: William B. Eerdmans Publishing Company, 1990.

Enzler, Svante M. "Environmental Effects of Warfare." 2006. www.lennntech.com/environmental-effects-war.htm (accessed February 2, 2013).

Equal Justice Alliance. "Our allies." n.d. http://www.equaljusticealliance.org/allies.htm (accessed March 1, 2012).

Falck, A J., M. B. Escobedo, J. G. Baillargeon, L. G. Villard, and J. H. Gunkel "Proficiency of Pediatric Residents in Performing Neonatal Endotracheal Intubation." *Pediatrics, 112,* no. 6 (2003): 1242-1247.

Fang, Irving. "Alphabet to Internet: Mediated Communication in Our Lives." 2008. www.mediahistory.umn.edu/archive/PigeonPost.html

Felton, Debbie. *Haunted Greece and Rome: Ghost Stories from Classical Antiquity.* Austin: University of Texas Press, 1999.

Fernandez, Luis A. *Policing Dissent: Social Control in the Anti-Globalization Movement.* Piscataway, NJ: Rutgers University Press, 2008.

Filner, Bob. "The Battlefield Excellence Through Superior Training (BEST) Practices Act-H. R. 1417. *The PETA Files,* April 8, 2011. *www.peta.org/b/thepetafiles/archive/tags/BEST.../default.aspx* (accessed February 2, 2013).

Foster, Robert E., Ellen P. Embrey, David J. Smith, Annette K. Hildabrand, Paul R. Cordts, and Mark W. Bowyer. "Final Report of the Use of Live Animals in Medical Education and Training Joint Analysis Team." 2009. www.mediapeta.com/ulamet/ulamet_jat.pdf (accessed February 3, 2013).

Foucault, Michel. *The History of Sexuality, Volume 1: The Will to Knowledge.* London, UK: Penguin, 1988.

Fox News. "Afghan Police Stop Bombing Attack From Explosives-laden Donkey." June 8, 2006. http://www.foxnews.com/story/2006/06/08/afghan-police-stop-bombing-attack-from-explosives-laden-donkey/

Frank, Joshua. "Bombing the Land of the Snow Leopard: The War on Afghanistan's Environment." *Counterpunch,* January 17, 2010. http://www.counterpunch.org/2010/01/07/the-war-on-afghanistan-s-environment/ (accessed February 2, 2013).

Frankel, Rebecca "War Dog." *Foreign Policy,* May 4, 2011. www.foreignpolicy.com/articles/2011/o5/04/war_dog (accessed February 4, 2013).

Fuentes, Gidget. "Navy's Underwater Allies: Dolphins." *North Country Times,* May 6, 2001. http://simonwoodside.com/content/writing/dolphins/2001-05-06-nctimes.txt (accessed February 4, 2013).

Gabriel, Richard A. *The Ancient World: Soldiers' Lives Through History.* Westport, CT: Greenwood Publishing Group, 2007a.

___. *Muhammad: Islam's First Great General.* Norman, OK: University of Oklahoma Press. 2007b

Gala, Shalin G., Goodman, Justin R., Murphy, Michael P., & Balsam, Marion J. (2012). "Use of Animals by NATO Countries in Military Medical Training Exercises: An International Survey." *Military Medicine,* 177(8), 907-910.

Gallagher, Carole. *American Ground Zero: The Secret Nuclear War.* Cambridge, MA: Massachusetts Institute of Technology, 1993.

Galtung, John, and Carl G. Jacobsen. *Searching for Peace: The Road to TRANSCEND.* London, UK: Pluto Press, 2000.

Gandhi, Mohandus K. *Gandhi, an Autobiography: The Story of My Experiences with Truth.* Boston, MA: Beacon Press, 1993.

Gardiner, Juliet. *The Animals' War: Animals in Wartime from the First War to the Present Day.* London, UK: Portrait, 2006.

Wilhelm (Trans). *Culavamsa: Being the More Recent part of the Mahavamsa,* Asian Educational Services: Chennai, 2003.

Ghebrehiwet, Teame. "The Camel in Eritrea: An All-Purpose Animal." *World Animal Review,* 91, no. 2. 1998. www.fao.org/docrep/W9980T/w9980T6.htm (accessed January 30, 2013).

Gianoli, Luigi, and Mario Monti. *Horses and Horsemanship Through the Ages.* New York: Crown Publishers, 1969.

Gibson, J. W. "The New War on Wolves." *Los Angeles Times,* December 8, 2011. http://articles.latimes.com/2011/dec/08/opinion/la-oe-gibson-the-war-on-wolves-20111208 (accessed February 19, 2013).

Gilbert, Scott. "Environmental Warfare and U.S. Foreign Policy: The Ultimate Weapon of Mass Destruction." *Global Research.* January 1, 2004. http://www.globalresearch.ca/environmental-warfare-and-us-foreign-policy-the-ultimate-weapon-of-mass-destruction-2/5357909 (accessed January 30, 2013).

Goodman, Jared S. "Shielding Corporate Interests from public dissent: An examination of the undesirability and unconstitutionality of 'eco-terrorism' legislation. *Journal of Law and Policy*, 16, no. 2 (2008): 823-875.

Gouveia, Lourdes, and Arunas Juska. "Taming Nature, Taming Workers: Constructing the Separation Between Meat Consumption and Meat Production in the U.S." *Socologica Ruralis*, 42, no. 4 (2002): 370-390.

Gowers, Sir Willia. "The African Elephant in Warfare." *African Affairs*. 46, no. 182 (1947): 42-49

Grandin, Temple, and Catherine Johnson. *Animals in Translation: Using the Mysteries of Autism to Decode Animal Behavior*. New York: Simon & Schuster, 2005.

Greenhalgh, P. A. L. *Early Greek Warfare: Horsemen and Chariots in the Homeric and Archaic Ages*. Cambridge: Cambridge University Press, 2010.

Grichting Anna. "From Military Buffers to Transboundary Peace Parks: The Case of Korea and Cyprus." Paper presented at the Parks, Peace and Partnership Conference, Waterton, Montana, September 9-11, 2007. http://www.beyondintractability.org/citations/9976 (accessed February 3, 2013).

Griffith, Samuel B. *On Guerilla Warfare*. Chicago, IL: University of Illinoise Press, 2000.

Grossman, Dave. *On Killing: The Psychological Cost of Learning to Kill in War and Society*. New York: Back Bay Books, 2009.

Guardian/UK, February 1 2003. "War: Hell for Animals." http://www.animalaid.org.uk/h/n/NEWS/archive/ALL/882/ (accessed April 29, 2013).

Guizzo, Erico. "Moth Pupa + MEMS Chip = Remote Control Cyborg Insect." IEEE Spectrum: Automaton. February 17, 2009. spectrum.ieee.org/automaton/robotics/robotics-software/moth_pupa_mems_chip_remote_controlled_cyborg_insect (accessed February 3, 2013).

Haddon, Celia. "So Can a Dog Really Die of a Broken Heart?" *Daily Mail*, March 4, 2011. www.dailymail.co.uk/femail/article-1362789/So-dog-really-die-broken-heart.html (accessed February 4, 2013).

Haggis, Jane. "Thoughts on a Politics of Whiteness in a (Never Quite Post) Colonial Country: Abolitionism, Essentialism and Incommensurability." In *Whitening Race: Essays in Social and Cultural Criticism*, edited by Aileen Moreton-Robinson. Canberra, AUS: Aboriginal Studies, 2004.

Hall Andrew B. "Randomized Objective Comparison of Live Tissue Training Versus Simulators for Emergency Procedures." *The American Surgeon*, 77 no 5 (2011): 561-565.

Hambling, David. "U.S. Denies Incendiary Weapon Use in Afghanistan." May 15, 2009. www.wired.com/dangerroom/2009/05/us-incendiary-weapon-in-afghanistan-revealed (accessed February 3, 2013).

Hamilton, Jill. *Marengo – The Myth of Napoleon's Horse*. Toronto: Harper Collins Canada/Fourth Estate, 2000.

Hanson, Thor, Thomas M. Brooks, Gustavo A. B. Da Fonseca, Michael Hoffman, John F. Lamoreux, Gary Machlis, Cristina G. Mittermeier, Russell A. Mittermeier, and John D. Pilgrim. "Warfare in Biodiversity Hotspots." *Conservation Biology,* 23, no 3 (2009): 578-587.

Harding, Lee E., Omar F. Abu-Eld, Nahsat Hamidan, and Ahmad al Sha'Ian. "Reintroduction of the Arabian oryx *Oryx leucoryx* in Jordan: war and redemption" *Oryx*. 41, no. 4 (2007): 478.

Hardt, George L., and Hank Heifetz, translators. *The Four Hundred Songs of War and Wisdom: An Anthology of Poems from the Classical Tamil (The Purananuru)*. New York: Columbia University Press, 1999.

Hardt, Michael, and Antonio Negri. *Multitude: War and Democracy in the Age of Empire*. New York: Penguin, 2004.

Harris, Robert, and Jeremy Paxman. *A Higher Form of Killing: The Secret History of Chemical and Biological Warfare*. New York: Random House, 1983.

Hatton, J., M. Couto, and J. Oglethorpe. *Biodiversity and War: A Case Study from Mozambique. 2001*. www.worldwildlife.org/bsp/publications/Africa/146/Mozambique.pdf (accessed October 12, 2012).

Hausman, Gerald, and Loretta Hausman. *The Mythology of Dogs: Canine Legend*. New York: Macmillan, 1997.

Hofmeister, Erik H., Cynthia M. Trim, Saskia Kley, and Karen Cornell. "Traumatic Endotrachial Intubation in the Cat." *Veterinary Anaesthesia and Analgesia,* 34, no 3 (2007): 213-216.

Hogsed, Sarah. "Live Goats Used in Fort Campbell Medic Training." *Eagle Post,* January 20, 2010. www.theeaglepost.us/fort_campbell/article_4da5e92f-10d9-513e-ad61-19157ad63a29.html (accessed February 3, 2013).

Holmes, Bob. "New Tools Fuel Progress on Development of Genetically Engineered Farm Animals." *Health,* July 14, 2010. www.ihavenet.com/Health-New-Tools-Fuel-Progress-on-Development-of-Genetically-Engineered-Farm-Animals-New-Scientist.html (accessed December 31, 2010).

hooks, bell. *Teaching to Transgress: Education as the Practice of Freedom*. New York: Routledge, 1994.

Hotakainen, Rob. "Is Navy Plan a Threat to World's Oldest Killer Whales?" *McClatchy Newspapers,* December 24, 2010. article.wn.com/view/2010/12/24/Environmentalists_fear_Navy_plan_could_harm_whales/ (accessed October 14, 2012).

Hribal, Jason. *Fear of the Animal Planet: The Hidden History of Animal Resistance*. Oakland, CA: AK Press.

Huff, Mickey, Andrew Lee Roth, and Project Censored. *Censored 2011*. New York: Seven Stories Press, 2010.

Hui, Sylvia. "Films Tell Story of WWII Elephant Rescue in Burma." *Guardian,* November 1, 2010. www.guardian.co.uk/workd/feedarticle/9339643 (accessed February 3, 2013).

Human Rights Watch, July 24, 1990. "Ethiopia 'Mengistu has Decided to Burn Us like Wood' Bombing of Civilians and Civilian Targets by the Air Force." http://www.hrw.org/reports/archives/africa/ETHIOPIA907.htm

Hussain, Farooq. "Whatever Happened to Dolphins?" *New Scientist* (January 25, 1973): 182-184.

Hyland, Ann. *The Warhorse: 1250-1600*. Stroud, UK: Sutton, 1998.

___. *The Horse in the Middle Ages*. Stroud, UK: Sutton, 1999.

Hyland, Ann and Lesley Skipper. *The warhorse in the modern era : the Boer War to the beginning of the second millennium*. Stockton-on-Tees: Black Tent Publications, 2010.

Institute for War and Peace Reporting, August 1, 2011. "Report Spurs Action on Afghan Bird Poaching." http://iwpr.net/report-news/report-spurs-action-afghan-bird-poaching-0

International Campaign to Ban Landmines (ICBL). "What is a Landmine?" n.d. www.icbl.org/index.php.icbl/Problem/Landmines/What-is-a-Landmine (accessed October 14, 2012).

International Coalition to Ban Uranium Weapons (ICBUW). "A Concise Guide to Uranium Weapons, the Science Behind Them, and Their Threat to Human Health and the Environment." n.d. www.bandepleteduranium.org/en/i/77.html#1 (accessed October 12, 2012).

Intergovernmental Panel on Climate Change. "Climate Change 2013: The Physical Science Basis, 2013." http://www.climatechange2013.org (accessed November 13, 2013)

Jager Theodore F. *Scout, Red Cross and Army Dogs: A Historical Sketch of Dogs in the Great War and a Training Guide for Rank and File of the United States Army*. Rochester, NY: Arrow, 1917.

Jenson, Eric T. "The International Law of Environmental Warfare: Active and Passive Damage During Times of Armed Conflict." *Vanderbilt Journal of Transnational Law, 38* (January 2005): 145. papers.ssrn.com/so13/papers.cfm?abstract_id=987033 (accessed October 14, 2012).

Johnston, Steven. "Animals in War: Commemoration, Patriotism, Death." *Political Research Quarterly*, 65, no. 2 (2012): 359-371.

Joy, Melanie. *Why We Love Dogs, Eat Pigs and Wear Cows*. San Francisco, CA: Conari Press, 2010.

Judy, Jack. "Hybrid Insect MEMS (HI-MEMS) Programs." *Microsystem Technology Office,* March 5, 2010. www.derpa.mil/mto/programs/himems/indes.html#content (accessed December 20, 2012).

Kailasapathy, Kanakacapapati. *Tamil Heroic Poetry.* Clarendon, UK: Oxford University Press, 1968.

Katagiri, Nori. "Containing the Somali Insurgency: Learning from the British Experience in Somaliland." *African Security Review,* 19, no. 1 (2010): 33-45.

Katzman, Gerald H. "On Teaching Endotracheal Intubation." *Pediatrics,* 70, no. 4 (1982): 656.

Keegan, John. *A History of Warfare.* New York, First Vintage Books, 1994.

Keesler Air Force Base. "Protocol #FKE20070008A Endotracheal Intubation Training Exercise Using a Ferret Model." July 26, 2007. (Private Resource)

Kelly, Jeffrey A. "Alternatives to Aversive Procedures with Animals in the Psychological Teaching Setting." In *Advances in Animal Welfare Science,* edited by Michael W. Fox and Linda D. Mickley. Washington, DC: The Humane Society of the United States (1985): 165-184.

Kennedy, Phoebe. "Why Burma's Dictatorship Is Desperately Hunting for a While Elephant." *Independent,* April 2, 2010. http://www.independent.co.uk/news/world/asia/why-burmas-dictatorship-is-desperately-hunting-for-a-white-elephant-1934018.html (accessed February 3, 2013).

Kenner, Charles L. *Buffalo Soldiers and Officers of the Ninth Cavalry, 1867-1898: Black and White Together.* Norman: University of Oklahoma Press, 1999.

Kimberlin, Joanne. "Military contractor cited for treatment of goats." *The Virginian Pilot,* June 30, 2012. http://hamptonroads.com/2012/06/military-contractor-cited-treatment-goats

King, Jessie. "Vietnamese Wildlife Still Paying a High Price for Chemical Warfare." *The Independent,* June 8, 2006. http://www.independent.co.uk/environment/vietnamese-wildlife-still-paying-a-high-price-for-chemical-warfare-407060.html (accessed February 2, 2013).

Kirkham, Sophie. "Training Day for the Dog Soldiers." *Sunday Times,* December 15, 2002. http://www.sundaytimes.lk/021215/index.html (accessed October 12, 2012).

Kistler, John M. *Animals in the Military: From Hannibal's Elephants to the Dolphins of the U. S. Navy.* Santa Barbara, CA: ABC-CLIO, 2007.

Klein, Naomi. *The Shock Doctrine: The Rise of Disaster Capitalism.* London, UK: Routledge, 2008.

Knapp-Fisher, Harold C. *Man and His Creatures.* London, UK: Routledge & Sons, 1940.

Kovach, Bob. "Riderless Horse Adds Poignancy to Military Burials." *CNN.com.* March 23, 2008. http://www.cnn.com/2008/LIVING/05/23/arlington.riderless.horse/

Kovach, Gretel C. "Marine Corps Expands Infantry Bomb Dog Program: Camp Pendleton Handlers Tout Results." *UT San Diego News,* June 16, 2010. www.signonsandiego.com/news/2010/ddec/04/marine-corps-expands-infantry-bomb-dog-program (accessed February 4, 2013).

Kristof, Nicholas D. "Dad Will Really Like This." *New York Times,* June 16, 2010. http://www.nytimes.com/2010/06/17/opinion/17kristof.html (accessed February 4, 2013)

Lackland Air Force Base. "Protocol #FWH20090154AT Intubation Instruction and Training Using a Ferret." (July 27, 2009): Private Resource.

Langley, Andrew. *Ancient Egypt.* Chicago, IL: Raintree, 2005.

LaPrensa. "El Giobierno Prohibe a los Militaires Sacrificat Animales." *FM Bolivia,* March 31, 2009. www.fmbolivia.com/noticia10332-el-gobierno-prohibe-a-los-militares-sacrificar-animales-html (accessed October 12, 2012).

Last, Alex. "Victory on the Back of a Donkey." *BBC News,* 2000. http://news.bbc.co.uk/2/hi/africa/755624.stm (accessed February 12, 2013).

Lawrence, Thomas E. *Seven Pillars of Wisdom.* New York: Penguin, 1997.

Le Chene, Evelyn *Silent Heroes: The Bravery and Devotion of Animals in War.* London, UK: Souvenir Press, 1994.

Lederach, John P. *Preparing for Peace: Conflict Transformation Across Cultures.* Syracuse, NY: Syracuse University Press, 1995.

Leighton, Albert C. "Secret Communication Among the Greeks and Romans." *Technology and Culture,* 10, no. 2 (1969): 139-154. www.jstor.org/discover/10.2307/3101474?uid=3739256&uid=2129&uid=2&uid=70&uid=4&sid=21101750261877 (accessed February 3, 2012).

Lemish, Michael. *War Dogs: A History of Loyalty and Heroism.* Dulles, VA: Potomac Books, 1996.

Lendman, Stephen. "Depleted Uranium—a Hidden Looming Worldwide Calamity." *Global Research,* January 19, 2006. depleteduraniumthechildkiller.com/depleted_uranium_a_worldwide_calamity.htm (accessed February 4, 2013).

Leopold, Aldo. *The Land Ethic: In a Sand County Almanac.* Oxford, UK: Oxford University Press, 1966.

Levy, Debbie. *The Vietnam War.* Minneapolis, MN: Lerner Publishing Group, 2004.

Liddick, Donald. *Eco-Terrorism: Radical Environmental and Animal Liberation Movements.* Westport, CT: Praeger Publishers, 2006.

Lin, Guy, Yahav Oron, Ron Ben-Abraham, Dafna Barsuk, Haim Berkenstadt, Amitai Ziv, and Amir Blumenfeld. (2003). "Rapid Preparation of Reserve Military Medical Teams Using Advanced Patient Simulators." *TraumaCare* 13(2): 52

Lilly, John C. *The Scientist: A Metaphysical Autobiography.* Berkley, CA: Ronin Publishing, 1996.

Lin, Guy, Yahav Oron, Ron Ben-Abraham, Dafna Barsuk, Haim Berkenstadt, Haim Ziv, and Amir Blumenfeld "Rapid Preparation of Reserve Military Medical Teams Using Advanced Patient Simulators." *International Trauma and Anesthesia and Critical Care Society Conference,* May 15, 2003. www.itaccs.com/traumacare/archive/spring_03/Friday_pm.pdf (accessed February 4, 2013).

Linden, Annette, and Klandermans, Bert. "Stigmatization and repression of extreme-right activism in the Netherlands." *Mobilization,* 11, no 2 (2006), 213-228.

Lindow, Megan. "The Landmine Sniffing Rats of Mozambique." *Time,* June 2, 2008. http://www.time.com/time/world/article/0,8599,1811203,00.html (accessed February 3, 2013).

Little, Robert. "Army's Claims for Survival Rate in Iraq Don't Hold Up." *Baltimore Sun,* Narcg 29, 2009. www.baltimoresun.com/news/nation-world/bal-military-medicine-statistics-0329,0,1407580.story (accessed February 4, 2013).

Long, Douglas. *Ecoterrorism.* New York: Facts on File, 2004.

Looking-Glass. n.d. *Animals in War.* www.looking-glass.co.uk/animalsinwar/ (accessed February 20, 2009).

Loretz, John "The Animal Victims of the Gulf War." *PSR Quarterly,* (1991): 221-225. fn2.freenet.edmnton.ab.ca/~puppydog/gulfwar.htm (accessed February 4, 2013).

Lousky, Tamir. "Training, Research and Testing in Israel." *Alternatives to Animal Testing and Experimentation,* 14, Special Issue (August 2007): 261-264. altweb.jhsph.edu/bin/s/q/paper261.pdf (accessed February 4, 2013).

Love, Ricardo M. "Psychological Resistance: Preparing Our Soldiers for War." 2011. msnbcmedia.msn.com/i/.../120103_PTSD_Army_Paper.pdf (accessed February 4, 1013).

Lovley, Erika. "Lawmaker Says DOD 'Tortures' Animals." *Politico,* February 3, 2010. www.politico.com/news/stories/0210/32496.html (accessed February 4, 2013).

Lovitz, Dara. "Animal Lovers and Tree Huggers Are the New Cold-Blooded Criminals?" *Journal of Animal Law,* 3 (2007): 79-98. http://www.animallaw.info/articles/arus3janimall79.htm (accessed February 4, 2013).

___. *Muzzling a Movement: The Effects of Anti-Terrorism Law, Money, & Politics on Animal Activism.* New York: Lantern Books, 2010.

Lubow, Robert E. *The War Animals*. Garden City: Doubleday, 1977.

Lucas, Alfred. *Ancient Eyptian Materials and Industries*. London, UK: Arnold Publishers, 1962.

Mabry, Robert L. "Use of a Hemorrhage Simulator to Train Military Medics." *Military Medicine*, 170, no 11 (2005): 921-925.

MacDonald, Mia. "War News: Animals in Afghanistan." *Satya*, February 15, 2002. www.miamacdonald.com/a.php?id=16 (accessed February 4, 2013).

Madigan Army Medical Center. "Department of Clinical Investigation: Annual Research Progress Report: Fiscal Year 2006." 2007. www.dtic.mil/cgi-bin/GetTRDoc?AD=ADA492477 (accessed February 4, 2013).

Majumdar, Ramesh C., Hem Chandra Raychaudhuri, and Kalikincar Datta. *An Advanced History of India*. London, UK: Macmillan Publishers India LTD, 1950.

Mallawarachi, Bartha. "Sri Lankan War Zone to Become Wildlife Sanctuary." *Seattle Times*, December 1, 2010. http://seattletimes.com/html/nationworld/2013560287_apassrilankawildlife.html (accessed February 4, 2013).

Maps of World. "Wildlife in Marshall Islands." n.d. travel.mapsofworld.com/marshall-islands/marshall-islands-tours/wildlife-in-marshall-islands.html (accessed February 4, 2013).

Margawati, Endang T. "Transgenic Animals: Their Benefits to Human Welfare." *Action Bioscience*, January 2003. www.actionbioscience.org/biotech/margawati.html?ref-Klasistanbul.Com (accessed February 4, 2013).

Marshall, S. L. A. "Slam." *Men Against Fire: The Problem of Battle Command*. Norman: University of Oklahoma Press, 2000.

Martin, Brian. *Social Defense, Social Change*. London, UK: Freedom Press, 1993.

Mayor, Adrienne. *Greek Fire, Poison Arrows, and Scorpion Bombs: Biological and Chemical Warfare in the Ancient World*. New York, Overlook, 2003.

McCabe, Richard E. *Prarie Ghost: Pronghorn and Human Interaction in Early America*. Boulder: University of Colorado Press, 2004.

McCarthy, Colman. *All of One Peace: Essays on Nonviolence*. New Brunswick, NJ: Rutgers University Press, 1999.

McCoy, Kimberley E. "Subverting Justice: An Indictment of the Animal Enterprise Terrorism Act." *Animal Law Journal*, 14 (2008): 1-18.

McCrummen, Stephanie. "After War, Wildlife Returns to the Sudan." *Boston Globe*, October 11, 2009. www.boston.com/news/world/Africa/articles/2009/10/11/after_war_wildlife_returns_to_sudan (accessed February 4, 2013).

McDonald, Mia. "War News: Animals in Afghanistan." *Satya*, February 15, 2002. http://www.miamacdonald.com/a.php?id=16 (accessed February 4, 2013).

McLaughlin, Elliott C. "Giant Rats Put Noses to Work on Africa's Land Mine Epidemic." *CNN.com,* September 8, 2010. www.cnn.com/2010/WORLD/Africa/09'07/herorats.detect.landmines/index. html (accessed February 4, 2013).

Mendoza, Monica. "Man's Best Friend Not Immune to Stigmas of War; Overcomes PTSD." *Official Website of the U. S. Airforce,* July 27, 2010. http://www.af.mil/news/story.asp?id=123215014 (accessed February 4, 2013).

Miller, Lloyd E. *Lyme Disease: General Information and FAQ.* n.d. www.cs.cmu.edu/afs/cs.cmu.edu/usr/jake/mosaic/lyme.html (accessed February 4, 2013).

Miller, Joseph A., and R. M. Miller. *Eco-Terrorism and Eco-Extremism Against Agriculture.* Arlington, VA: Joseph A. Miller, R. M. Miller, 2000.

Mills, C. Wright. *The Power Elite.* New York, Oxford University Press, 1999.

Milstein, Mati. "Lebanon Oil Spill Makes Animals Casualties of War." *National Geographic News,* July 31, 2006. http://news.nationalgeographic.com/news/2006/07/060731-lebanon-oil.html (accessed February 4, 2013).

Mohanty, Chandra Talpade, Pratt, Minnie Bruce, Riley, Robin L. "Introduction: feminism and US wars—mapping the ground. In *Feminism and War: Confronting U.S. Imperialism,* edited by Robin L. Riley, Chandra Talpade Mohanty, and Bruce Pratt. Zed Books, 2008, 1-16.

Moore, Andrew N. I. "Caging Animal Advocates' Political Freedoms: The Unconstitutionality of the Animal and Ecological Terrorism Act." *Animal Law,* 11 (2005): 255-282. http://www.animallaw.info/articles/arus11animall255.htm (accessed February 4, 2013).

Morehouse, David. "Live Tissue Training Point Paper. bloximages.chicago2.vip.townnews.com/nctimes.com/content/tncms/assest/v 3/editorial/2/0c/20c128fa-83ab-11de-b0a8-001cc4c002e0/20c128fa-83-ab-11de-b0a8-001cc4c002e0.pdf (accessed December 20, 2012).

Moret, Leuret. "U.S. Nuclear Policy and Depleted Uranium." Testimony at the International Criminal Tribunal for War Crimes in Afghanistan. Chiba, Chiba Prefecture, JP: June 28, 2003. http://www.grassrootspeace.org/TribTest062803.html. (accessed February 4, 2013).

Morillo, Stephen. "The Age of Cavalry Revisited." In *The Circle of War in the Middle Ages: Essays on Medieval Military and Naval History,* edited by Donald J. Kagay and L.J. Andrew Villalon. Rochester: Boydell Press, 1999, 45-58.

Morris, Ruth. *Stories of Transformative Justice.* Toronto, CA: Canadian Scholars Press, 2000.

MSNBC. "More bird fall from the sky – this time in Louisiana." *MSNBC,* January 24, 2011.
http://www.msnbc.msn.com/id/40904491/ns/us_news-environment/ (accessed March 12, 2011)

Munson, Mary. "There Ought to Be a Law to Protect Animals." *Miami Herald,* November 24, 2008. https://www.commondreams.org/view/2008/11/24-2 (accessed February 4, 2013).

Muwankida, Vincent B., Silvester Nyakaana, and Hans R. Siegismund. "Genetic Consequences of War and Social Strife in Sub-Saharan Africa: The Case of Uganda's Large Mammals." *African Zoology,* 40, no. 1 (2005): 107-113. http://www.nbi.ku.dk/english/staff/publicationdetail/?id=4737b700-74c3-11db-bee9-02004c4f4f50 (accessed February 4, 2013).

Mydans, Seth. April 17, 2003. "Researchers Raise Estimate on Defoliant Use in Vietnam War." *New York Times.* http://www.nytimes.com/2003/04/17/world/researchers-raise-estimate-on-defoliant-use-in-vietnam-war.html

National Army Museum. "Boney's Mount." April 20, 2011. http://www.nam.ac.uk/exhibitions/permanent-galleries/changing-world-1784-1904/gallery-highlights/boneys-mount (accessed February 20, 2013).

National Museum of Denmark. "Weapons, Violence and Death in the Neolithic Period." *Historic Viden, Danmark.* n.d. oldtiden.natmus.dk/udstillingen/bondestendlaeren/slebne_oekser_af_flint/va aben_vold_og_doed_i_bondestenalderen/language/uk (accessed February 4, 2013).

Nautilus Institute for Security and Sustainability. "Toxic Bases in the Pacific." 2005. nautilus.org/apsnet/toxic-bases-in-the-pacific/ (accessed February 4, 2013).

Naval Medical Center, Portsmouth. "Protocol # NMCP.2008.A034. Pediatric Intubation Training Using the Ferret Model." 2008. http://www.dtic.mil/dtic/brd/2008/34672.html (accessed February 4, 2013).

Naval Medical Center, Portsmouth. February 23, 2009. Internal Memorandum. (Private Resource).

New Scientist. "Mongoose-Robot Duo Sniff Out Landmines." April 26, 2008. http://www.newscientist.com/article/mg19826535.900-mongooserobot-duo-sniffs-out-landmines.html (accessed February 4, 2013).

Nibert, D "Conflict, Violence, & the Domestication of Animals." Paper Presented at the 10th Annual North American Conference for Critical Animal Studies, Brock University, Ontario, Canada: March 31, 2011.

Nichols, Bob. "D.I.M.E. Bombs: Closer to Fallujua's Puzzle." *Veterans Today: Military and Foreign Affairs Journal,* October 30, 2010. www.veteranstoday.com (accessed February 4, 2013).

Nocella, A. J. II. "An Overview of the History and Theory of Transformative Justice," *Peace and Conflict Review*, 6, no. 1 (2011). http://www.review.upeace.org/index.cfm?opcion=0&ejemplar=23&entrada= 124 (accessed February 19, 2013).

Noske, Barbara. *Beyond Boundaries: Humans and Animals.* New York: Black Rose Books, 1997.

O'Donnell, John E. *None Came Home The War Dogs of Vietnam.* Bloomington: Authorhouse, 2001.

Olson, Lacie. "Analysis of FY 2012 Budget Request. The Center for Arms Control and Non-Proliferation." *Washington, DC Center for Arms Control and Non-Proliferation,* 2011. http://armscontrolcenter.org/issues/securityspending/articles/fy_2012_briefin g_book/ (accessed February 4, 2013).

___. "Fiscal Year 2012 Defense Spending Request Briefing Book." *Washington, DC Center for Arms Control and Non-Proliferation,* February 14, 2011. http://armscontrolcenter.org/issues/securityspending/articles/fy_2012_briefin g_book/ (accessed February 4, 2013).

Ornes, Stephen. "The Pentagon's Beetle Borgs." *Discover,* May, 2009. http://discovermagazine.com/2009/may/30-the-pentagons-beetle-borgs#.URFy_-goXeY (accessed February 4, 2013).

Padilla, Abel. "The Mighty M4." *War Wolf,* September 21, 2009. http://themightym4.blogspot.com/2009/09/war-wolf.htmln (accessed February 4, 2013).

Parenti, Christian. *The Soft Cage: Surveillance in America from Slavery to the War on Terror.* New York: Basic Books, 2003.

Parenti, Michael. *Against Empire.* San Francisco, CA: City Lights Publishers, 1995.

Paul, E. S., and Anthony L. Podberscek "Veterinary Education and Students' Attitudes Toward Animal Welfare." *Veterinary Record,* 146, no. 10 (2000): 269-272.

Pearl, Mary C. "Natural Selections Roaming Free in the DMZ." *Discover,* November 13, 2006. http://discovermagazine.com/2006/nov/natural-selections-dmz-animals (accessed February 4, 2013).

Pearn, John, and David Gardner-Medwin. "An Anzac's Childhood: John Simpson Kirkpatrick (1892-1915)." *The Medical Journal of Australia*, 178, no. 8 (2003): 400-402.

People for the Ethical Treatment of Animals (PETA). *Military Stabbing Live Dogs.* Online Video. n.d. http://www.peta.org/tv/videos/peta2-investigations/959533349001.aspx (accessed February 4, 2013).

People for the Ethical Treatment of Animals (PETA). "Victory! Army to Discharge Monkeys from Lab." October 13, 2011. www.peta.org/b/thepetafiles/archive/2011/10/13/victory-army-to-discharge-monkeys-from-lab.aspx (accessed February 6, 2013).

People for the Ethical Treatment of Animals (PETA). "Peta's Caring Consumer Program: Companies That Do Tests on Animals." www.mediapeta.com/peta/PDF/companiesdotest.pdf (accessed February 6, 2013).

Peterson, Dale. *The Moral Lives of Animals.* New York: Bloomsbury Press, 2011.

Pfohl, Stephen. *Images of Deviance and Social Control: A History.* New York: McGraw-Hill, 1994.

Phillips, Gervase. "'Who Shall Say That the Days of Cavalry are Over?' The Revival of the Mounted Arm in Europe, 1853-1914." *War In History.* 18, no. 1 (2011):5-32.

Phillips, Michael M. "Shell-Shocked Dog of War Finds a Home with the Family of a Fallen Hero. Jason's Death in Iraq Left Room for a Marine at the Dunhams' House; Gunner Fit the Bill." *Wall Street Journal,* October 6, 2010.

Phillips, Peter, and Project Censored. *Censored 2000: The Year's Top Censored Stories.* New York: Seven Stories Press, 2003.

Physicians Committee for Responsible Medicine. "Frequently Asked Questions: Implementing Non-Animal Training Methods in U.S. Military Medical Courses." n.d. http://www.pcrm.org/research/edtraining/military/faqs-implementing-nonanimal-training-methods (accessed February 6, 2013).

____. "New Videos and Website Expose Cruel Military Training." 2009. http://www.pcrm.org/good-medicine/2009/summer/new-videos-and-web-site-expose-cruel-military (accessed February 6, 2013).

____. "Live Animal Use in Advanced Trauma Life Support Courses in the U.S. and Canadian Programs: An Ongoing Survey." April 26, 2012. http://www.pcrm.org/pdfs/research/education/pcrm_survey_list_us_canada_atls_programs.pdf (accessed February 6, 2013).

____. "Live Animal Use for the Teaching of Endotracheal Intubation in Pediatrics Residency Programs in the United States." August 6 ,2012. www.pcrm.org/.../EthicsinPediatricsTrainingSurveyResults.pdf (accessed February 6, 2013).

Physicians for Human Rights. "Physicians for Human Rights Calls for Pentagon Inspector General Inquiry Into Alleged "No-Bid" Contract to Dr. Martin Seligman." October 14, 2010. http://physiciansforhumanrights.org/press/press-releases/news-2010-10-14-seligman.html (accessed February 6, 2013).

Pickrell, John. "Dolphins Deployed as Undersea Agents in Iraq." 2011. *National Geographic News,* March 28,2003. news.nationalgeographic.com/news/2003/03/0328_030328_wardolphins.html (accessed February 6, 2013).

Piggot, Stuart. "Chariots in the Caucasus and China." *Antiquity.* 48, no. 89 (1974):16-24

Pilger, John, and Alan Lowery. *The War You Don't See,* Film, directed, written and produced by John Pilger and Alan Lowery; (2010; London, UK: Dartmouth TV1).

Plato. *The Republic,* translated by Christopher Rowe. New York: Barnes & Noble, 2004 (original work 380 B.C.).

Plumwood, Val. *Feminism and the Mastery of Nature.* London, UK: Routledge, 1993.

Poole, R "By the Law of the Sword: Peterloo Revisited." *History,* 91, no 302 (2006): 254-276.

Potter, Will. *Green is the New Red: An Insiders Account of a Social Movement Under Siege.* San Fancisco, CA: City lights Books, 2011.

Quade, Alex. "Monument Honors U.S. 'Horse Soldiers' Who Invaded Afghanistan." *CNN.com.* October 6, 2011.
http://www.cnn.com/2011/10/06/us/afghanistan-horse-soldiers-memorial/

Radhakrishnan, Sarvepalli, and Charles A. Moore. *A Source Book: Indian Philosophy.* Princeton, NJ: Princeton University Press, 1989.

Ramanthapillai, Rajmohan. "Modern Warfare and the Spiritual Disconnection From Land." *Peace Review,* 2, no. 1 (2008): 113-120.
www.tandfonline.com/doi/abs/10.1080/10402650701873825
(accessed February 6, 2013).

Rance, Philip. "Elephants in Warfare in Late Antiquity." *Acta Antiqua,* 43, no. 3-4 (2003): 355-384.
http://www.akademiai.com/content/p427216360x17417/
(accessed February 6, 2013).

Ravitz, Jessica. "War Dogs Remembered, Decades Later." *CNN.com.* February 12, 2010. http://www.cnn.com/2010/LIVING/02/12/war.dogs/

Read, Donald. *Peterloo: The Massacre and Its Background.* Manchester, UK: Manchester University Press, 1958.

Resner, Benjaman I. "Rover @ Home: Computer Mediated Remote Interaction Between Humans and Dogs." *Massachusetts Institute of Technology,* 2001. http://dspace.mit.edu/handle/1721.1/62357 (accessed February 6, 2013).

Resources News, n.d. "Birds Also Victims in Afghan War."
http://www.mts.net/~dkeith2/dec-5.html

Rice, Rob S., Simon Anglim, Phyllis Jestice, Scott Rusch, and John Serrati *Fighting Techniques of the Ancient World: 3000 B.C. – 500 A. D. Equipment, Combat Skills, and Tactics.* New York: Thomas Dunne Books, 2006.

Richardson, Edwin H. *British War Dogs: Their Training and Psychology.* London, UK: Skeffington & Son, 1920.

Ritter, Matt E., and Mark Bowyer "Simulation for Trauma and Combat Casualty Care." *Minimally Invasive Therapy & Allied Technologies,* 14, no. 4 (2005): 224-234.

Roberts, Adam M., and Kevin Stewart "Landmines: Animal Casualties of the
    Underground War." *Animals' Agenda,* 18, no. 2 (1998): 224-234.
    http://ecn.ab.ca/~puppydog/aa-art.htm (accessed February 6, 2013).
Robles De-La-Torre, Gabriel. "Haptic Technology, an Animated Explanation."
    n.d. http://www.isfh.org/comphap.html (accessed February 6, 2013).
Robson, Seth, and Marcus Kloeckner. "Army Looking to Conduct Combat
    Medic Training on Live Animals in Germany." *Stars and Stripes,* June 2,
    2010. http://www.stripes.com/news/europe/army-looking-to-conduct-
    combat-medic-training-on-live-animals-in-germany-1.105621
    (accessed February 6, 2013).
Routley, Richard. "Is There a Need for a New Environmental Ethic?"
    Proceedings of the XV World Congress of Philosophy, Volume 1 (1973):
    205-210.
Routley, Richard, and Val Routley. "Against the Inevitability of Human
    Chauvinism." In *Ethics and Problems of the 21ˢᵗ Century,* edited by Kenneth
    E. Goodpaster and Kenneth M. Sayre, 36-58. Notre Dame, IN: University of
    Notre Dame Press, 1979.
___. "Human Chauvinism and Environmental Ethics. In *Environmental
    Philosophy,* edited by Mannison McRobbie and Richard Routley, 96-189.
    Canberra, AUS: Australian National University Press, 1980.
Rupert, Mark E. "Academia and the Culture of Militarism. In *Academic
    Repression: Reflections from the Academic Industrial Complex,* edited by
    Anthony J. Nocella, II, Steven Best, and Peter McLaren, 428-436. Oakland,
    CA: AK Press, 2010.
Saenz, Aaron. "Free Flying Cyborg Beetles." *Singularity Hub,* October 7, 2009.
    http://singularityhub.com/2009/10/07/free-flying-cyborg-beetles/
    (accessed February 6, 2013).
___. "Eye Popping Pics of Cyborg Animals from Photoshop Contest."
    Singularity Hub, March 15, 2010. http://singularityhub.com/2010/03/15/eye-
    popping-pics-of-cyborg-animals-from-photoshop-contest/
    (accessed February 6, 2013).
Sanbonmatsu, John. "Blood and Soil: Notes on Leirre Keith, Locavores, and
    Death Fetishism."*Upping the Anti,"* no. 12 (2011).
___. "John Snabonmatsu Replies to Derrick Jensen." *Upping the Anti,* no. 13
    (2011).
Sanders, Barry. *The Green Zone: The Environmental Impact of Militarism.*
    Oakland, CA: AK Press, 2009.
Sanua, Victor D., Editor. *Fields of Offering: Studies in Honor of Raphael Patai.*
    Cranbury: Associated University Press, 1983.
Saunders, John Joseph. *The History of the Mongol Conquests.* Philadelphia:
    University of Pennsylvania Press, 2001.
Saunders, Nicholas J. *Ancient Americas: The Great Civilisations*, Sutton
    Publishing Limited: United Kingdom, 2004.

Sawyer, Taylor, Agnes Sierocka-Castaneda, Debora Chan, Benjamin Berg, and Mark W. Thompson "High Fidelity Simulation Training Results in Improved Neonatal Resuscitation Performance." *American Academy of Pediatrics National Conference,* October 1, 2010.

Scahill, Jeremy. *Blackwater: The Rise of the World's Most Powerful Mercenary Army.* New York: Nation Books, 2008.

Schafer, Edward H. "War Elephants in Ancient and Medieval China." *Oriens,* 10, no. 2 (1957): 289-291.

___. *Ancient China.* New York: Time-Life Books, 1967.

Schaffer, E. *Animals, World War!"* Encyclopedia S-z (Volume 4).

Scharrer, Gary. "Indian Group Objects to Buffalo Soldier Plates." *Houston Chronicle,* November 26, 2011. http://www.chron.com/news/houston-texas/article/Indian-group-takes-issue-with-Buffalo-Soldier-2293128.php (accessed February 6, 2013).

Schirch, Lisa. *The Little Book of Strategic Peacebuilding.* Intercourse, PA: Good Books, 2004.

Science Clarified. "Agent Orange." n.d. http://www.scienceclarified.com/A-Al/Agent-Orange.html (accessed February 6, 2013).

Scigliano Eric. *Love, War, and Circuses: The Age-Old Relationship Between Elephants and Humans.* Boston, MA: Houghton Mifflin Co., 2002.

Seligman, Martin. "Learned Helplessness." *Annual Review of Medicine.* 23, no. 5 (1972):407-412.

Shambaugh, James, Judy Oglethorpe, and Rebecca Ham. *The Trampled Grass: Mitigating the Impacts of Armed Conflict on the Environment.* Washington, DC: Biodiversity Support Program, 2001. pdf.usaid.gov/pdf_docs/PNACN551.pdf (accessed February 6, 2013).

Shaw, J. C. *The Paston Papers Siam 1688,* Craftsman Press: Bangkok, 1993.

Shelton, Jo-Ann. "Elephants as Enemies in Ancient Rome." *Concentric: Library and Cultural Studies,* 32, no 1 (2006): 3-25.

Shiva, Vandana. *Biopiracy: The Plunder of Nature and Knowledge.* Boston, MA: Southend Press, 1995.

Singer, Peter. *Biopiracy: The Plunder of Nature and Knowledge,* London, UK: Pimlico Press, 1975.

Singer, Peter W. *Wired for War: The Robotics Revolution and Conflict in the Twenty-First Century.* New York: Penguin Books, 2009.

Singh, Upinder. *A History of Ancient and Early Medieval India: From Stone Age to the 12th Century.* New Delhi, IN: Dorling Kindersley, 2008.

Singleton, John. "Britain's Military Use of Horses 1914-1918." *Past and Present.* 193, no. 1 (1993):178-203.

Skocpol, Theda. *Social Revolutions in the Modern World.* Cambridge, UK: Cambridge University Press, 1994

Society for the Prevention of Cruelty to Animals (SPCA). "Retired Working
     Dogs Stranded in Iraq." March 12, 2011.
     http://www.spcai.org/index.php/news-and-blog/spcai-news/item/522-retired-
     working-dogs-stranded-in-iraq.html (accessed February 6, 2013).
South, Nigel. "Corporate and State Crimes Against the Environment:
     Foundations for a Green Perspective in Europe." In *The New European
     Criminology: Crime and Social Order in Europe*, 443-461. New York:
     Routledge, 1998.
Spielberg, Steven. *War Horse*, Film directed by Steven Spielberg (2011;
     Burbank, CA: Walt Disney).
Stannard, David E. *American Holocaust*. New York: Oxford University Press,
     1992.
Stanton, Doug. *Horse Soldiers: The Extraordinary Story of a Band of US
     Solders Who Rode to Victory in Afghanistan*. New York: Scribner, 2009.
Starhawk. "Feminist Voices for Peace." In *Stop the Next War Now: Effective
     Responses to Violence and Terrorism*, edited by Jodie Evans and Medea
     Benjamin, 84-86. Novato, CA: New World Library, 2005.
Stockholm International Peace Research Institute (SIPRI). *Warfare in a Fragile
     World: Military Impact on the Human Environment*. New York: Crane,
     Russak, 1980.
____. *Background paper on SIPRI Military Expenditure Data*. April 11, 2010.
     http://www.sipri.org/databases/milex (accessed February 6, 2012).
Stuart, Hunter. "Sharktopus Trailer Released and It Is Awesome." *Huffington
     Post*, September 16, 2010.
     http://www.huffingtonpost.com/2010/07/17/sharktopus-trailer-
     releas_n_650081.html (accessed February 6, 2013).
Sulfigar, Ali. "PESHAWAR: Wildlife Too Bearing the Brunt." *Dawn*,
     November 5, 2011. http://archives.dawn.com/2001/11/05/local28.htm
     (accessed February 21, 2013).
Sullivan, Shannon, and Nancy Tuana, Editors. *Race and Epistemologies of
     Ignorance*. Albany: State University of New York (SUNY) Press, 2007.
Sutherland, Donald M. G. *The French Revolution and Empire: The Quest for a
     Civic Order*. Oxford, UK: Blackwell, 2003.
Swart, Sandra. "Horses in the South African War, c. 1899-1902." *Society &
     Animals* 18, no. 4 (2010a): 348-366.
____. "'The World the Horses Made': A South African Case Study of Writing
     Animals into Social History." *International Review of Social History*. 55, no.
     2 (2010b): 241-263
Tait, Cindy. "On the Differences Between a Child and a Kitten." *Journal of
     Emergency Nursing*, 36, no. 1 (2010): 78-80.
Tan, Michelle. "Dogs Bring Home Stress Too." *Army Times*, December 30,
     2010.

Teh, Kong Soon, Shang Ping Lee, and Adrian David Cheok. "Poultry Internet: A Remote Human-Pet Interaction System." In *CHI '06 Extended Abstracts on Human Factors in Computing Systems,* (2006): 251-254.http://dl.acm.org/citation.cfm?id=1125505&dl=ACM&coll=DL&CFID =274800838&CFTOKEN=87688175 (accessed February 7, 2012).

Telegraph. "Terrorists Tie Bomb Belt to Dog in Iraq." May 27, 2005. http://www.telegraph.co.uk/news/worldnews/middleeast/iraq/1490888/Terro rists-tie-bomb-belt-to-dog-in-Iraq.html

Thomas, William. *Scorched Earth: The Military Assault on the Environment.* Philadelphia, PA: New Society Publishers, 1995.

Tier One Group. "Instructing Combat Trauma Mangement to Trainees." March 16, 2008. (Private Resource).

Tilly, Charles. *From Mobilization to Revolution.* New York, NY: McGraw-Hill Publishing, 1978.

Torres, Bob. *Making a Killing: The Political Economy of Animal Rights.* Oakland, CA: AK Press, 2007.

Tsolidis, Georgina. (2010) "Simpson, His Donkey and the Rest of Us: Public Pedagogies of the Value of Belonging." *Educational Philosophy and Theory,* 42, no. 4 (2010): 448 - 461.

Tucker, Spencer C. *Almanac of American Military History: Volume One, 1000-1830.* Santa Barbara, CA: ABC-CLIO, 2012.

Twine, Richard. *Animals as Biotechnology: Ethics, Sustainability and Critical Animal Studies.* Oxford, UK: Routledge, 2010.

___. "Revealing the 'Animal-Industrial-Complex': A Concept and Method for Critical Animal Studies." *Journal for Critical Animal Studies,* 10, no. 1 (2012): 12-39.

Ulansey, David, *Call of Life: Facing the Mass Extinction,* Film directed by Monty Johnson (2010; New York: Species Alliance.) DVD.

Uniformed Services University of the Health Sciences. "Live Animal Purchases for Use in Student Education." Washington, DC: n.d.

United Nations. "End Nuclear Testing." *International Day Against Nuclear Tests.* n.d. www.un.org/en/events/againstnucleartestsday/history.shtml (accessed February 6, 2013).

University of Kansas Natural History Museum. "Comache Preservation." n.d. http://naturalhistory.ku.edu/explore-topic/comanche-preservation/comanche-preservation (accessed February 21, 2013).

U.S. Army Europe Command Surgeon. Internal Memorandum, 2010. (Private Resource).

U.S. Army Medical Department, Office of the Surgeon General. "HQDA EXORD 096-09, "Mandatory Pre-Deployment Trauma Training (PDTT) for Specified Medical Personnel." 2009. www.documbase.com/HQDA-Exord-048-10.pdf (accessed October 12, 2012).

U. S. Army Medical Research Institute of Chemical Defense. "Chemical Casualty Care Resuscitation Practical Exercise Using the Nonhuman Primate Model." 2005a. http://www.gevha.com/home/51-general/821-pcrm (accessed October 12, 2012).

____. "Medical Management of Chemical Casualties, Laboratory Exercise Worksheet." 2005b. video.onset.freedom.com/nwfdn/kf8sgk-18pigs.pdf (accessed February 7, 2013).

U.S. Department of Agriculture. "Memo: Complaint #E10-197 Tactical Medics International." July 29, 2010. (Private Resource).

U.S. Department of Army, Navy, Air Force, Defense Advanced Research Projects Agency, and Uniformed Services University of Health Sciences. "The Care and Use of Laboratory Animals in DOD Programs." 2005. www.apd.army.mil/pdffiles/r40_33.pdf (accessed February 7, 2013).

U.S. Department of Defense. "DOD Biomedical Research Database (BRD)." 2010. http://www.dtic.mil/biosys/brd/index.html (accessed February 6, 2013).

U.S. Department of Justice Federal Bureau of Investigation. "Terrorism: 2002-2005." n.d. http://www.fbi.gov/stats-services/publications/terrorism-2002-2005 (accessed February 6, 2013).

U.S. Medicine Institute for Health Studies. December 3, 2002. "Computer, Robots, and Cyberspace: Maximizing the Cutting Edge."

Vandiver, John, and Marcus Kloecker. "German Ruling Puts USAREUR Plans for Live-Animal Medical Training on Hold." *Stars and Stripes,* August 17, 2010. www.stripes.com/news/german-ruling-puts-usareur-plans-for-live-animal-medical-training-on-hold-1.114989 (accessed February 6, 2013).

Van Strum, Carol. "Action Alter: Pacific NW Residents—Stop the Navy's Coastal Weapons Testing." *Daily Kos,* Ocober 21, 2010. http://www.dailykos.com/news/coastal%20protection# (accessed February 6, 2013).

Varner, John G., and Jeannette J. Varner. *Dogs of the Conquest.* Norman: University of Oklahoma.

Vastag, Brian. "Army to Phase Out Animal Nerve-Agent Testing." *Washington Post,* October 13, 2011. articles.washingtonpost.com/2011-10-13/national/35277114_1_green-monkeys-nerve-gas-vervet (accessed February 6, 2013).

Waisman, Amir, Mor, Mimouni "Pediatric Life Support (PALS) Courses in Israel: Ten Years of Experience." *Israel Medical Association Journal,* 7, no. 10 (2005): 639-642. (accessed February 6, 2013).

Walmsley, Robert. *Peterloo.* Manchester, UK: Manchester University Press, 1969.

War Resisters League. "Where Your Income Tax Money Really Goes: U.S.
    Federal Budget 2012 Fiscal Year." 2011.
    www.warresisters.org/sites/default/files/FY2012piechart-color.pdf
    (accessed February 6, 2013).
Webb, Robin. "Animal Liberation—By 'Whatever Means Necessary.' In
    Terrorists or Freedom Fighters: Reflections on the Liberation of Animals,
    edited by Steve Best Anthony J. Nocella. Lantern, 2004, 75-80.
Weiss, Rick. "Dragonfly or Insect Spy? Scientists at Work on Robobugs." *The
    Washington Post*, October 9, 2007.
    http://www.washingtonpost.com/wp-
    dyn/content/article/2007/10/08/AR2007100801434.html (accessed 4
    November 2013).
Westing, Arthur H. "Environmental Warfare II: 'Levelling the Jungle.'" *Bulletin
    of Peace Proposals*, 4, no. 38 (1973a).
___. "Environmental Warfare II: 'The Big Bomb.'" *Bulletin of Peace Proposals*,
    4, no. 40 (1973b).
___. "Environmental Consequences of the Second Indochina War: A Case
    Study." *Ambio*, 4, no 5 (1975): 216-222.
White, Rob. *Crimes Against Nature: Environmental Criminology and
    Ecological Justice*. Portland: William, 2008.
White, Thomas I. *In Defence of Dolphins: The New Moral Frontier*. Oxford,
    UK: Blackwell Publishing, 2007.
Whitehouse, David. "Here Come the Ratbots." BBC News, May 1, 2002.
    http://news.bbc.co.uk/2/hi/science/nature/1961798.stm
    (accessed February 6, 2013).
Wildlife Conservation Society. "Afghanistan's First National Park." 2009.
    www.wcs.org/conservation-challenges/local-livelihoods/recovering-from-
    conflict-and-disaster/afghanistan-first-national-park.aspx
    (accessed February 6, 2013).
Wildlife Extra. "Pigmy Hippos Survive Two Civil Wars in Liberia's Sapo
    National Park." 2008. http://www.wildlifeextra.com/go/news/pygmy-
    hippos872.html#cr (accessed February 6, 2013).
___. Wildlife Extra. "Sierra Leone & Liberia Create Major Trans-Boundary
    Park." 2009. http://www.wildlifeextra.com/go/news/leone-
    liberia009.html#cr (accessed February 6, 2013).
    Wilcox, Fred. *Scorched Earth: Legacies of Chemical Warfare in Vietnam.*
New York: Seven Stories, 2011.
Wincer, Simon. *The Lighthorsemen,* Film written by Ian Jones and directed by
    Simon Wincer. (1987; Sydney, AU: Hoyts). DVD.
Winterfilm Collective. *Winter Soldier.* Film produced by the Winterfilm
    Collective. (2008; United States: Millarium Zero). DVD.

Women's International League for Peace and Freedom. "Chemical Weapons." *Reaching Critical Will,* n.d. www.reachingcriticalwill.org/legal/cw/csindex.html (accessed October 14, 2012).

Woolf, Marie. "Military Lab Tests on Animals Double in Five Years." *Independent,* May 14, 2006. http://www.independent.co.uk/news/uk/politics/military-lab-tests-on-live-animals-double-in-five-years-478165.html (accessed February 21, 2013).

World Health Organization/Food and Agriculture Organization. "Human Vitamin and Mineral Requirements." 2010. www.fao.org/docrep/004/Y2809Ey2809e00.htm (accessed January 18, 2012).

World Society for the Protection of Animals. "Situation Critical for Gaza's Animals." January 23, 2009. http://www.wspa-international.org/latestnews/2009/animal_welfare_gaza.aspx (accessed February 6, 2013).

Wylie, Dan. *Elephant.* London, UK: Reaktion Books, 2008.

Wynter, Philip. "Elephants at War: In Burma, Big Beasts Work for Allied Army." *Life,* April 10, 1944. http://www.lifemagazineconnection.com/LIFE-Magazines-1940s/LIFE-Magazines-1944/1944-April-10-WWII-LIFE-Magazine-Burma-Cassino (accessed February 6, 2013).

Yager, Jordy. "A Nose for Explosives." *The Hill,* May 25, 2010. http://thehill.com/capital-living/cover-stories/99617-a-nose-for-explosives (accessed February 6, 2013).

Yale Peabody Museum. "Fossil Fragments: The Riddle of Human Origins." New Haven, CT: Permanent Exhibit, n.d.

Young, Iris M. *Justice and the Politics of Difference.* Princeton, NJ: Princeton University Press, 1990.

CONTRIBUTORS

Julie Andrzejewski, Ed.D. is a professor, activist scholar, and co director of the Social Responsibility Masters Program at St. Cloud State University in Minnesota. She is the initiator and first editor of *Social Justice, Peace, and Environmental Education* (Routledge, 2009). Her co-authored chapter on Interspecies Education for Humans, Animals, and the Earth (with Helena Pedersen and Freeman Wicklund) in this volume situates animal oppression and speciesism as foundational to a fully comprehensive understanding of global social responsibility and education. Other books include: *Oppression and Social Justice: Critical Frameworks; and Why Can't Sharon Kowalski Come Home?* (with co author Karen Thompson) which received the national Lambda Literary Award. Andrzejewski has also founded a women's center, organized nationally on LGBT, feminist, and disability issues, supported legal actions against discriminatory institutions, served as union president, initiated program development and curriculum transformation for global social responsibility, and directed grants on peace, environment, women, and social justice. She taught the first course on animal rights at St. Cloud State University. Based on her work teaching these courses, she wrote: "Teaching animal rights at the university: Philosophy and practice" in the *Journal of Animal Liberation Philosophy and Policy*. She can be reached at jrandrzejewski@stcloudstate.edu.

Judy K. C. Bentley, Ph.D., is an associate professor in the Department of Foundations and Social Advocacy at the State University of New York College at Cortland, and editor-in-chief of *Social Advocacy and Systems Change*, a peer-reviewed social justice journal. Her research interests include Symbolic Inclusion, critical animal studies, and the wisdom and competence of children with disabilities as architects of their own education. Recent publications include *Earth, Animal and Disability Liberation: The Rise of the Eco-Ability Movement (Co-Editor/Author)* (2012, Peter Lang).

Shalin Gala received a bachelor's degree in Anthropology from the University of Washington in St. Louis and currently works as a laboratory methods specialist in the Laboratory Investigations Department at People for the Ethical Treatment of Animals (PETA). He talks directly with corporate executives in a variety of industries—running the gamut from the developers of medical devices to the makers of food and beverage products—promoting sophisticated non-animal research methods and how companies can implement these technologies in place of cruel experiments on animals. He also works on changing regulations around the world, which has involved writing detailed technical dossiers to Indian and Taiwanese officials in order to reform inhumane medical education curricula, submitting a detailed brief to the U.S. Department of Defense regarding alternatives to mutilating animals in crude combat trauma training exercises, and flying to Bolivia to testify before a congressional commission in favor of a national draft animal welfare law.

Justin Goodman is the associate director of Laboratory Investigations at People for the Ethical Treatment of Animals, where he directs campaigns against animal experimentation. He holds a master's degree in Sociology from the University of Connecticut where he studied and researched the use of non-violent direct action in the animal rights movement. Goodman is also an adjunct faculty member in the Department of Sociology and Criminal Justice at Marymount University (Arlington, VA). He has published scores of opinion articles on animal experimentation issues. His work to end animal experimentation has been covered in a variety of national publications, including the *New York Times*, the *Chronicle of Higher Education*, and *The Scientist*.

Elliot M. Katz, DVM, is the president of In Defense of Animals (IDA), which he founded in 1983. He is a graduate of Cornell University's College of Veterinary Medicine, and practiced veterinary medicine in Brooklyn, New York before moving to California. IDA is an international animal protection organization dedicated to ending the abuse and exploitation of animals by protecting their rights, welfare and habitats, and by raising their status beyond that of mere commodities, property, objects or things. Through investigative and advocacy work and through their chimpanzee sanctuary in Cameroon, Africa, veterinary clinics in Mumbai, India, and their sixty-four acre sanctuary for abused and abandoned animals in rural Mississippi, IDA has been a powerful voice and force for change. Dr. Katz is the father of daughters Danielle and Raquel, and lives in Corte Madera, California, with his beloved rescue dog Charlie.

Colman McCarthy, a syndicated columnist for the *Washington Post* from 1969 to 1998, is the director of the Center for Teaching Peace, a Washington nonprofit he founded in 1985 and which helps schools at all levels begin or expand academic programs in the philosophy of pacifism and the methods of nonviolent conflict resolution. He is the author of several books, including *All of One Peace, I'd Rather Teach Peace, Disturbers of the Peace, At Rest With the Animals* and is the editor of two anthologies of peace essays titled *Solutions to Violence* and *Strength Through Peace: The Ideas and People of Nonviolence*. Since 1982, he has been teaching courses on nonviolence in high schools, colleges and graduate school. He is currently on the adjunct faculty at Georgetown University Law Center, American University, the University of Maryland, the Washington Center for Internships, Bethesda-Chevy Chase High

School and Wilson High School in Washington. He has had more than 8,000 students in his classes. He is a regular speaker at U.S. campuses.

Ana P. Morrón is a scholar and an activist from Queens, New York. As a child, she formed strong relationships with her companion animals, relationships which inspired her to lead a more compassionate lifestyle. After graduating from Williams College (Williamstown, MA) in 2009 as a Mellon Mays Fellow with a B.A. in English and Religion, she went on to Yale Divinity School (New Haven, CT) to pursue a master's degree in Religious Studies. She is primarily interested in the study of animal ethics, writing passionately on the subject for newspapers, conferences, as well as her blog. Someday she hopes to conduct higher level graduate work on the human-animal bond and the animal rights/welfare movement. She is equally dedicated to raising awareness of animal and environmental justice issues, engaging in grassroots activism as well as state level legislative advocacy. Finally, her faith is ecumenical and deeply influenced by her humane practices.

Anthony J. Nocella II, award-winning author, educator, and peacemaker, is a Visiting Professor at Hamline University in the School of Education. He received his Ph.D. from the Maxwell School at Syracuse University in Social Science. Nocella is a leading scholar in the fields of critical animal studies, disability studies, environmental ethics, urban education, peace and conflict studies, critical pedagogy, and anarchist studies. He is also interested in critical media studies, critical criminology, inclusive education, Quaker pedagogy, urban education, and hip-hop studies. He is also an associate with the Program for the Advancement of Research on Conflict and Collaboration (PARCC). Nocella holds an MA in Peacemaking and Conflict Studies, and a graduate certificate in mediation from Fresno Pacific University, and an MS in Cultural Foundations of Education, an Advanced Certificate in Women's Studies, and an Advanced Certificate in Transnational Conflicts from Syracuse University. He has taught workshops in mediation and tactical analysis, and assisted in a number of legal committees in North and South America, including working with the Mennonite Central Committee (MCC), American Friends Service Committee (AFSC), and Christian Peacemaker Teams (CPT) in Colombia between 2000 and 2003. He is on the regional board, programming committee, and international board of the Noble Peace Prize-winning AFSC. Nocella has provided conflict management and negotiation workshops to NGOs, ROTC, U.S. military, law enforcement, as well as in prisons, juvenile halls, and middle and high schools, in hopes of building peace and providing skills to revert violent conflicts to nonviolent transformation. Nocella's website is www.anthonynocella.org

Rajmohan Ramanathapillai is a native of Sri Lanka and he is currently serving as an assistant professor of Philosophy and Peace and Justice and the coordinator of Peace and Justice Studies program at Gettysburg College, Pennsylvania. He worked with victims of torture in Sri Lanka and recorded human rights violations in art form with his students. This work has been on exhibit at National Civil Right Museum in Memphis and Royal Ontario Museum in Toronto. Human Rights, Beyond Terrorism, Gandhi, War and the Environment and Human and Elephant Conflict are some of the courses he taught. He has published a wide range of articles including Gandhi, human rights, war trauma, war on nature and religion in interdisciplinary journals. He served as Program Director of M.K. Gandhi Institute at Christian Brother University in Memphis and directed a program named "Kindness is Contagious" with African American children. Also designed and directed a "Culture of Peace" childrens program with Diaspora community in Toronto, Canada.

Colin Salter teaches in the Faculty of Arts, Law and Creative Arts at the University of Wollongong, following an appointment as assistant professor in the Centre for Peace Studies at McMaster University. He holds a BE (hons), a BA (hons) and a PhD. As an environmental engineer, he worked on the design and monitoring of socially, culturally, and environmentally appropriate technology projects in Australia and the Pacific. On returning to the university sector, Dr Salter has expanded on more than a decade-long research interest, exploring the efficacy of grassroots campaigns and movements seeking to foster peace and justice. He has presented papers and published research on movements supporting respect and recognition of First Peoples, the strategies and tactics of contemporary animal-environmental-social justice movements and the intersections between masculinity, exceptionalism, violence and nonviolence. He is the author of *Whiteness and Social Change: Remnant Colonialisms in Australia and Canada* (2013).

Ian Smith has been an animal liberation activist for several years. He earned a master's degree in philosophy at the University of Connecticut where he focused on ethics and political theory. In addition to working toward animal liberation, Smith has been involved in the labor movement as a union organizer and has served as a student board member for the New York Public Interest Research Group (NYPIRG). He has worked on numerous environmental, anti-nuclear, and student rights campaigns througout New York State. He is currently a research associate in the Laboratory Investigations Division of People for the Ethical Treatment of Animals (PETA).

John Sorenson has a background in anthropology and received a PhD from York University's Social and Political Thought Programme. He has conducted field research in Eritrea, Ethiopia, Sudan and Pakistan. He was associated with the Disaster Research Unit (University of Manitoba), the Centre for Refugee Studies (York University) and worked with the Eritrean Relief Association in Canada. His books include *Imagining Ethiopia: Struggles for History and Identity in the Horn of Africa*; *Disaster and Development in the Horn of Africa*; *African Refugees; Ghosts and Shadows* and *Culture of Prejudice*. Currently, he is writing on the experience of women in the Eritrean liberation struggle and after independence. His interests are in the area of social justice generally, with special concern for animal liberation and the environment.

INDEX